TEMPLE THEMES IN
CHRISTIAN WORSHIP

TEMPLE THEMES IN CHRISTIAN WORSHIP

MARGARET BARKER

t & t clark

Published by T&T Clark International
A Continuum Imprint
The Tower Building, 11 York Road, London SE1 7NX
80 Maiden Lane, Suite 704, New York, NY 10038

www.continuumbooks.com

British Library Cataloguing-in-Publication Data
A catalogue record for this book is available from the British Library.

Typeset by Fakenham Photosetting, Fakenham, Norfolk
Printed on acid-free paper in Great Britain by Cromwell Press Ltd, Trowbridge, Wiltshire

ISBN 10:   0567031551 (Hardback)
            0567032760 (Paperback)
ISBN13 :   9780567031556 (Hardback)
            9780567032768 (Paperback)

For
Bishop Basil of Amphipolis

CONTENTS

PREFACE

A full treatment of Temple Themes in Christian Worship would run to many volumes, and the realities of time and publishing make that impossible. This is a sketch book, not looking at early Christian worship as a whole, but at those elements which seem to have temple roots.

These proved to be more extensive than I had realised when I embarked on the project, and so writing a short book was not easy. There were constant temptations to explore very nook and cranny and to engage with every theory; there was the frustration of being unable to cite more examples and quote more authorities. Several aspects of early Christian worship will have to wait for another book: the art and architecture, and, above all, the role of Mary.

The temple was a world of its own, with its own language, its own symbols and stories. The literalism that we consider accuracy was alien to this way of thinking and being, where talking snakes and seven horned lambs were the sophisticated symbolic theology of a non-philosophical culture. The message was communicated by sounds that were sometimes heard as one word and sometimes as another. The balance of creation was expressed in the balance of literary and poetic forms, and was influenced by human action and attitudes. Worship was part of the balancing system, and this temple worship became the worship of the Church.

I should like to thank all who make my writing possible: my family and my friends who help in so many ways. I should like to dedicate this book to a scholar and teacher from whom I have learned much.

Margaret Barker
Pentecost 2007

We have not deemed it necessary to give a tithe of the various readings, but have confined ourselves to those that seem important.

James Donaldson, Introduction to *The Apostolic Constitutions*, Ante Nicene Christian Library vol XVII, Edinburgh T & T Clark, 1870.

Chapter 1

THE TEMPLE TRADITION

Of these things we cannot now speak in detail.

Hebrews 9.5

St Basil the Great (330–379 CE) was bishop of Caesarea in Cappodocia, now central Turkey. He was a towering figure in the history of the Church, and one of the great liturgies, still used ten times a year by the Orthodox Churches, is ascribed to him. Basil, together with his brother Gregory of Nyssa and his friend from student days Gregory of Nazianzus, are known as the Cappodocian Fathers, three men who were a formative influence in developing the understanding of the Trinity. The Liturgy of St Basil used today incorporates some later material, but there is no doubt that Basil did produce the liturgy used by Christians speaking Greek, Syrian, Armenian, Ethiopian, Egyptian, Arabic, Old Slavonic, Georgian and Romanian. Since he helped to form Christian thinking about their fundamental doctrine — the Trinity — and shaped the worship of countless eastern and oriental churches, *it is very significant indeed that he claimed to know of authentic Christian traditions not recorded in the Bible.*

Basil spoke of two ways in which Christian teaching had been handed down: 'Of the dogma and kerygma which are preserved in the Church, we have some from teachings in writing, and the others we have received from the tradition of the apostles, handed down in a mystery' (*On the Holy Spirit* 66). He said that they were of equal importance, and that rejecting the unwritten customs reduced the gospel. He gave many examples: signing with the cross (at baptism), blessing the water of baptism, threefold immersion at baptism, blessing the oil for anointing, anointing itself, facing east to pray, and the words of epiclesis at the Eucharist. *All these concern worship.* He stated that 'The apostles and fathers who prescribed from the beginning the matters that concerned the Church, guarded in secret and unspoken, the

1

holy things of the mysteries.' Basil distinguished between doctrine and proclamation, between the deepest theology and what was given as public teaching, believing that one form of this silence was the obscurity of some passages of Scripture, which held the theology, but not obviously. There were meanings in Scripture apart from what was obvious. Basil gave some examples: where the proclamation and public practice was to pray facing east, the theology underlying this, but less widely known, was that Christians were looking towards their old home, Paradise, the garden in the east. He said: 'A whole day would not be long enough for me to go through all the unwritten mysteries of the Church' (*On the Holy Spirit* 67).

These 'unwritten mysteries' were both unwritten and mysteries. The word 'mysteries', in this context, meant aspects of the faith that were not fully open to human language and logic. They were beyond words, ineffable, and in this sense *could not* be adequately or completely expressed in words because they derived from, and represented something beyond, the material world in which language and logic function. The Old Testament visionaries were conscious of this when they tried to describe what they had seen, Ezekiel's account of the throne chariot being a good example. The Hebrew text is impossible to translate. Ezekiel was overwhelmed and struggled for words: 'something that looked like burning coals'; 'the likeness of a throne in appearance like sapphire'; 'the appearance of the likeness of the glory of the LORD' (Ezek. 1.13, 26, 28). John also struggled to describe the throne: 'the one who sat there appeared like jasper and carnelian, and round the throne a rainbow that looked like an emerald' (Rev. 4.3, 6). Both Ezekiel and John were describing what they saw in the holy of holies; in Ezekiel's case, the chariot throne had left the holy place, and he saw it in Babylon (Ezek. 1.3); in the Book of Revelation, John had been summoned to enter heaven, which the holy of holies represented, and he stood before the throne (Rev. 4.1–2). Peter said that Christians had had revealed to them 'the things into which angels long to look' (1 Pet. 1.12).

Jesus spoke of mysteries, and the Gospels mention teaching given in private. When he was alone with his disciples, Jesus explained the parables: 'To you has been given the secret (*musterion,* the word used by Basil) of the kingdom of God, but for those outside, everything is in parables' (Mark 4.11). Now the Kingdom of God was the holy of holies, the place of the throne, and all the early Christian beliefs and hopes about the Kingdom derived from traditional lore about the holy of holies. The Kingdom was 'in the midst' (Luke 17.21), just as the holy of holies had represented God at the heart of the visible creation. The LORD in the midst was a recurring theme in the Old Testament: 'Great in your midst is the Holy One of Israel' (Isa. 12.6; also Hos. 11.9; Joel 2.27); 'Thou O LORD art in the midst of us' (Jer. 14.9; Zeph. 3.5, 15, 17). The Kingdom was also 'at hand', because the LORD would emerge on the Day of the LORD and bring judgement: 'The Day of the LORD is near' (Isa. 13.6; Joel 1.15; Zeph. 1.7). The secret of the Kingdom — that it was already present in the midst and yet to come forth in the future — was fundamental to Christian worship, which was set in the holy of holies, in the present Kingdom that was also to come.[1]

Occasionally, the Gospels record the meaning of the parables (e.g. Matt. 13.36ff., where Jesus explained the parable of the wheat and the weeds), but, in general, there is no public record of this private teaching, the mystery. The early Church continued to restrict what was said in public discourse, as we see in the *Clementine Homilies*, writings attributed to Clement, bishop of Rome at the end of the first century CE, but probably from a later hand. They record debates between Peter and Simon Magus. Peter said to Simon at one point: 'We remember that our LORD and teacher gave us a command and said, "Keep the mysteries for me and the sons of my house."[2] That is why he explained to his disciples privately the mysteries of the kingdom of heaven. But to you who oppose us and examine nothing but our statements, to see if they be true or false, it would be impossible to state the hidden truths'(Homily 19.20).

The date of this text is uncertain, but it shows how people imagined the early years of the Church: there had been hidden truths that could not be examined by worldly methods. Clement of Alexandria, writing early in the third century, also knew this, saying: 'It is for only a few to comprehend these things. It was not out of envy that the LORD said in one of the gospels: "My mystery is for me and the sons of my house"' (*Miscellanies* 5.10).

This saying known to Peter and to Clement is not in the New Testament, and this is another sense in which the word 'unwritten' is used. Teachings of Jesus not written in the New Testament are called

---

[1] See my book *The Hidden Tradition of the Kingdom of God*, London: SPCK, 2007. In Hebrew there was wordplay: *qereb* meant 'in the midst' and *qarob* meant 'at hand, coming'.

[2] This is how the Targum and some versions of the Greek Old Testament understood Isaiah 24.16 — it was about a mystery that was revealed.

the *agrapha,* the 'unwritten' sayings. They were not necessarily an oral tradition. Several ancient texts quote teachings of Jesus not found in the New Testament. The Gospel of Thomas, rediscovered in 1945 and almost certainly an authentic early record of Jesus' teaching, includes many sayings not in the New Testament, as well as many that are. Irenaeus, at the end of the second century, knew that Jesus had taught about the great fertility of the land in the time of the Kingdom: 'Vines shall grow each having ten thousand branches, and on one branch ten thousand shoots, and on every shoot ten thousand clusters' (*Against Heresies* 5.33). Origen, a generation later, had heard the saying: 'He that is near me is near the fire. He that is far from me is far from the Kingdom', but he was not convinced that the saying was authentic (Homily 20, *On Jeremiah*). Origen also quoted sayings from gospels that are now lost, for example: 'My mother the Holy Spirit took me by one of my hairs and carried me to Mount Tabor', which he found in the Gospel of the Hebrews (Homily 15, *On Jeremiah*). The Hebrew Christians knew the Holy Spirit as Jesus' heavenly mother.

When Basil wrote of matters 'guarded in secret and unspoken, the holy things of the mysteries', there was probably something of all these in his mind: teachings that could not be put into words, teachings that had not been put into written words, teachings that were not written in the Scriptures, and teachings that were not obvious in the surface meaning of the Scriptures. His examples of practices not mentioned in the Bible suggest that these Christian worship customs derived from temple practice, but not the temple that Jesus knew. The second temple, built in the sixth century BCE when the exiles returned from Babylon, was very different from Solomon's original. Memories persisted, as we shall see, of how the new temple — deemed impure by many — had changed the rituals and lacked traditional furnishings.

Ezekiel, a priest in the first temple (Ezek. 1.3), described people facing east to pray towards the rising sun (Ezek. 8.16). He condemned them, but this sunrise prayer continued for centuries among the most conservative priestly groups, even though it was rejected by the leaders of the second temple. They had a prayer during the Feast of Tabernacles: 'Our fathers, when they were in this place turned ... and they worshipped the sun towards the east, but as for us, our eyes are turned upon the LORD' (Mishnah Sukkah 5.4). In the first century CE, Josephus said of the Essenes: 'Before the sun is up they utter no words on mundane matters, but offer to him certain prayers which have been handed down from their forefathers as though entreating him to rise' (*Jewish War* 2.128). They had strict criteria for admission, and, according to the material found in the Slavonic text of Josephus but not in the Greek, a new member swore a tremendous oath 'invoking the living God and calling to witness his almighty right hand, and the Spirit of God, the incomprehensible, and the Seraphim and Cherubim, who have insight into all, and the whole heavenly host' (*War* 2.138). The living God, his almighty right hand and the Spirit sound remarkably like the Trinity. The Essene swore that he would reveal none of their secrets, even under torture, and that he would preserve their books and the names of the angels (*War* 2.141–2). Philo, an older contemporary, described a monastic community in Egypt, the Therapeuts, who were similar if not identical: 'At sunrise they pray for a fine bright day, fine and bright in the true sense of the heavenly daylight which they pray may fill their minds' (*Contemplative Life* 27). Matthew described the wise ones who saw the king's star rising *in the east*, and came to worship (Matt. 2.2). The faithful in the Book of Revelation watched for the angel to appear *in the sunrise*, bearing the seal of the living God to mark the faithful (Rev. 7.2). They were all facing east to wait for the Messiah, the Morning Star (Rev. 22.16).

Ezekiel knew the angel with the seal. He saw a man[3] clothed in linen going through Jerusalem, marking the faithful with a cross to protect them from the imminent judgement. He put on their foreheads the letter *tau*, which in the time of Ezekiel was a diagonal cross (Ezek. 9.4; the English versions say 'mark' but it is *tau*). They had been marked with the sign of the Name of the LORD, just as the faithful in the Book of Revelation were marked with the seal on their foreheads to protect them from the judgement (Rev. 7.3). They wore the Name (Rev. 14.1). Basil gave signing with the cross as an example of an 'unwritten' custom. His other examples, as we shall see, also had roots in the *first* temple. This will be important for tracing the temple themes in Christian worship. *They were from the earlier temple.*

It is also possible that the practices themselves were preserved without always keeping their original meaning. A ritual or symbol was re-explained, perhaps when the Church was losing touch with its Hebrew roots. Basil's explanation of facing east towards the lost Eden was, as we have seen, different from the original temple reason for facing east. It was a perfectly reasonable explanation, but not the

---

[3] In temple discourse, a 'man' means an angel, and humans are represented by an animal.

original.[4] The Church continued to have allusions to the sunrise, but they had lost their context: the star in the east; the 'dawn from on high' as a title for the Messiah (Luke 1.78), the angel appearing in the sunrise with the seal of the living God. The originally diagonal cross of the *tau* sign became the upright cross of the crucifixion, and 'the Name' of the LORD on the forehead became a problem. Again, the new explanation was perfectly reasonable, but not the original one.

Basil compared these mysteries to the rituals and divisions in the temple. Moses decreed that ordinary people should not enter the temple itself: only the Levites could enter, and only the high priest, once a year, could enter the holy of holies to see the mysteries. Restricted access to the holy places symbolized limited access to the teaching and understanding represented by them, and appears in the original biblical laws for the priesthood: 'The LORD said to Aaron, "You and your sons with you shall attend to your priesthood for all that concerns the altar and that is within the veil; and you shall serve"' (Num. 18.7). Anyone else who came near would die. The Greek Old Testament, but not the Hebrew, has this commandment also at Numbers 3.10. The mysteries of the holy of holies were entrusted only to the high priests, and Basil implied that something similar was true in the Church. There were sources, which he described as 'unwritten traditions', 'the unwritten witness of the fathers', 'the unwritten teachings', 'the unwritten customs', 'the unwritten mysteries', and 'the unwritten doxologies', which he said were universally accepted. *All concerned liturgy and worship,* and he argued from this to justify his theology of the Holy Spirit: there were rites and practices that implied a certain theology. This was temple theology.

Basil knew the works of Origen, a native of Alexandria who had worked in Palestine early in the third century, one hundred years before the time of Basil. It is likely that when Basil was thinking about the unwritten traditions, he had in mind Origen's *Homilies on Numbers,* which are said to be the key to his spirituality. Origen compared the temple vessels to knowledge — presumably they represented this knowledge in some way — and said that the knowledge had to be kept veiled, just as the temple treasures had been kept from public view: 'If one is a priest to whom the sacred vessels, that is, the secrets

---

[4] For detail of facing east to pray, and its place in current church debate about liturgy, see U. W. Lang, *Turning Towards the Lord. Orientation in Liturgical Prayer,* San Francisco: Ignatius Press, 2004.

of mysterious Wisdom have been entrusted, he must keep them veiled and not produce them easily for the people' (Origen, Homily 4, *On Numbers*). He found this teaching implicit in the instructions for transporting the tabernacle in the desert (Num. 4.1–15). The tabernacle was the Church of the living God, and seven objects had to be kept from sight: the ark, the table, the lamp stand, the golden altar, the temple vessels, the covering of the altar and the bronze sea. Only the sons of Aaron saw these holy things, and they had to wrap them before allowing the sons of Kohath to carry them. The ark and the table were wrapped in three coverings, the other vessels in two. Thus most of the custodians of the tabernacle, (and so also of the temple) did not see what it represented, but carried the veiled teaching on their shoulders.

When Philo described the Essenes in Palestine — the group who prayed towards the rising sun and swore a 'Trinitarian' oath — he said they abandoned as unnecessary to the acquisition of virtue the logical aspects of philosophy (in this context we should understand 'theology') and left it to people who liked playing with words (literally hunting for words). They concentrated instead on 'that part which treats philosophically of the existence of God and the creation of the universe' (Philo, *Every Good Man is Free*, 80). On the Sabbaths they met in their synagogues to hear readings from Scripture and then an exposition in secret codes or allegory 'in the ancient manner' (*Every Good Man*, 82). The Damascus Document found at Qumran says that the leader of that community (the $m^c baqqer$, bishop/guardian) had to 'recount before them the things of eternity, and their interpretation' (CD XIII). 'Eternity' here is *'olam'*, literally the hidden place, and so the 'bishop' was probably expounding the lore of the holy of holies. In the mid fourth century, teaching attributed to Cyril of Jerusalem observed the same distinction: when the bishop instructed the catechumens, baptism, anointing and the Eucharist were not expounded until after their baptism, after they had become part of the community.[5] These are what Cyril's contemporary Basil called the 'mysteries': the things handed down unwritten.

Philo also described a group in north Egypt, the Therapeuts, who were very like the Essenes. They prayed towards the sunrise and read the Scriptures as a secret code, in the manner of their ancestors: 'They think that the words of the literal text are symbols of something

---

[5] The *Mystagogical Lectures*, usually published as the last five of the *Catecheses* of Cyril of Jerusalem, but thought by some to be the work of his successor, John.

whose hidden nature is revealed by studying the underlying meaning'
(*On the Contemplative Life* 28). The founders of their community, he
said, had left writings that treated Scripture as a code to be interpreted, and they followed that pattern. Nothing is known of the
fate of the Therapeuts. Eusebius said they were a Christian monastic
community, and wondered whether Philo had invented the name
for them, as 'Christian' was not then in general use. Whether or not
Eusebius was correct to identify them as Christian, it is significant
that a learned bishop, writing in Palestine early in the fourth century
CE — a generation before Basil — identified this way of reading the
Scriptures as characteristic of the Christians.

What Philo says of the Therapeuts' worship is like the worship of
the saints in the Book of Revelation. He described their chief feast,
Pentecost, when the whole community of men and women assembled
in white robes (*Contemplative Life* 65–6). They shared a meal of bread
and water, abstaining from wine as did the priests when they entered
the tent of meeting or the inner court of the temple (Lev. 10.9; Ezek.
44.21), but the Therapeuts observed this priestly discipline for their
whole life (*Contemplative Life* 74). Before the meal, their president
expounded the Scriptures, looking for the inner meaning, 'bringing
to light the veiled and enfolded secret symbols ... so that they could
discern the invisible in the visible' (*Contemplative Life* 78). This was two
centuries before Origen wrote about the secrets that were concealed
when the temple furnishings were wrapped. After the evening meal,
they held a sacred vigil and sang hymns until dawn, when they turned
towards the east and prayed. When the Book of Revelation described
an elder interpreting a vision (Rev. 5.5; 7.14) this too was followed by
a hymn, and the saints were clothed in white. The Book of Revelation
described the kingdom of priests, the original Church.

Origen, who came from Alexandria, adopted the lifestyle of the
Therapeuts (Eusebius, *Church History* 6.3). He abandoned the study
of literature and gave away his precious library, in order to live a life of
self-denial and study of the Scriptures. The books of the Therapeuts
are lost, but much of Origen's vast output has survived and, with it, a
glimpse of how he understood the Old Testament. It could be read on
several levels, he taught, corresponding to body, mind and spirit, and
it was the spiritual that dealt with the unspeakable mysteries (*On First
Principles* 4.2.7). In this respect he followed Philo who had worked
in Alexandria in the middle of the first century CE, and Eusebius
says that Origen had also been a pupil of Clement (Eusebius *Church
History* 6.6). He went to live in Palestine in 230 CE, and established

himself in Caesarea, where he would have come across Jewish beliefs very similar to his own about interpreting Scripture.

There is a story told about two rabbis in Palestine at that time: Rabbi Simeon ben Jehozadak asked Rabbi Samuel ben Nahman to explain Genesis 1.3: 'Let there be light.' Rabbi Samuel spoke in a whisper about the Holy One wrapping himself in light, but Rabbi Simeon observed: 'There is a verse which says that openly: "Who coverest thyself with light as with a garment" (Ps. 104.2), so why speak in a whisper?' Rabbi Samuel replied: 'I heard it in a whisper, so I have told it to you in a whisper.' Rabbi Berekiah then explained: 'If Rabbi Isaac had not taught this openly, could we have spoken of it?' What Rabbi Isaac had taught must once have been secret lore, and it concerned the origin of light in the temple: 'The light was created from the place of the temple, as it is said: "And behold the Glory of the God of Israel came from the east"' (Ezek. 43.2, in Genesis Rabbah III.4). In other words, temple tradition about the light from the east was being discussed by Jewish scholars in Palestine early in the third century CE.

Another contemporary who studied at Sepphoris in Palestine before returning to Babylon was Abba Arika, usually known as Rab, meaning 'great' because of his great learning. He founded the academy at Sura where the Talmud was developed, and he died in 247 CE. Rab was much concerned with mystical lore — the account of the creation, the throne chariot that Ezekiel saw (Ezekiel 1), and the mystery of the Divine Name. He taught that the world was created by ten things: by wisdom, understanding, reason, strength, rebuke, might, righteousness, judgement, loving kindness and compassion (Babylonian Talmud Hagigah 12a). These are very similar to the ten *sefiroh*, the powers that are central to Kabbalah, a temple-based tradition about the creation that emerges in written form many centuries later. The powers were located around the great Sefirotic Tree, at the tips of its branches and at their intersections, and the tree was a stylized form of the menorah, the seven-branched temple lamp. Nobody can know the age of the oral tradition that was eventually committed to writing, but it is entirely possible that this temple tradition goes back to the time of the temple.

Rab also taught about the 42 letters of the Divine Name, and who could be entrusted with this knowledge (Babylonian Talmud Kiddushin 71a). The letters of the Name were the powers that created the universe, as can be seen in 3 Enoch, a collection of temple mysteries compiled by later Jewish scholars in Babylon. Enoch/

Metatron, the great angel who was also the high priest, wore the letters on his crown: '... the letters by which heaven and earth were created, the letters by which seas and rivers were created, the letters by which mountains and hills were created, the letters by which stars and constellations, lightning and wind, thunder and thunderclaps, snow and hail, hurricane and tempest were created; the letters by which all the necessities of the world and all the orders of creation were created' (3 Enoch 13.1). These letters were later to appear in the consecration ceremony for a church. The Greek and Roman alphabets were written by the bishop diagonally across the floor of the new nave. This custom was known in the time of Pope Gregory I, who died in 604 CE, and is now said to represent the teaching given to the newly baptized. Its origin, however, lay in the belief that the great hall of the temple (corresponding to the nave of a church) represented the visible creation that was created by the letters of the Name and 'sealed with thy terrible and glorious Name'; that is, sealed with a diagonal cross (Prayer of Manasseh 3). Justin, in the mid second century knew that the bonds of creation had been sealed with a cross, the sign of the Name (*Apology* 1.60), but he linked this to Plato's *Timaeus*. Temple lore was in the Church from the beginning, but time and again, its forms acquired new meanings as the Church grew away from its Hebrew roots.

It is interesting that the Hebrew Scriptures give no explanation of the furnishings required for the tabernacle. They represented, in some way, what Moses had seen in his vision on Sinai (Exod. 25.9, 40), but he was not simply copying a heavenly archetype. Although there is some evidence for Moses having seen a heavenly temple, the dominant tradition is that he saw the six days of creation during his six days on Sinai (Exod. 24.15–16), and so the tabernacle furnishings in some way represented this. Why, then, did the lamp have to have seven branches and be made like an almond tree (Exod. 26.1–39)? Could it be that the Kabbalah has preserved the original significance of the temple lamp and the pattern of creation? Why were there two cherubim on something we cannot identify that was described simply as the *kapporet*, the atoning place where the LORD spoke to Moses (Exod. 25.17–22)? Why was the veil of the temple made of four prescribed colours — red, blue, purple and white linen — and of a particular type of fabric — skilled work, *hošeb*, (Exod. 26.31)? Why did the high priest, and nobody else, wear a vestment made of exactly the same fabric (Exod. 28.5–6)? 'Because the LORD commanded it' would have been the public explanation, but there are hints outside the Bible that there were reasons for all these specifications.

A detailed explanation of temple symbolism does not appear until Josephus, at the end of the second temple period. He was from a high priestly family, and so knew the 'inner' teachings. The crucial question is whether the earlier silence was because the high priests protected the knowledge, as commanded, or because there was no secret meaning and Josephus made it up. Since Josephus was a traitor to his people and worked for the Romans, it is not impossible that he betrayed their secrets also. It is likely that Josephus was the false prophet mentioned in Revelation 16.13, who worked for the dragon and the beast when armies were attacking Jerusalem. He did claim to be a new Jeremiah called by God to tell his people that the Romans were divinely appointed agents of the wrath of God. 'A priest himself and of priestly descent, he was not ignorant of the prophecies in the sacred books', and he interpreted them as favourable to the Romans (*War* 3.351–54). He saw the Christians as false prophets, possibly even John himself: they read the prophecies, but read them wrongly (*War* 6.312–13).[6] Josephus, for all his treachery, may have done us a service, in showing us what the temple furnishings meant.

The shape of the temple was the shape of the early Christian world view. In his six days on Sinai (Exod. 24.16), Moses has a vision of the creation which became the six days of Genesis 1.[7] He was told to replicate this as the tabernacle (Exod. 25.9, 40). Day One was the state of unity underlying and sustaining the whole creation, represented by the angels and the throne of God, and in the tabernacle/temple it was the holy of holies. The second day was the firmament separating what is above from what is below (Gen. 1.6), represented by the veil that separated the holy of holies from the hall of the tabernacle/temple. On the third day the plants were created, represented by the table with offerings of cereal, wine and incense. On the fourth day, the lights of heaven were created, represented by the seven-branched lamp. Thus far the ancient pattern is clear in the Old Testament texts: when Moses assembled the tabernacle, he did so in stages corresponding to the days of creation (Genesis 1 cf. Exod. 40.16–25). After the fourth day the pattern is disrupted due to problems in the Greek and Hebrew texts at this point, but later Jewish and Christian

---

[6] See my book *The Revelation of Jesus Christ*, London: T&T Clark, 2000, pp. 237–9.

[7] For detail see my book *The Great High Priest*, London: T&T Clark, 2003, pp. 152–9.

tradition remembered the sequence. When God created the human on the sixth day, he created the high priest for his temple, the one who had access to the presence of God at the heart of creation.

Christians were the new royal high priesthood, said Origen, and thus worthy to see the Word of God and the mysteries of Wisdom, in other words, to understand the temple (Homily 5, *On Numbers*). The tent of witness was the company of saints; the apostles were the lamp; the holy table was those who distribute; the ark, which held the tablets of the Law and the insignia of high priesthood (Heb. 9.4), was those to whom the mysteries were entrusted; the cherubim over the ark were those with the greatest knowledge. Long before Basil, Origen knew there were some Christian customs observed without everyone knowing why: 'It is the same among the observances of the Church, where there are things that everyone does, without everyone knowing the reason. Bending the knee, facing east, the ritual of the Eucharist, the rites and ceremonies of baptism, the questions and answers at baptism … [all done] according to the way in which they have been revealed and entrusted to us by the great high priest and his sons' (Homily 5.1). Like Basil, Origen knew the distinction between teaching given publicly and other doctrines: 'The holy apostles, when preaching the faith of Christ, took certain doctrines, those they believed to be the necessary ones, and gave them in plain language to believers, even to those who appeared to be rather dull in their investigation of divine knowledge … but there were other doctrines about which the apostles simply said that they were so, and kept silence as to how or why' (Preface to *On First Principles*). Origen also saw the unwritten teaching of Jesus as part of the unwritten tradition of prophecy, symbolized by eating a scroll: 'The Jews used to tell of many things in accordance with secret tradition reserved to a few, for they had other knowledge than that which was common and made public' (*Commentary on John* 19.92); 'Our prophets did know of greater things than any in the Scriptures, which they did not commit to writing. Ezekiel, for example, received a scroll written within and without … but at the command of the Word he swallowed the book so that its contents might not be written and so made known to unworthy persons' (*Against Celsus* 6.6).

When the mighty angel, wreathed in a rainbow and wrapped in a cloud, appeared to John, he gave him a scroll to eat (Rev. 10.1–11). This must have been secret teaching, and the command to 'write what you see' (Rev. 1.11, 19) could imply that such visions were not normally recorded. John was seeing the secrets of the holy of holies.

The whole vision was set in the heavenly temple, with angels and incense, the ark and the golden altar. John began in the outer part of the temple and then was summoned to enter and stand before the throne (Rev. 4.1–2). There, everything was revealed to him, as it had been to the ancient prophets: 'I will take my stand to watch, and station myself on the tower,[8] and look forth to see what he will say to me and what I will answer concerning my complaint. And the LORD answered me: "Write the vision, make it plain upon tablets"' (Hab. 2.1–2). The Christians remembered John as a prophet and as a high priest (Eusebius, *Church History* 3.31).

Origen was much influenced by a man he called simply 'the Hebrew', a Jewish scholar who had become a Christian and fled his native land for Alexandria. Together with the Therapeuts, 'the Hebrew' is an obvious source of what he knew about unwritten traditions and the inner meaning of the Hebrew Scriptures. In the time of Jesus, the true meaning of Scripture had been contested. Among the Dead Sea Scrolls were pieces from a commentary on Habakkuk, describing a Teacher of Righteousness to whom 'God made known all the mysteries of the words of his servants the prophets' (1QpHab VII). The implication is that there were other teachers who did not understand the mysteries in Scripture. A secret book, the Apocryphon of James, was attributed to James, another high priest of the Jerusalem church. Dated to the early second century CE, it has the form of a letter to someone who had asked about the secret teaching: 'You asked me to send you the secret teaching that was revealed to me and Peter by the LORD ... Be careful and do not repeat to many this writing which the Saviour did not wish to divulge even to all the twelve disciples.' The text may not be genuine, but forgeries imitate, and so it must have represented something known in the early Church.

Christian teaching came from the great high priest and his 'sons' that is, his successors: 'My mystery is for me and the sons of my house.' While the Christians were claiming to have the true temple tradition, the Jews were basing their claims on the transmission of the Law of Moses: 'Moses received the Law from Sinai, and committed it to Joshua, and Joshua to the elders, and the elders to the prophets and the prophets committed it to the men of the Great Synagogue. They said three things: be deliberate in judgement, raise up many disciples, and make a fence around the Law' (Mishnah Pirke Aboth 1.1, compiled about 200 CE). The men of the Great Synagogue were

---

[8] A traditional description of the holy of holies.

defined as 'a body of 120 elders, including many prophets, who came up from exile with Ezra; they saw that prophecy had come to an end, and that restraint was lacking. Therefore they made many new rules and restrictions for the better observance of the Law'.[9] In the period when Jews and Christians were each establishing their distinctive identity, the Jews emphasized a tradition that had no place for the temple and priesthood, whereas the Christians claimed consistently that their beliefs had been taught by the Great High Priest and his heirs.

Irenaeus (died 202 CE), writing some fifty years before Origen, and on the other side of the Mediterranean world, also used temple imagery not obviously in the New Testament. He wrote a handbook of fundamental Christian teaching, *The Proof of the Apostolic Preaching*, which was lost for centuries and then rediscovered in 1904 in an Armenian translation. He saw himself as the guardian of true teaching, and wrote a huge five-volume work *Against Heresies*. It is interesting to see what he regarded as the fundamentals. Early in his list was a description of the seven heavens, which he related to the sevenfold Spirit prophesied by Isaiah (Isa. 11.2): 'As the pattern of this, Moses received the seven branched lamp [the menorah] that shines continually in the holy place.' The highest heaven was Wisdom and encompassed all the rest; then there were the heavens of understanding, counsel, might, knowledge, godliness. 'The seventh, this firmament of ours, is full of the fear of that Spirit that gives light to the heavens' (*Proof* 9). These seven for which the menorah was the pattern are remarkably similar to Rab's account of the ten powers of creation and thus of the later sefirot: wisdom, understanding, reason, strength, rebuke, might, righteousness, judgement, loving kindness and compassion. It is not immediately obvious why the menorah should be linked with the powers and process of creation, and so this cannot be coincidence. Now Irenaeus had an impeccable pedigree: he had been a disciple of Polycarp in Asia Minor, and from him had learned the teachings of John, the writer of the Book of Revelation. Where had this guardian of the truth acquired all his knowledge about the menorah, the seven heavens and temple symbolism?

Irenaeus' contemporary, Clement of Alexandria, was another great teacher who knew and used temple symbolism in his exposition of

---

[9] Quoted in H. Danby, *The Mishnah*, Oxford: Oxford University Press (1933) 1989 p. 446n.

Christianity. He gave a detailed account of the meaning of temple furnishings (*Miscellanies* 5). In refuting heretics, he declared that they had no knowledge of the truth: 'They do not enter in as we enter in, through the tradition of the LORD, by drawing aside the curtain' (*Miscellanies* 7.17). Knowledge learned 'beyond the curtain' must have been knowledge from the holy of holies, the knowledge reserved for the high priests. This knowledge concerned the vision of God, and had been transmitted by a few 'having been imparted unwritten by the apostles' (*Miscellanies* 6.7). The high priestly knowledge was unwritten, and Clement's friends insisted that he commit to writing the oral traditions he had learned from the earliest authorities of the Church (Eusebius, *Church History* 6.13).[10]

Earlier still, at the beginning of the second century CE, when the leaders of the Church could have known eyewitnesses of Jesus' ministry, there were similar hints that temple tradition had played a major part in transmitting Christianity. Ignatius, bishop of Antioch in the earliest years of the second century CE, died as a martyr in Rome. Nothing else is known of him, except that he wrote to several churches as he travelled to Rome. His main concern was the unity of the churches, each with its own bishop, but among the images and phrases he used, the temple appears. Some people had told him that they would not believe anything that was not found in the ancient Scripture. He replied that these things — he did not reveal what they were — were indeed in the Scriptures. For him, the true record was the death and resurrection of Jesus and the faith that came through him. Then he implied that he knew teaching not in the ancient Scriptures: 'The priests of old, I admit, were, estimable men, but our own high priest is greater, for he has been entrusted with the Holy of Holies, and to him alone are the secret things of God committed' (Letter to the Philadelphians 9). Jesus had taught the secret knowledge of the holy of holies, the secrets of the Kingdom.

Elsewhere Ignatius implied that he too had the temple knowledge, although he emphasized that it was not the knowledge that made him a disciple. He knew 'celestial secrets and angelic hierarchies, and the dispositions of the heavenly powers, and much else both seen and unseen' (Letter to the Trallians 5). The holy of holies, as we shall see, was the world of the angels,[11] and so these celestial secrets could have

---

[10] According to 1 Enoch 69.9, it was the evil angels who taught people to write, which led to many errors.

[11] See below pp. 89ff; 123ff.

been the knowledge imparted by the Great High Priest. He told the church at Ephesus that they were 'initiates of the same mysteries as Paul' (Letter to the Ephesians 12), and one wonders what was in his mind when, earlier in the same letter, he wrote this: 'You are pilgrims in the same great procession, bearing your God and your shrine and your Christ and your sacred treasures on your shoulders, every one of you arrayed in the festal garments of the commandments of Jesus Christ' (Letter to the Ephesians 9). Was he just thinking of the great processions in Ephesus, or was he also remembering the words of Psalm 68: 'Thy solemn processions are seen, O God, the processions of my God, my King, into the sanctuary'? (Ps. 68.24). One hundred years later, Origen would use exactly the same image of carrying the sacred treasure to describe preserving the true teaching that the temple treasure represented, and this was the context of Ignatius' words here. There had been pernicious teachers from elsewhere, but the faithful Ephesians had been deaf to their message and had proved themselves true stones for the Father's temple, carrying their sacred treasures (Letter to the Ephesians 9).

Clement, bishop of Rome a few years before the death of Ignatius (about 88–97 CE), had to write to the turbulent church in Corinth. He had studied the Scriptures, and it was clear, he said, that the LORD had set down clear regulations for orderly worship: the high priest, the priesthood, the Levites and the laity all have their roles assigned: 'And in the same way, when we offer our own Eucharist to God, each one of us should keep to his own degree' (1 Clem. 40–41). Christian worship was modelled on temple worship.

The Letter of Barnabas, attributed to the Barnabas who was sent to calm the troubles in Antioch (Acts 11.22) and who later accompanied Paul on the first missionary journey (Acts 13.2), recognized that temple themes were central to Christianity, but not the literal building of a temple. The temple in Jerusalem had been destroyed, he wrote, and some were foolishly trying to rebuild it, not knowing the nature of the true temple that the LORD would build in the last days: 'His own very presence, inwardly inspiring us and dwelling within us ... It is in these ways that he admits us, the bondsmen of mortality, into the temple that is immortal' (Barn. 16). These must have been the living stones of the spiritual temple (1 Pet. 2.5). The rest of his letter dealt with many temple themes, showing how they were adapted and transformed in Christian practice: purification, fasting, Sabbath observance, and above all, sacrifice. He prayed: 'May the God and LORD of all the world grant you wisdom, understanding and knowledge, together with true comprehensions of his ordinances, and the gift of perseverance' (Barn. 21).

His prayer for 'wisdom, knowledge and understanding' has echoes in another almost contemporary text, one that deals with secret teaching. The book, known variously as 4 Ezra and 2 Esdras, is a much reworked Jewish text that originated after the destruction of Jerusalem in 70 CE, but, as was the fashion of the times, was set in the years immediately after the destruction of the first temple. The main character is the biblical Ezra, one of whose tasks was to restore the holy writings lost in the disaster. The LORD spoke to Ezra from a bush, and recalled how he had given Moses certain teachings, some to reveal and some to keep secret: 'These words you shall publish openly, and these you shall keep secret' (2 Esdras 14.6). At the end of the first century CE, then, people knew there was more to the teaching of Moses than what was in Hebrew Scriptures. Ezra was told to take five scribes and wait in a field for the LORD to reveal all the holy books. These he dictated to his scribes for forty days. At the end of that time they had written ninety-four books, and Ezra was told: 'Make public the twenty four books you write first, and let the worthy and the unworthy read them; but keep the seventy that were written last in order to give them to the wise among your people. For in them is the spring of understanding, the fountain of wisdom and the river of knowledge' (2 Esdras 14. 45–47). Wisdom, understanding and knowledge — exactly what Barnabas had prayed for his people. The earliest eucharistic prayers outside the New Testament are similar: 'Over the particles of bread, say "We give thanks to thee, our Father, for the life and knowledge thou hast made known to us through thy servant Jesus"' (Didache 9). 'When all have partaken sufficiently, give thanks in these words, "Thanks be to thee holy Father, for thy sacred Name which thou hast caused to dwell in our hearts, and for the knowledge and faith and everlasting life which thou hast revealed to us through thy servant Jesus"' (Didache 10).

Since Ignatius, Clement, Barnabas and the Didache have taken us almost back to the New Testament writers, the secret teaching associated with the temple may account for some enigmatic words in Hebrews. After a list of the temple furnishings — the curtain, the altar, the ark, the urn of manna, Aaron's rod, the tablets of the Law and the mercy seat — we find: 'Of these things we cannot now speak in detail' (Heb. 9.5). What detail? The passage goes on to explain the meaning of the inner and outer tents (Heb. 9.8). Might there have been similar meanings for the temple furnishings, which could not be revealed, just as Origen and Basil would teach several centuries later?

There is little doubt that there was a tradition of temple teaching known only to a few. It is not clear whether it was unwritten in the sense that it was oral tradition, or in the sense that it was not in the public scriptures. It may have been both — texts and interpretation not openly read and taught. The hidden tradition concerned the mysteries, and among these Basil included baptism, anointing and the Eucharist, practices at the very heart of Christian worship. There were certain passages even in the Hebrew Scriptures that were forbidden as public readings for Jews (Mishnah Megillah 4.10, compiled about 200 CE), and among them were two of special interest for Christian origins: one was the chapter of the chariot, the description of the throne of God in Ezekiel 1; another was the blessing given by the high priests, which could be read out but not interpreted:[12] 'the LORD make his face to shine upon you' (Num. 6.24–26).

The picture of Christian worship that closes the Book of Revelation is based on these two forbidden passages (Rev. 22.3–5). All the servants of the LORD stand before the throne, which John has described in great detail, and they see the face of the LORD. The LORD God is their light, and they reign for ever and ever. In other words, these are the ones who see the throne, and on whom the light of the LORD's face shines. Early Judaism banned these topics from public discourse. Why?

---

[12] Another version of the text says that the blessing could be neither read out nor interpreted.

Chapter 2

TEMPLE AND SYNAGOGUE

They will put you out of the synagogues.

John 16.2

The origin of Christian worship is usually located in the synagogues rather than the temple. Statements such as: 'The temple worship left little mark on Christian worship'[1] or 'For the purposes of this study [on the origins of Christian worship] we shall omit consideration of the Temple'[2] are all too easy to find. Several reasons are given for looking elsewhere than the temple: the Jews who lived outside Palestine had never seen the worship of the temple, and even in Palestine, the real centre of Jewish worship was the synagogue; Gentile converts to Christianity would have had no link to the temple at all; or 'There is very little literary evidence which provides reliable details of the [temple] cult at this period.'[3] The earliest known complete Jewish prayer book, however, was compiled about 875 CE by Rabbi Amran Gaon, and so any reconstruction of synagogue worship, like any reconstruction of temple worship, has to rely on fragments, either embedded in other texts or surviving independently. When there is so little hard evidence, imagination and guesswork play a large part in any reconstruction, whether of temple or synagogue, and scholars often suggest that forms used in later synagogue worship derived from the temple. Thus, in the confession found in Amran's prayer book, 'one sees at once that it goes, in part, back to the time

---

[1] W. D. Maxwell, *An Outline of Christian Worship. Its Development and Forms,* Oxford: Oxford University Press, 1936, p. 2.

[2] P. F. Bradshaw, *The Search for the Origins of Christian Worship,* London: SPCK, 1992, p. 15.

[3] Ibid., p. 15.

19

of the temple service; for example, "And for the sins for which we owe an offering, varying according to our means ..."[4]

Any investigation of the origin of Christian worship must take into account the fact that Jesus was proclaimed as the Great High Priest (e.g. Heb. 4.14), and the high priest did not function in a synagogue; that the central message of Christianity was the atonement, a ritual at the heart of temple worship; that the hope for the Messiah was grounded in the royal high priesthood of the original temple; and that the Christians thought of themselves as a kingdom of priests (1 Pet. 2.9). The great high priest and his royal priests would have been out of place in a synagogue, and a large number of priests joined the church in Jerusalem (Acts 6.7). The disciples in Jerusalem attended the temple 'day by day' (Acts 2.46), they were 'continually in the temple blessing God' (Luke 24.53). The earliest picture of Christian worship is found in the Book of Revelation, set in the temple. This is how the first Christians imagined their worship; they joined, as we do today, with the angels and archangels. The great throne scenes of the Book of Revelation are often assumed to be modelled on the Roman imperial cult, without considering how a Christian from Palestine might have witnessed such rituals.

Early Christian worship, as described in the New Testament, was 'attending the temple together day by day', and 'the apostles' teaching and fellowship, the breaking of bread and the prayers' (Acts 2.42). They fasted on Wednesdays and Fridays, to distinguish themselves from Jews who fasted on Mondays and Thursdays (Didache 8). They prayed at the times of temple prayer: at the third, sixth and ninth hour (Acts 2.15; 10.9; 3.1), examples cited by Tertullian to explain why Christians prayed at those times (*On Fasting* 10). The Didache emphasized that the prayers, though said three times a day, should be different from the Jewish prayer; Christians should say the LORD's Prayer (Didache 8). R. Gamaliel, who lived at the end of the first century CE, taught that Jews should say the Eighteen Benedictions three times a day, but R. Akiba, a generation later, said that a shorter version was permitted (Mishnah Berakoth 4.1, 3). The LORD's Prayer does resemble a short version of the Eighteen Benedictions: blessing the LORD, the God of their fathers, declaring that his Name is holy (corresponding to 'Our Father in heaven, Hallowed be thy Name'), and then a series of petitions for knowledge of the Law and resto-

---

[4] W. O. E. Oesterley, *The Jewish Background of the Christian Liturgy*, Oxford: Oxford University Press, 1925, reprinted Gloucester, Mass.; Peter Smith, 1965, p. 79.

ration of the Kingdom ('Thy Kingdom come'), for forgiveness ('Forgive us our trespasses'), for healing and redemption, and for good crops ('Give us this day our daily bread'). The LORD's Prayer is essentially a Jewish prayer that was modified for Christian use, and Jesus' command to be brief in prayer (Matt. 6.7), followed by teaching the LORD's Prayer, could indicate that he was giving the short form his disciples were to use.

The early Church also had public reading of Scripture, preaching and teaching (1 Tim. 4.13). Since the canon of the Hebrew Scriptures was not determined until the end of the first century CE, we cannot be certain what the first Christians considered as Scripture. Jude, after all, quoted Enoch as a prophet, and was not referring to the Enoch verses in Genesis (Jude 14 cf. Gen. 5.21–24). He was paraphrasing the opening chapter of 1 Enoch, the LORD coming with his angels to bring the judgement. This, as we shall see, became an important hope in the early Church that was preserved in the liturgy. 1 Enoch was found among the Dead Sea Scrolls and was used by other early Christian writers, but is not in the Bible today. Paul's letters were read out (Col. 4.16; 1 Thess. 5.27). The church at Corinth assembled for a hymn, a lesson, a revelation, a tongue or an interpretation (1 Cor. 14.26). Paul preached long sermons and sent people to sleep (Acts 20.7–9). They had collections, and sent the money to other churches or to support mission (Rom. 15.26; 1 Cor. 16.2; 2 Cor. 9.9–15). All this is very familiar, as is the distinction between dress for men and dress for women. Men prayed and prophesied with their heads uncovered, while women prayed or prophesied with their heads covered, exactly the opposite of synagogue practice today (1 Cor. 11.4–5).

The reason for women covering their heads, however, is less familiar. It was 'because of the angels' (1 Cor. 11.10). The early Christians lived in a world full of angels, and knew the story of the fallen angels in 1 Enoch who looked down from heaven and were tempted by the beautiful women. Looking down from above, they must have seen their hair, and this was the first temptation (1 Enoch 6.2). The angels came to earth to take human wives, and brought with them the knowledge that corrupted the earth. So women had to cover their heads in future, to avoid any further problems.

The early Christians assembled to break bread. This could have been just a shared meal, but Paul seems to discourage this. When they assembled for a meal, he wrote, eat at home first, and then go to eat the bread and drink the wine (1 Cor. 11.23–31). The 'LORD's Supper', as he called it, had to be different (1 Cor. 11.20–22). He compared the wine and the bread to the sacrifices of Israel: 'Are not those who eat the sacrifices partners in the altar?' This is not the language of the synagogue, where there were no sacrifices. The only place of sacrifice was the temple. Even if they were not in the temple, they were thinking 'temple' as they met together. Jesus established the meal as a covenant ritual sealed with his blood, according to Paul, who had received this teaching from the LORD (1 Cor. 11.23–25). 'Blood' implies a temple setting.

The Gospel accounts are similar (Mark 14.24, Matt. 26.28), but the earliest texts of Luke's Gospel did not mention a covenant cup that was the blood of Jesus. At the Last Supper, Jesus took bread and simply said 'This is my body' (Luke 22.19a).[5] There was the earlier cup, over which Jesus had said, 'I shall not drink of the fruit of the vine until the kingdom of God comes' (Luke 22.18), but there was no reference in the earlier texts to blood and covenant. Luke's Last Supper did not have this temple imagery. The verses that make Luke's text similar to Matthew's and Mark's must have been added later to harmonize the accounts; one could understand the need for that, whereas there could have been no reason to remove the verses about the covenant blood.[6] Luke's temple imagery was carried by the bread alone, which in temple tradition was associated with Wisdom, the mother of the Messiah.[7] This is consistent with other characteristics of his Gospel: his concern for the women of the gospel story, and his account of the Nativity which probably came from Mary.

So what was the Last Supper? Paul used Passover imagery: 'For Christ, our paschal lamb, has been sacrificed' (1 Cor. 5.7); and John agreed with this: Jesus died when the Passover lambs were sacrificed in the temple (John 19.31, 36). The Synoptic Gospels set the events one day earlier, and so the Last Supper, not the crucifixion, was on the first day of Passover, when they should have eaten unleavened bread, *azumos* (Matt. 26.17; Mark 14.12; Luke 22.7). During the supper, however, unleavened bread is not mentioned: Jesus takes a loaf, *artos*, and breaks it. This is strange if the Last Supper was a Passover meal. There are other Passover and Exodus images too: Hebrews drew the parallel between the rebellious Israelites in the desert who did not live

---

[5] Thus the text of the Greek and Latin Codex Bezae, the Western text.

[6] B. D. Ehrman *The Orthodox Corruption of Scripture. The Effect of Early Christological Controversies on the Text of the New Testament*, Oxford: Oxford University Press, 1993, pp. 197–209.

[7] See below, Chapter 8.

to see the Promised Land, and those, presumably in the Church, who were in similar danger (Heb. 3.16–19). Jesus described himself as the true bread from heaven that would give life, reminding the Jews that their ancestors had eaten manna in the desert, but had died (John 6.48–50). Paul compared crossing the Red Sea to being baptized into Moses (1 Cor. 10.1–5). The Passover and Exodus were given as two examples among many of the faith of their forefathers (Heb. 11.28–9). Jerusalem was allegorically called 'Sodom' and 'Egypt' (Rev. 11.8), presumably because the Christians had escaped. Given the central importance of Jesus' death at the time of the Passover, there is surprisingly little built on this in the New Testament.

Few scholars now accept that the Last Supper was just a Passover meal. In fact, the New Testament source texts are very difficult to evaluate: there has been alteration and harmonization, and it is no longer easy to see a direct line between the Last Supper and what the Eucharist came to be. Early texts outside the New Testament make no link between the Eucharist and the Last Supper, as we shall see. Was the Last Supper, perhaps, one of Jesus' fellowship meals with his friends, special because it was on the evening before he died? Was it, perhaps, his anticipation of the messianic banquet, the great feast in Jerusalem when death would be swallowed up, tears wiped away, and the LORD revealed on Mount Zion (Isa. 24.23–25.9)? The Targum (the Aramaic version of the Scriptures) gives an idea of how this passage in Isaiah was understood in the time of Jesus. The LORD reigning in Jerusalem and revealing his glory was the revelation of the Kingdom, and the banquet was part of the celebration.[8] Did the Eucharist acquire its sacrificial elements among the earliest Gentile converts, for whom worship without sacrifices was unthinkable? Since they were uncircumcised they would have been barred from the temple, and perhaps their sacrificial Eucharist was a substitute. Were the Christians barred from the temple? All these possibilities have been suggested, and all have some evidence to support them.

There can, therefore, be no certainty about the origin of the Eucharist. The later liturgies of the Church seem more akin to the Day of Atonement than to Passover, and it may be that the Day of Atonement was the context from the beginning, even though the date was Passover. *There can be no certainty that what the Eucharist became*

---

[8] The enigmatic description in Exodus 24.9–11 probably recalls the temple antecedent of this idea: the elders saw the God of Israel enthroned and then feasted.

was different from Jesus' original intention. The problem again is lack of real sources for the early period — as opposed to sources that have been harmonized by later scribes — and so much reconstruction has to rely on imagination. Another problem arises over what is admitted as evidence, and how that evidence is evaluated. Data becomes significant only in context, and if a synagogue context is assumed because Christians called their assemblies 'synagogues' (Jas 2.2), or a Passover context is assumed, because Jesus was crucified at Passover, data can be put into those frameworks, and a picture constructed which may be inaccurate because it is based on false assumptions. If other contexts are considered, then the same data can convey something very different, because a different set of associations is implicit in the proposed contexts.

One passage describing worship will illustrate the point. A group of people praise and thank the LORD with their music; they call upon him and they invoke him — *but the verb also means 'to remember'.* Is this early Christian worship, when they met together to remember — or was it to invoke? — the presence of the LORD with 'psalms and hymns and spiritual songs, singing and making melody to the LORD with all your heart' (Eph. 5.19)? Paul described the Corinthian church meeting together for hymns, revelations, and prophecy (1 Cor. 14.26), *exactly like the worship of the Levites in the temple.* Praising the LORD with music, thanking him and invoking/remembering him was David's command to the Levites when he established them as ministers before the ark in Jerusalem (1 Chron. 16.4). There had just been a communal meal there (1 Chron. 16.3). The passage about the Levites' worship could, out of context, have been describing the worship of the early Church. On one occasion in the temple, when the people of Judah were assembled, the Spirit of the LORD came upon Jahaziel, one of the Levites, and he prophesied (2 Chron. 20.13–17). On another occasion, the Spirit of God 'clothed itself with' Zechariah, a priest, and he too prophesied (2 Chron. 24.19–20, translating literally). Ecstatic prophecy belonged in the temple, but also in early Christian worship. What little we know of early Christian worship fits as well in a temple context as in a synagogue, and sometimes rather better. The Christians may not have been literally in the temple, but they thought of themselves as a spiritual house, a holy priesthood (1 Pet. 2.5). Proposing a temple context might reveal other aspects of early Christian life and belief, other connections. Paul himself reminded the church at Corinth: 'If I do not know the meaning of the language, I shall be a foreigner to the speaker and the speaker a foreigner to me' (1 Cor. 14.11).

The Passover

The earliest *interpretations* of the death of Jesus — apart from 'Christ our Passover' — suggest that the theological context was the Day of Atonement. Atonement and dying 'for our sins' (1 Cor. 15.3) are not obviously Passover themes. The shape of the Christian liturgy, with a 'blood' offering on the inner altar, is not the shape of a Passover, where the blood was never taken into the temple but splashed on the outdoor altar. The Passover was offered by all the people; it was not a high priestly or even a priestly sacrifice. The men were required to kill their own lambs in the temple court and pass the blood to the priests for sprinkling on the altar (Mishnah Pesaḥim 5.5). Ascension, enthronement and 'coming again' to establish the Kingdom are not obviously Passover themes. The early Eucharistic prayer in the Didache gives thanks for life and knowledge, the Name 'dwelling in our hearts', and 'everlasting life revealed to us through thy Servant Jesus'. These are not Passover. Nor do the themes attached to Passover discourse itself in the early Church derive from Passover; *they seem to be imported from the Day of Atonement.*

The ancient Passover was a blood ritual to protect Israel from the destruction of the last plague (Exod. 12.13), and as such was similar to atonement, which renewed the covenant bonds with blood and thus protected all those within the covenant.[9] Passover as described in Exodus was a domestic and pastoral feast, but it became a temple festival in the seventh century BCE, when Josiah purged and changed the old religion of Israel and centralized Passover in Jerusalem (2 Chron. 35.1–19). When Ezekiel had a vision of the ordinances of the future temple, he described Passover and the Day of Atonement as similar festivals. He prescribed the blood of a bull to cleanse the temple on the first day of the new year, putting blood on the doorposts, the altar and the gateposts to atone the temple, and then at Passover, the fourteenth day of the first month, another bull for a sin offering. In the seventh month there was to be a similar unnamed festival, at a time when we should expect the Day of Atonement (Ezek. 45.18–25). Ezekiel's is not the Passover we know: there is no link to Moses and the Exodus. The association of atonement and Passover however, was to recur in Christian texts. Ezekiel implies that the two festivals were temple cleansings that marked the equinoxes. There were also different calendars current in the time of Jesus: the

---

[9] See below, p. 176.

one assumed by the Temple Scroll found at Qumran had a year of 364 days, exactly 52 weeks, such that Passover always fell on a Tuesday and, interestingly, the Day of Atonement on a Friday.

At the end of the second temple period, the name Passover was still said to mean 'passing over' (Exod. 12.27), but this was understood in different ways. Josephus kept the original meaning, 'passing over', because on that day 'God passed over our people when he smote the Egyptians' (*Antiquities* 2.313). Philo had a different explanation: 'The festival is a reminder and thank offering for that great migration from Egypt which was made by more than two million men and women' (*Special Laws* 2.146). It was the time when Israel passed over the sea. The oldest Palestinian Targums[10] show what the ordinary person in the synagogue associated with Passover, possibly as early as the time of Jesus, but neither the Targums nor their component parts can be dated with certainty. It is entirely possible that Christian interpretations of Passover influenced Jews: Jewish festivals continued to attract Christians, so much so that 'Judaizers' were frequently condemned. John Chrysostom, at the end of the fourth century CE, condemned his own church in Antioch for having too close a relationship with the Jews.[11] The exposition of Passover in the Palestinian Targums, with its extraordinary associations, could reflect Christian interpretations. The Targum links Exodus 12.42, the night of watching, to the night of the creation of the world, to the LORD appearing to Abraham 'between the pieces'; that is, to make a covenant with him (Gen. 15.7–20), to the binding (Akedah) of Isaac (Gen. 22.1–18) and to the end of the world when King Messiah would appear. Of these, there is pre-Christian evidence to link Isaac to Passover; according to the Book of Jubilees,[12] which was known in the time of Jesus, the Akedah took place at Passover (Jub. 17.15–18.3). In the Targum, Passover is linked to covenant — but the Abraham covenant was not the covenant of the Last Supper and had nothing to do with remission of sins. There was the clear link to the sacrifice of the beloved son (Gen. 22.2), but a ram was offered instead of Isaac. This *may* be what Paul had in mind when he wrote: 'He who did not spare his own son but gave him up for us all' (Rom. 8.32). The Targum's link to the coming of King Messiah may have derived from the LORD coming to smite Egypt at midnight (Exod. 12.29). The Egyptian Jewish community

---

[10] Neofiti and the Fragment Targums.

[11] His eight sermons *Against Judaising Christians*.

[12] An alternative version of Genesis found at Qumran.

in the time of Jesus said that the Word appeared at Passover: 'Thy all powerful Word leaped from heaven, from the royal throne, into the midst of the land that was doomed ... and touched heaven while standing on the earth' (Wisdom of Solomon 18.15). This *may* underlie Jesus' warning: 'The kingdom of God is not coming with signs to be observed' (Luke 17.20).[13] There is insufficient evidence to know who influenced whom.

Since the Akedah took place at Passover, Jewish understanding of Isaac may have influenced Christian interpretations of Passover. Neither Philo nor Josephus, however, made any link between Isaac and atonement, so the influence may have been the other way: Christians influencing Jews, since atonement was central to Christianity from the beginning. The earliest Jewish interpretation was that the LORD would *remember* the binding of Isaac and protect his descendants in the future. It was a promise that the protection of Passover would continue. The Palestinian Targums had Abraham give thanks and pray: 'I beseech ... when the children of Isaac my son enter into a time of distress, remember them and answer them and redeem them' (Tg. Pseudo-Jonathan Gen. 22.14; Tg. Neofiti is similar). An early Jewish explanation of the Passover blood — 'When I see the blood, I will pass over you, and no plague shall fall upon you to destroy you' (Exod. 12.13) — did suggest that Isaac's was an atoning sacrifice insofar as it protected from the plague.[14] 'When I see the blood, I will pass over you, I see the blood of the binding of Isaac' was linked to the account of David's sin that nearly destroyed Jerusalem. 'The LORD saw' — but the text of Chronicles does not say what he saw when the angel was about to destroy Jerusalem (1 Chron. 21.15). The explanation was that the LORD had seen the blood of the binding of Isaac, and this was protection for the city. The plague stopped.[15]

There was also the parallel tradition that Isaac had been sacrificed and raised again, which was still known in Europe in the thirteenth century.[16] Genesis does not say that Isaac returned with his father, only that Abraham returned to his waiting servants (Gen. 22.19), and one of the Palestinian Targums[17] at this point says the angels on high took Isaac for three years. This cannot be dated, but there is a fresco

[13] The Greek word *parateresis* can also mean looking for signs or observing rules.

[14] See below p. 182ff.

[15] Mekhilta on Exod. 12. 13, a commentary on Exodus compiled in the third century CE but incorporating material from a century earlier.

[16] See S. Spiegel *The Last Trial*, New York: Schocken Books, 1967.

[17] Pseudo-Jonathan.

in the synagogue of Dura Europas, completed in 244 CE, that shows the Akedah, with Abraham holding up the knife, a ram caught in a bush, and a figure going up behind a curtain held open by a disembodied hand — the symbol of the LORD. Since the temple curtain represented access to the presence of God, this seems to depict Isaac going to heaven. Given this other possibility, some early Christian texts might be referring to Isaac's resurrection: 'By faith Abraham, when he was tested, offered up Isaac ... he considered that God was able to raise men even from the dead; hence, figuratively speaking, he did receive him back' (Heb. 11.17, 19); 'Was not Abraham our father justified by works, when he offered[18] his son Isaac upon the altar?' (Jas. 2.21). Two texts from the end of the first century CE also seem to know that Isaac was sacrificed. Barnabas linked Isaac to the Day of Atonement: 'In time to come, He would be sacrificing the vessel of his Spirit for our sins — whereby the type created in Isaac, when he was sacrificed on the altar, would be fulfilled' (Barn. 7). The text continues with a detailed explanation of the Day of Atonement and eating the flesh of the sin offering,[19] an unmistakable reference to the Eucharist. Clement wrote to Corinth: 'Was it not Abraham's faith that prompted him to acts of righteousness and truth? And it was Isaac's confident faith in what would follow that stretched him on the altar with a light heart' (1 Clem. 31).

There were references to Passover in early Christian writings that simply compared Jesus to the Passover lamb. Justin in the mid first century CE compared the blood that saved Israel in Egypt to the blood of Christ (*Trypho* 111), and, on a less theological note, he compared the specially shaped spit used for the Passover lamb to the shape of the cross (*Trypho* 40). Ephrem, in the mid fourth century, wrote: 'Our LORD ate the little Pascha and became himself the great Pascha' (*Hymns on the Crucifixion* 3). There was, however, no emphasis on the suffering of the Passover lamb in Jewish tradition nor on its being a sin-bearer, and so the Christian emphasis on suffering and sin bearing introduced new elements into the interpretation of Passover. This was done by making the suffering Servant of Isaiah 'a lamb that is led to the slaughter' (Isa. 53.7), a reference to the Passover lamb, and by linking this to John the Baptist's recognition of Jesus: 'Behold, the Lamb of God, who takes away the sin of the world!' (John 1.29).

---

[18] The verb is *anaphero*, used of priests offering sacrifice, whence the *anaphora*, the offertory prayer of the Eucharist.

[19] See below, p. 198.

Origen used this interpretation and said of the Pascha: 'Here you see the true lamb, "the lamb of God who takes away the sins of the world", and say "Christ our Paschal lamb has been sacrificed" (1 Cor. 5.7). Let the Jews eat the flesh of the lamb in a carnal way, but let us eat the flesh of the Word of God' (Homily 23, *On Numbers*).

The suffering was read into Passover by mean of false etymology. Melito, bishop of Sardis in Asia Minor in the late second century CE, introduced a new explanation for Pascha: it meant suffering, he said, because the Greek verb *paschein* means to suffer. He made a whole series of comparisons, not all of which had a Passover basis: [Christ says] 'I am your forgiveness; the Pascha that saves, the lamb slain for you, your ransom, your life, your light, your salvation, your resurrection, your King' (*On the Pasch* 103). This suggests that Easter themes such as light and life that had no Passover basis, had to be included. Melito's is the earliest surviving explanation of Paschal symbolism: 'The Scripture of the Hebrew Exodus has been read, and the words of the mystery have been plainly stated, how the sheep is sacrificed and the people is saved' (*On the Pasch* 1). He understood the Servant prophecy 'led like a lamb to the slaughter' (Isa. 53.7) as a reference to Jesus the Passover lamb (*On the Pasch* 4), and he applied the Jewish Passover thanksgiving to Jesus: 'He delivered us from slavery to liberty, from darkness to light, from death to life ...' (*On the Pasch* 68, quoting Mishnah Pesaḥim 10.5). Origen, in the mid third century, criticized Melito's explanation of Pasch: 'Most, if not all, of the brethren think that Pascha is named from the passion of the Saviour ... If any of our people in the company of Hebrews makes this rash statement ... they will ridicule him for being completely ignorant of the meaning of the name' (*On the Pasch*, 1). The link between suffering and Pascha continued: Eutychus, Patriarch of Constantinople in the late sixth century said: 'Before he suffered he ate the Pascha, the mystical Pascha, of course. For it would not be called Pascha without the passion. And so he sacrificed himself in mystic fashion' (*Sermon on the Pasch and the Eucharist*).

Philo's understanding of 'Passover' — that it was the people passing over to a new life — was developed in many ways, notably by Origen, a fellow Alexandrian. The Christian life was a continual Passover, a constant moving over to better things. There is not a moment when a Christian is not 'keeping the feast'. 'He is always passing over in thought and word and deed from the affairs of this life to God and hastening towards his city' (*Against Celsus* 8.2). Eusebius, like many in the fourth century, wanted to separate the Christian Pascha from the

Jewish Passover: the people of the New Testament, he said, perform the Pascha every LORD's day. 'We are always departing from Egypt, ... we are always celebrating the crossing feast ... Every week we are performing the mysteries of the true sheep though whom we have been purified ...' (*On the Paschal Solemnity* 7). John Chrysostom, writing in 387 CE, made the same point when warning his church in Antioch against celebrating a Jewish-style Passover: 'The Pascha comes three times a week, even four. For the Pascha is not fasting, but offering the sacrifice that takes place at every synaxis' (*Against the Judaising Christians* 3). It is interesting that the liturgy attributed to him has only one possible reference to Passover and Exodus, namely deliverance from slavery to the enemy. This emphasis on deliverance was also linked to the custom of Easter baptism. Gregory of Nazianzus, at Easter 362 CE, described the Christians' escape from Egypt as their feast of departure, and linked it to dying and rising with Christ: 'Yesterday I died with him; today I am brought to life with him' (Oration 1 *On the Pascha*).

Passover as the time of creation was used by Cyril of Jerusalem to show how the resurrection linked to Passover: 'At what season does the Saviour rise? ... This is the time, the first month among the Hebrews, in which is celebrated the feast of the Pasch, formerly the figurative Pasch, but now the true. This is the season of the creation of the world' (*Catecheses* 14). This understanding of Passover, combined with the 'passing over', is best known from the Easter hymn of St John of Damascus:

> The day of resurrection, Earth tell it out abroad,
> The Passover of gladness, the Passover of God!
> From death to life eternal, from earth unto the sky,
> Our God hath brought us over, with hymns of victory.

The Passover as the coming of the Messiah was mentioned by Lactantius early in the fourth century CE as the reason for the Easter vigil: 'This is the night that we celebrate by watching until morning on account of the coming of our King and God. There are two meanings for this night: in it he received life when he had suffered, and afterward he is to receive the kingship over the world' (*Divine Institutes* 7.19). Jerome related this to the coming of the Bridegroom. Expounding Matthew 25.6: 'At midnight there was a cry, "Behold, the Bridegroom! Come out to meet him"', he wrote: 'Perhaps it will help the reader to know that Jewish tradition tells us that the Messiah will come at midnight, as happened in Egypt when they celebrated the Pascha, and the Exterminator came, and the LORD passed over the dwellings' (Exod. 12.29) (*Commentary on Matthew*, Book 4). The earliest record of this seems to be the Gospel of the Hebrews, now lost apart from references and quotations in other works: 'The eight days of the Pascha, on which Christ the Son of God rose, signify the eight days after the remission of the Pascha, when the whole seed of Adam will be judged, as is told in the Gospel of the Hebrews. For this reason, wise men are of the opinion that the day of Judgement will come in the time of the Pascha, inasmuch as Christ rose on that day so that the saints in turn might rise on it.'[20]

The story of the Akedah was important for the Church: the earliest surviving lectionaries show that it was read on Maundy Thursday,[21] or on Good Friday.[22] It was not given special emphasis, however, in the Liturgy of St Basil, which mentions Abraham's sacrifice, along with those of Abel, Noah, Moses, Aaron and Samuel. Some texts compared the death and resurrection of Jesus to Isaac; others contrasted the death of Jesus and the Akedah, because Abraham offered a ram in his place, implying that Isaac did not die. The earliest of these came from Melito, bishop of Sardis: 'In place of Isaac the just, a ram appeared for slaughter, in order that Isaac might be liberated from his bonds. The slaughter of this animal redeemed Isaac from death. In like manner, the LORD being slain, saved us' (*Catena on Genesis*). Athanasius, writing in 334 CE, said that Abraham 'saw Christ in the ram which was offered instead of Isaac as a sacrifice to God' (*Festal Letter* 6). Origen saw both Isaac and the ram as foreshadowing the crucifixion: 'Christ underwent death in the flesh prefigured here by the ram ... but the Word remained for ever incorruptible, that is Christ according to the Spirit, of whom Isaac is the image.' Origen linked this to the Day of Atonement, since the intended victim carried the wood, a priestly duty, and so he was both priest and victim in the manner of the high priest making atonement (*On Genesis*, Homily 8).

Given that Jesus died at Passover, and so Good Friday was bound to be linked to Passover, it is surprising how few references there are in the New Testament to the characteristically Passover theme of release

---

[20] Cited in R. Cantalamessa, *Easter in the Early Church*, tr. J. M. Quigley and J. T. Lienhard, Collegeville, Minn.: The Liturgical Press, 1993, p. 38, citing the Codex Vaticanus Reginensis Latinus 49.

[21] The Old Armenian Lectionary used in Jerusalem 417– 439 CE.

[22] The earliest Syriac lectionary, and the early Western lectionary, the Liber Comes, often attributed to Jerome.

from slavery, or to the accompanying foods and rituals of Passover such as the bitter herbs or the *haroseth*.[23] Eating the sacrifice was a Passover theme, and the link to Isaac was pre-Christian, but how the Akedah was interpreted and by whom and when is not clear. The resurrection could have been a Passover theme, and the coming of the Messiah could have been a Passover theme, but the sin bearing, the suffering, the LORD as both priest and victim, the love, light, life, knowledge and healing that were to characterize Christian liturgy have no basis in Passover. It is entirely possible that the Last Supper should be set in another context, the Day of Atonement, where all these themes, and many more, naturally belong.[24]

EXPULSION?

How Christian worship related literally to the temple and the synagogues is not clear. Jesus taught in synagogues and was well received (Luke 4.15), until he claimed to be the long-expected Messiah: 'The Spirit of the LORD ... has anointed me ... Today this scripture has been fulfilled in your hearing' (Luke 4.16–30). Then he was cast out. He predicted persecution for his followers in the years until the temple was destroyed: 'You will be beaten in synagogues' (Mark 13.9). Since Mark's Gospel is said to be the memoirs of Peter (Eusebius, *Church History* 2.15), it is unlikely that Peter would have attributed such a warning to Jesus had it not been both genuine and fulfilled in his experience. The Beatitudes in Luke have a similar warning that may refer to expulsion from the synagogue: 'Blessed are you when men hate you, and when they exclude you and revile you, and cast out your name as evil, on account of the Son of man!' (Luke 6.22). John, whose Gospel was written later than the Synoptic Gospels (Eusebius *Church History* 3.24) and independently of them, says that people were excluded from the synagogue even during Jesus' lifetime, if they recognized Jesus as the Messiah: 'The Jews had already agreed that if anyone should confess (Jesus) to be Christ, he was to be put out of the synagogue (John 9.22): 'Many even of the authorities believed in [Jesus], but for fear of the Pharisees they did not confess it, lest they should be put out of the synagogue' (John 12.42); (Jesus said) 'They will put you out of the synagogues; indeed,

---

[23] A mixture of fruits and nuts that sweetened the bitterness of the herbs.
[24] See below pp. 197ff.

the hour is coming when whoever kills you will think he is offering service to God' (John 16.2).

The pattern throughout Paul's journeys, as described in Acts, is of conflict with Jews and expulsion from synagogues (Acts 13.50; 14.5–6; 17.5, 13; 18.6; 19.9; 20.3, 19). There may be more to this than simply hostility from Jews. There was hostility towards Paul himself from the Jerusalem church (e.g. Acts 9.23–30), and Paul in his turn reacted strongly to them. His letter to the Galatians was full of anger against Christians who persisted in their Jewish ways (Gal. 2.1–14), and the 'Jews' who pursued him on his travels could have been envoys of the Jerusalem church — Jews who had become Christian, but who did not like Paul's gospel for the Gentiles. If so, then the Jerusalem Christians would have been in good standing in those synagogues, and not expelled. The picture is complex. Christians who kept Jewish customs were hostile to Paul, and yet John, a pillar of the Jerusalem church, called one group a 'synagogue of Satan' (Rev. 2.9). The Roman Christians called their meeting place a synagogue, according to the Shepherd of Hermas, a book of visions and prophecies written there in the early second century CE: 'When the man who has the Divine Spirit comes to a synagogue of righteous men, who have the faith of the Divine Spirit, and intercession is made to God from the synagogue of those men ...' (The Shepherd, Mandate 11.9, also 13, 14).

If the Christians assembled in their own synagogues, this only complicates the matter of 'expulsion from synagogues', which is a fiercely debated topic, some scholars doing their best to deny the validity of evidence, or to read it in another way.[25] Justin, writing in Rome in the mid second century CE, had no doubt that Jews cursed both Jesus and his followers. 'You curse in your synagogues', said Justin to Trypho, the Jew with whom he was debating, 'all those who are called from him Christians, and other nations effectively carry out the curse by putting to death those who simply confess themselves to be Christians. (Justin, *Trypho* 96). 'You curse him [Jesus] without ceasing, as well as those who side with him, while all of us pray for you and for all men, as our Christ and LORD has taught us to do (*Trypho* 133; see also 16, 47, 93, 95, 108, 123, 137).

Expulsion from the community was symbolically, and often literally, a sentence of death. This may explain a plot against Paul's life when

[25] For example, R. Kimelman 'Birkat Ha Minim and the Lack of Evidence for Anti-Christian Jewish Prayer in Late Antiquity', in E. Sanders, ed., *Jewish and Christian Self Definition*, vol. 2, London: SCM press, 1981, pp. 226–44.

he returned to Jerusalem, and some forty Jews, with the knowledge of the chief priests and elders, took an oath to kill him. Paul's nephew heard of the plot, and Paul was saved (Acts 23.12–16). The Jews of Damascus tried to kill him immediately after his conversion (Acts 9.23). The main persecutors of the early Church in Jerusalem were the Jews. The charge against Stephen was that he spoke blasphemously against Moses and against God (Acts 6.11). Saul of Tarsus supervised his stoning (Acts 7.59), something he later described as extreme zeal for the traditions of his fathers (Gal. 1.14). King Herod 'laid violent hands' on some of the Jerusalem Christians and had James son of Zebedee executed. 'When he saw that it pleased the Jews' he arrested Peter also (Acts 12.1–3).

There are other stories of early persecution by the Jews. The *Clementine Recognitions* are 'Clement's' account of his travels with Peter, and, whatever the actual date of the text, they show how the early days in Jerusalem were remembered. The *Recognitions*, like the Acts of the Apostles, describe how the Christians preached and taught in the temple. James, the leader of the Church, after seven days discussing the prophecies of the Messiah, had almost persuaded a group of people, including the high priest, to be baptized. 'An enemy' — clearly Saul — then entered the temple court and began inciting the crowd against the Christians: 'Why do we not lay hands on them and pull all these men to pieces?' James was set upon by 'the enemy', who clubbed him and then threw him down some steps, where he was left for dead. James' disciples carried him home, and early next morning, 5,000 Christians fled the city before dawn and went to Jericho. The enemy then received authority from Caiaphas, the high priest, to arrest all who believed in Jesus (*Clem. Rec.* 1.70–71). Whatever lies behind this story, it does suggest that the Christians were not welcomed in the temple.

Expelling misfits from the community, and thus from the temple, was an established custom. The harsh measures adopted by the returned exiles in the late sixth century, when they excluded those not deemed fit under the more rigorous purity laws, were to have serious consequences, as we shall see.[26] Eunuchs were cut off from the temple and foreigners excluded, a reference to the laws in Deuteronomy 23.1–8 (Isa. 56.1–8). There were 'brethren' who hated other brethren and cast them out for the sake of the Name (Isa. 66.5). Ezra had expelled people and confiscated their property (Ezra 10.8).

---

[26] See below pp. 53ff.

The community expelled all those of foreign descent, and Nehemiah expelled even the grandson of the high priest because he deemed his wife unsuitable (Neh. 13.3, 28). The Qumran community excluded anyone who uttered the Name improperly: 'He shall be dismissed and return to the Council of the Community no more' (1 QS vii.1).

'Cutting off' was the punishment for breaking the covenant laws. Anyone who did not observe correctly the feast of unleavened bread was 'cut off' from Israel (Exod. 12.15). This 'cutting off' meant more than just exclusion from the covenant community — it meant death: 'everyone who profanes [the Sabbath] shall be put to death; whoever does any work on it, that soul shall be put to death' (Exod. 31. 14). Anyone who sinned deliberately 'with a high hand', was cut off: 'But the person who does anything with a high hand, whether he is a native or a sojourner, reviles the LORD, and that person shall be cut off from among his people' (Num. 15.30). Anyone who copied temple incense or temple anointing oil for private use was cut off (Exod. 30.33, 38). Anyone who touched a sacrifice in an unclean state, or who consumed blood, was cut off from his people (Lev. 7.20, 21, 25, 27). The Psalmist knew that the wicked would be cut off: 'The wicked shall be cut off; but those who wait for the LORD shall possess the land ... Those blessed by the LORD shall possess the land, but those cursed by him shall be cut off' (Ps. 37.9, 22, also vv. 28, 38).

'Cutting off' followed the cursing, another ritual associated with breaking the covenant law. The Levites uttered solemn curses against anyone who made an image or dishonoured his parents, removed a landmark or misled the blind, had forbidden sexual relations, perverted justice, accepted a bribe or committed murder (Deut. 27.11–16). At some stage, though, cutting off came to mean expulsion rather than death. The Qumran community advocated exclusion where the Law had prescribed death: 'No man who strays so as to profane the Sabbath and the feasts shall be put to death' (CD XII), despite the ruling in Numbers 15.32–6, that anyone who did this should be put to death by stoning. Those who preached apostasy, however, were treated like mediums and wizards, and put to death (CD XII; Lev. 20.27). Philo interpreted the laws of exclusion — no eunuchs, bastards, Ammonites or Moabites to join the congregation (Deut. 23.1–8) — as excluding also those with comparable intellectual conditions: atheists and polytheists (Philo, *Special Laws* 1.324–45). The Hebrew Christians also had strict rules for exclusion, but we do not know how they enforced them: 'It is impossible to restore again to repentance those who have once been enlightened ... if they then commit apostasy, since they crucify the Son of God on their own account and hold him up to contempt (Heb. 6.4–6).

Death for apostasy may explain the harsh treatment of apostates in Egypt. When the Jewish community in Egypt were persecuted by Ptolemy IV Philopator, (221–204 BCE), some of them agreed to save themselves by participating in the cult of Dionysus. The faithful despised them, and excluded them from the community (3 Maccabees 2.29–33). When the fortunes of the Jews changed, the same king permitted them to destroy all those Jews who had been unfaithful. 'They put to a public and shameful death any whom they met of their fellow-countrymen who had become defiled. In that day they put to death more than three hundred men, and they kept the day as a joyful festival, since they had destroyed the profaners' (3 Maccabees 7. 14–15). There is no way of knowing exactly when this book was written, but scholars suggest the first century CE, that is, in the time of the early Church. It gives a glimpse of what apostates could expect from those who had remained faithful, and sets in context Justin's words to Trypho: 'You curse in your synagogues all those who are called from him Christians, and other nations effectively carry out the curse by putting to death those who simply confess themselves to be Christians (Justin, *Trypho* 96). It gives a context too for Paul's impassioned outburst at the end of Romans 8: 'Who shall bring any charge against God's elect? Who shall separate us from the love of Christ? Neither death, nor life, nor angels, nor principalities, nor things present, nor things to come, nor powers, nor height, nor depth, nor anything else in all creation, will be able to separate us from the love of God in Christ Jesus our LORD' (Rom. 8.33, 35, 38). The verb 'separate', *chorizein,* is the one used in the Greek version of Nehemiah 13.3:[27] 'They *separated* from Israel all those of foreign descent.' It meant expulsion. Presumably Paul had been expelled from some community: the synagogue? Or the temple? Or even the Jerusalem church?

There is a third word linked to 'expulsion' and 'cutting off' — *ḥerem,* a word not easy to translate, but the range of meaning can be seen from the Greek words chosen to translate *ḥerem.* Any idolater was *ḥerem,* (Exod. 22.20); the Greek is 'shall be put to death'. Items that were *ḥerem* in Greek were under a curse, *anathema* (Deut. 7.26; 13.17). Jericho and everything in it was to be *ḥerem*; in the Greek, everything was *anathema,* cursed, and to be burned (Josh. 6.17, 18; 7.1, 11, 15).

---

[27] In the Greek Old Testament, this passage appears as 2 Esdras 23.3.

Edom was destined for the LORD's *herem*; the Greek says 'destined for destruction' (Isa. 34.5). The LORD delivered Jacob to *herem*; in Greek, to destruction (Isa. 43.28). The most significant *herem* text, for our purposes, is Zechariah 14.11. The whole chapter describes the Day of the LORD, when the LORD would become King over all the earth. Living waters would flow from Jerusalem, and everything in the temple would be holy (Zech. 14.8, 9, 20). Jerusalem would no longer be *herem* (Zech. 14.11). The Greek here is *anathema*, cursed. For whom had Jerusalem become 'cursed', destined for utter destruction that would be restored by the Day of the LORD? One of the earliest glimpses of Christian worship alludes to this verse. Using a synonym, *katathema*, John described the heavenly city, the holy of holies: he saw the river of life and the tree of life, and no more *katathema*, no more curse. (The English versions have: 'There shall no more be anything accursed', RSV; or 'There shall be no more curse' AV.) The faithful servants of the LORD would worship him and see his face, and reign for ever (Rev. 22.1–5). Does it mean that for the first Christians, the temple was *herem*, cursed, as implied by Jesus' prophecy that it would be destroyed (Mark 13.1–2). Or does it mean that the faithful servants would no longer be considered *herem* and banned from the temple?

The problem centres around the date of the twelfth of the Eighteen Benedictions, prayers recited by Jews three times a day in the synagogue. This is the version found in the Cairo Genizah, thought to represent Palestinian tradition: 'For apostates let there be no hope, and the dominion of arrogance do thou speedily root out in our days; and let Christians (*noṣrim*) and heretics (*minim*) perish as in a moment. Let them be blotted out of the book of the living and let them not be written with the righteous. Blessed art thou O LORD, who makes humble the arrogant.' There are further complications: not only is the date a problem but there is no agreement as to exactly who the *noṣrim* and *minim* were. Christians had been called the sect of the Nazarenes, possibly the *noṣrim*, from the earliest days in Jerusalem (Acts 24.5), but this may have meant the Gentile Christians, since they were identified as disciples of Paul. The *minim* could have been the Christians of Jewish origin. There are instructions to allow the books of the *minim* to burn if they caught fire on the Sabbath, even if they contained the sacred Name, and these books were probably the Hebrew texts of the early Palestinian Christians (Tosefta Shabbat 13.5). They were not sacred, and there was no obligation to save them. 'The *gilyonim* and the books of the *minim* do not defile the hands'; in other words, are not sacred (Tosefta Yadaim 2.13). The *gilyonim* were revelations, but probably here they were the Gospels, since there was a bitter pun on *evangelion*, the Greek word for 'gospel', and the similar sounding Hebrew *avon gilyon*, meaning 'iniquitous revelation' (Babylonian Talmud Shabbat 116a).[28] If these speculations are correct, the curse was against all the Christians, and it is unlikely they would have attended a synagogue to hear such a curse, had it been used during the earliest years.

Paul gives two hints — no more — that such a curse did exist in his time. He longed to see his fellow Jews recognize Jesus as the Messiah, and said he could wish himself under the curse and cut off from Christ for the sake of his kinsmen (Rom. 9.3). The sentence is curious, but could imply that there was a curse that cut the Christians off — presumably from the Jewish community. In Corinth, where Paul had testified 'to the Jews that the Christ was Jesus', they had opposed and reviled him (Acts 18.5). Writing to the Corinthians, he had contrasted two declarations: 'Jesus is cursed' and 'Jesus is the LORD'. One was the declaration of the Christian community, and presumably the other was the declaration of those opposed to them, the Jews. 'No one speaking by the Spirit of God ever says "Jesus be cursed!" and no one can say "Jesus is LORD" except by the Holy Spirit' (1 Cor. 12.3). Cursing was a test used by the Roman governor Pliny when he was trying to identify Christians in Bithynia in 112 CE. Writing to the Emperor Trajan, he described his policy: 'As for those who said they neither were nor ever had been Christians, I thought it right to let them go, since they recited a prayer to the gods at my dictation, made supplication with incense and wine to your statue … and moreover cursed Christ, things which, so it is said, those who are really Christians cannot be made to do' (Pliny, *Letter* 20.96). One generation later, this was Justin's accusation to Trypho about the Jews: 'You curse Jesus without ceasing.'

THE LIVING TEMPLE

Christianity and Judaism both claimed the Hebrew heritage, and after the tragedy of 70 CE, when the temple was destroyed, each developed its own style of worship. From the outset, the Christians had described themselves as the living stones of the spiritual temple (1 Pet. 2.5), a claim to be the true heirs to the temple tradition. The church at

---

[28] Another version in the same source was *aven gilyon*, worthless revelation.

Ephesus was reminded that it was being shaped into a holy temple for the LORD, built on the foundation of the apostles and prophets (Eph. 2.19–22). The risen LORD promised that the faithful Christian would be a pillar in the temple (Rev. 3.12), and the heavenly city, a giant golden cube representing the holy of holies, was built on twelve foundation stones, each bearing the name of an apostle (Rev. 21.14). This jewelled city had been inspired by Isaiah's vision of the restored Jerusalem, whose stones would be set in antimony, and its foundations set with sapphires. The pinnacles would be agate and the gates carbuncles, and the whole wall of precious stones (Isa. 54.11–12).

In the time of Jesus, these jewels symbolized the members of a priestly community, doubtless the origin of the early Church's claim to be the living temple. Fragments of a commentary on Isaiah found among the Dead Sea Scrolls interpret the sapphire foundations of the city as the priests and people who founded the Council of the Community. The pinnacles of agate were the twelve chief priests, and the gates of carbuncle were the chiefs of the tribes of Israel. The Council of the Community was the (living) holy of holies, their prayer was incense, 'the fragrance of righteousness', and their holiness of life was a free-will offering (Community Rule, 1 QS VIII, IX). This pure community would be a sanctuary for the LORD, offering the works of the Law like incense (4Q174). The Songs of the Sabbath Sacrifice, which have survived only as fragments, depict a living liturgy. The pillars, the corners and foundations of the holy of holies offer praise (4Q403), the engraved wall tiles are the holy angels, and the doors and gates proclaim the glory of God (4Q405).

Jesus himself may well have spoken of his followers as a living temple. When the Samaritan woman met him by the well and recognized that he was a prophet, she immediately asked him the pressing question of the time: which is the true temple? The Samaritan temple on Mount Gerizim or the Jewish temple in Jerusalem? Prophets were competent to pronounce on such matters. When Judas Maccabaeus regained possession of the temple in 164 BCE and drove out the occupying Syrians, he had the problem of what to do with the altar stones. They had been consecrated as an altar, but desecrated by the Syrians. He decided to store the stones 'until there should come a prophet to tell them what to do with them' (1 Macc. 4.46). Jesus was asked about the true temple, and he replied, in effect, that neither Samaritan nor Jew had the true temple: 'But the hour is coming, and now is, when the true worshippers will worship the Father in spirit and in truth, for such the Father seeks to worship him' (John 4.23).

There would be a spiritual temple, perhaps the origin of Peter's phrase: 'Like living stones, be yourselves built into *a spiritual house*, to be a holy priesthood, to offer spiritual sacrifices acceptable to God through Jesus Christ' (1 Pet. 2.5).

Thus the image of the spiritual temple came to describe the Christian lifestyle. 'Present your bodies as a living sacrifice, holy and acceptable to God, which is your spiritual worship,' wrote Paul (Rom. 12.1). The whole person sacrifice, as we shall see,[29] had been the original high priestly ritual of the Day of Atonement, and so Paul here says that Christian living must be one continuous act of atonement. The gift of money sent to Paul was described as 'a fragrant offering, a sacrifice acceptable and pleasing to God' (Phil. 4.18). The anointing that gave Christians their name had originally been the perfumed anointing oil used in the temple to consecrate the royal high priest. It was the sacrament of Wisdom and eternal life, as we shall see,[30] and opened the eyes of the anointed one to new ways of knowing. The Christians in Corinth must have been familiar with this transferred temple imagery, because Paul wrote to them: '[God] through us, spreads the fragrance of the knowledge [of Christ] everywhere. For we are the aroma of Christ ... (2 Cor. 2.14–15). The Christians, by their living, conveyed the transforming sacred chrism into the world.

The prophet Hermas also used temple imagery, which must have been familiar to his church in Rome, even *though they described themselves as a synagogue*. Hermas received several visions of a woman who showed him a tower being built by angels. The visions are followed by detailed explanations, showing that Hermas or his expositor knew far more temple tradition than appears in the Old Testament. Hermas saw an elderly lady clothed in shining robes, holding a little book, and a chair made of white wool. The lady began to teach Hermas, and then she read from the little book. She spoke of the power and wisdom of the Creator, and of the glory of creation, and then how all things were working together for the Church (Visions 1 and 2). The Lady was the Holy Spirit, but also the Son of God (Parable 9), a gender mixing that occurs also in the Book of Revelation, where the risen LORD spoke to John as Wisdom (Rev. 3.14–22).[31] Hermas has many other points of contact with the Book of Revelation.

---

[29] See below p. 180.
[30] See below p. 128.
[31] See my book *The Revelation of Jesus Christ*, Edinburgh: T&T Clark, 2000, pp. 112–3.

An angel came in a dream and told Hermas about the lady. He had thought the lady was the Sibyl, the great prophetess, but the angel said she was the Church. Why was she so old? 'Because she was created the first of all things, ... and for her sake was the world established.' Here, the Church has claimed temple tradition for itself — something that was to happen many times. Jewish tradition, of uncertain date, declared that six things had been created before the visible world, and the temple was one of them (Genesis Rabbah I.4). Here, that temple claim is made for the Church. The Book of Revelation shows the temple/holy city as a woman (Rev. 21.9) and the corrupted temple/city as the great harlot. The female figure who existed before the creation of the visible world was known as Wisdom (Prov. 8.22–31), and she made her throne in a pillar of cloud (ben Sira 24.4). The lady on the throne that looked like white wool was Wisdom.

'Ezra', a Jewish seer in Palestine at this time, also received visions of an old woman mourning the death of her son. Ezra rebuked her: 'You are sorrowing for one son, but the whole world is sorrowing for our mother' (2 Esdr. 10.8). Then the woman was transformed before his eyes into a great city, and the archangel Uriel explained that she was Zion. Paul had known the image of mother Zion: the present Jerusalem was enslaved by the Law, he wrote, 'but the Jerusalem above is free, for she is our mother' (Gal. 4.26). The woman Ezra saw was the genius of the city, known in the Old Testament as the Daughter of Zion, and linked there to the image of a tower and to the holy city. Micah had spoken of her and her tower: 'And you, O tower of the flock, hill of the Daughter of Zion, to you it shall come, the former dominion shall come, the kingdom of the daughter of Jerusalem' (Mic. 4.8). The Lady's tower was the Kingdom, and Ezra saw her mourning the death of her Son.

Isaiah tells more of her story: she had been abandoned by her LORD, but then restored. She had to rise from the dust and dress like a Queen (Isa. 52.1–2), no longer living as a widow (Isa. 54.1–4). Then, just as in Ezra's vision, the Queen became the city to be rebuilt with precious stones (Isa. 54.11–12), the mother of many more children (Isa. 66.7–14). She appears in the Book of Revelation as the bejewelled Bride of the Lamb, coming down from heaven (Rev. 21.10). John had first seen her clothed with the sun, about to give birth to her son and threatened by a great red dragon with seven heads (Rev.12.1–6). Hermas saw this same dragon in his fourth vision, a fearful beast that terrified him as it approached. He recalled the teaching of the Lady, 'Do not be double minded' — and the beast passed him by. This linking of the lady and the dragon shows that Hermas was living and thinking in the same world as John, that the temple visions of the Book of Revelation were shaping his world view (Vision 4).

In most of his visions, Hermas saw a tower. In the third vision, for example, he saw it being built from shining stones. Six young men were working on it, and countless other men were bringing stones up from the waters[32] on which the tower was built. The stones came out of the deep water around the tower and fitted perfectly without further shaping. So good was the fit that the tower looked like one stone. The lady told Hermas: 'The tower which you see being built is myself, the Church.' These were ancient images: the temple of Solomon was built with pre-hewn stones, so that they fitted perfectly on the site and no iron tool was used in the holy place (1 Kgs 6.7). The tower, especially the tower in the vineyard, had long been used as an image of the temple. There was a tower in Isaiah's vineyard parable (Isa. 5.2), and Habakkuk stood on a tower to watch what the LORD would show him (Hab. 2.1). There is no explanation of these towers in the Old Testament, but 1 Enoch describes the temple as a great and broad house, on which there is a lofty tower for the LORD of the sheep (1 Enoch 89.50), and rebuilding the temple after the exile is rebuilding the tower (1 En. 89.73). R. Yosi, a contemporary of Hermas, explained that the tower in Isaiah's parable of the vineyard was the holy of holies: 'He built a tower in the midst of it ... this is the sanctuary' (Tosefta Sukkah 3.15). The Lady 'was' the sanctuary.

Hermas was told that the six young men who built the tower were the archangels whom God had charged to complete the creation and build the Church. The other men were also angels, working together to build the Church, and the perfectly fitting stones were 'the apostles and bishops and teachers and deacons who walked according to the majesty of God and served the elect of God in holiness' (Vision 3). Since the original temple had represented the creation, the angels completing the creation and building the Church was a natural association of ideas. Philo understood that angels had helped with the creation: '[When] God said 'Let us make' (Gen. 1.26), this shows clearly that he was taking others as fellow workers' (*On the Creation* 75). 'He allowed his subject powers to have the fashioning of some

---

[32] An allusion to baptism, perhaps, as well as to the primeval waters over which the temple was believed to be built.

things, though he did not give them sovereign and independent knowledge for the completion of the task' (*The Confusion of Tongues* 174). In another vision, Hermas saw a great white stone that was the foundation of the tower (Parable 9.3). Again, the six men and a crowd of other men came to build the tower, and a glorious man, the LORD of the tower, appeared (Parable 9.7). The Shepherd angel explained that the glorious man was the Son of God, and that not even the angels could enter the tower without their LORD. Only those who wore the Name could enter the tower, here called the Kingdom (Parable 9.12).

Building the tabernacle/temple had been linked to the six days of creation at the beginning of each year, and so the dedication of the holy place was part of the autumn new year festival. Moses began to assemble the tabernacle at new year (Exod. 40.2); Solomon's temple was consecrated at the Feast of Tabernacles,[33] the fifteenth day of the year, (1 Kgs 8.2); and the returned exiles re-established worship in Jerusalem at the Feast of Tabernacles (Ezra 3.4). Hermas linked the building of the tower to the Feast of Tabernacles, and described the temple ritual of the willow branches, as it had been in the time of Jesus. The Mishnah gave these instructions: 'How was the rite of the willow branch fulfilled? There was a place below Jerusalem called Motza, where they went and cut themselves young willow branches. They came and set these up at the sides of the altar, so that their tops were bent over the altar … Each day (for the first six days of the festival) they went in procession a single time round the altar, saying "Save us [Hosanna!] we beseech thee O LORD! O LORD, we beseech thee, give us success!" [On the seventh day] they went in procession seven times around the altar' (Mishnah Sukkah 4.5). This is the psalm and the ritual of Palm Sunday,[34] but in the Christian calendar it moved from autumn to spring, just as the Day of Atonement moved to Passover. The willow branches had to meet certain conditions: 'If a willow branch was got by robbery, or was withered, it was not valid. If it came from an Asherah or from an apostate city, it was not valid. If its tip was broken off, or if its leaves were severed, or if it was a mountain willow, it was not valid. If it was shrivelled or had lost some of its leaves or had grown in a field (and not by a brook) it was not

---

[33] Here called the seventh month, because the post-exilic writer is thinking in terms of the later calendar that began in the spring.

[34] In the Tabernacles procession, a bundle of branches was carried: willow, myrtle and palm. Only the procedure for cutting the willow is described in the Mishnah.

valid' . People with such branches could not take part in the great procession.

Hermas described an angel of the LORD who stood by a willow tree, cutting branches from it and giving them to a crowd of people. The angel then received them back, and observed the condition of the branches. There were eleven conditions that showed signs of neglect, and meant that the branch and its bearer were not accepted: the branches might be dry, or half dry, or two-thirds dry, or any one of several similar states. Even branches that were still in their original green state were not acceptable. Only those whose branches had buds, or buds and fruit, were allowed into the tower wearing white robes (Parable 8.1–2). This echoes the story of Aaron's rod that budded and bore fruit, proof that he was the true high priest (Num. 17.1–11). Hermas has an elaborate account of the unacceptable states for branches: eleven states, just as there were eleven unacceptable states for the Tabernacles branches in the Mishnah. This cannot be coincidence — and yet this information cannot be found in the Bible, and it was compiled into the Mishnah almost a century after Hermas.

There are several indications that Hermas was drawing on material from the very earliest days of the Church. The glorious angel who cut the branches was called Michael (Parable 8.3), but later he was called the Son of God (Parable 9.12), similar to the double naming in the Book of Revelation: the armies of heaven are led by Michael (Rev. 12.7), but later they are led by the Word of God (Rev. 19.11–16). The earliest Christian theology emerged from the angel lore of the temple, as can be seen from the description of the Trinity in the Ascension of Isaiah, a pre-Christian text reworked by Christian scribes. The LORD, that is, Yahweh, sat at the right hand of the Great Glory, and the angel of the Holy Spirit sat at the left (Asc. Isa. 11.32). The Lady who spoke to Hermas as the Church had formerly been Wisdom, the Holy Spirit, the Mother of the LORD, the genius of Jerusalem, the Queen of Heaven. She 'was' the temple, just as the Lady 'was' the Church. Her theology, symbols and history were later attributed to Mary. The day commemorated as the birthday of Mary, 8 September, was very close to the autumn festival that celebrated the founding of the temple, and the date of her death, 15 August, the Dormition, was very close to 9 Ab, the day when the temple was destroyed.

Temple or synagogue? Where were the roots of Christian worship? No matter where the Christians actually assembled, or what they called those gatherings, they thought of themselves as the temple. *As far away as Rome, they could draw on temple traditions not recorded in the Bible.*

Chapter 3

SONS AND HEIRS

Do you see these great buildings?
There will not be left here one stone upon another, that will not be thrown down.

Mark 13.2

Jesus cleansed the temple. He drove out the traders and reminded them of the words of the prophets: 'My house shall be called a house of prayer for all the nations, but you have made it a den of robbers' (Mark 11.17 quoting Isa. 56.7 and Jer. 7.11). In the Synoptic Gospels, this marks the start of holy week, when the chief priests and scribes 'sought a way to destroy him' (Mark 11.18). John set the incident at the start of Jesus' ministry, symbolically setting the purification of the temple as the opening scene of the drama set mainly in the temple. When asked for a sign of his authority to act in this way, Jesus said: 'Destroy this temple, and in three days I will raise it up' (John 2.19).

Throughout the Fourth Gospel, 'the Jews' are the people who had lost touch with temple tradition and no longer understood their own heritage. Nicodemus, a good man and a teacher, did not understand what it meant to be born of the Spirit or born from above (John 3.2–10). In temple tradition, those born from above were the angels, the true teachers, and this is what the Christians claimed to be. 'The Jews' did not understand that the Sabbath signified the rest at the completion of the creation (John 5.16–18), the great 'tomorrow' that was central to the Christian hope. 'The Jews' had lost the original meaning of their Scriptures, which showed the LORD in human form (John 5.39; 8.39–41). 'The Jews' did not recognize the ancient belief in ascent to heaven (John 6.41–2; 7.35–6; 8.22), or that Wisdom fed her disciples with herself (John 6.52), and gave them sight (John 9.40–41). They had even forgotten that the LORD was their king (John 19.15). All these temple themes, and more, were to become fundamentals of Christian belief, expressed in their worship.

Jesus prophesied the destruction of the temple that had lost its way. There was even an inscription set up in the temple: 'Jesus the King did not reign but was crucified because he prophesied the destruction of the city and the devastation of the temple.'[1] Jesus often visited the temple and taught there, as the Fourth Gospel shows, but he knew it would be destroyed. The disciples asked him when this would happen, and he replied with dire warnings: there would be wars and rumours of wars, earthquakes and famines, persecution and false messiahs, and then the Son of man would appear (Mark 13.5–27). The 'Little Apocalypse', as this passage is called, is also in Matthew and Luke (Matt 24.4–31, Luke 21.8–28), but seems not to answer the disciples' question. They asked Jesus when his prophecy about the temple would be fulfilled, and he told them when the Son of man would appear: there would be clear signs, and then 'the Son of man coming in clouds with great power and glory' (Mark 13.26).

Why did Jesus link the coming of the Son of man and the destruction of the temple? When Jesus was arrested, he was accused of threatening to destroy the temple and build another (Mark 14.58). When the high priest questioned him, however, he did not ask about the threat to the temple, but said: 'Are you the Christ, the Son of the Blessed?' Destroying and rebuilding the temple, for the high priest, was the expected role of the Messiah. Jesus replied: 'I am; and you will see the Son of man seated at the right hand of Power, and coming with the clouds of heaven' (Mark 14.61–62). The Messiah was known as the Son of man. Jesus' answer to the disciples about the destruction of the temple was about the coming of the Messiah who would destroy it.

The title 'Son of man' has generated huge debate for years, especially after it was shown that 'son of man' could mean a human being when speaking impersonally, much as we might say '*One* does not do that.' The word 'man', however, had great significance for the visionaries, and their writings must be read with this in mind. To distinguish between earthly and heavenly characters in their visions, they adopted the convention of describing angels as 'men' and humans as animals. Thus, Jesus told the parable of the sheep and the goats — humans — judged by the Son of man and his angels (Matt. 25.31–46). Luke described two men 'in dazzling apparel' at the tomb on Easter morning (Luke 24.4), but the two on the road to Emmaus said the women had seen 'a vision of angels' (Luke 24.23). In the

---

[1] The Slavonic text of Josephus, *Jewish War*, 5.195.

Book of Revelation, a complex visionary text that was made public, John had to explain this convention to his readers. When the angel measured the heavenly city, it was 'a hundred and forty-four cubits by a *man's* measure, that is, an angel's' (Rev. 21.17). This was not a Christian innovation: Daniel was visited by 'the man Gabriel' whilst saying his afternoon prayers (Dan. 9.21). Once we know that the Man was the Great Angel, John's account of Good Friday regains its context: 'Jesus came out, wearing the crown of thorns and the purple robe. Pilate said to them, "Here is the man!"' (John 19.5).

Contemporary writings show that the Messiah, the Man, was expected to destroy and *rebuild* the temple. This was not, as some have suggested, the Gospel writers putting unlikely words into the mouth of the high priest. This role for the Messiah is found in 1 Enoch, in its stylized history of Israel, where humans are animals and angels are 'men'. After the great judgement, the LORD of the sheep — in the New Testament he is called the Good Shepherd — folded up the old house; everything was taken away and deposited in the south. Then he brought out a new house that was much bigger than the old one. The pillars, the beams and the furnishings were all new, and it was big enough for all the sheep who had survived the judgement (1 Enoch 90.28–29). The old temple was temporary, just as the taber- nacle in the desert had been temporary. In the parable of the sheep and the goats — Jesus' version of this story — those who survived the judgement did not enter the new temple, they entered the Kingdom. The Kingdom *was* the new temple, as implied by the visions of the Book of Revelation.

John said the heavenly city had no temple, presumably because the whole city was the temple, or rather, the whole city was the holy of holies. The city was a huge golden cube, and in it was the throne of God and the Lamb. This can only have been the holy of holies, which in the temple had been a golden cube of 20 cubits (1 Kgs 6.20). John said the golden holy of holies was where the servants of God worshipped him and saw his face; his name was on their foreheads; the LORD God was their light; and they reigned with him (Rev. 22.3–5). This is exactly how the ancient high priests were described: they alone could enter the holy of holies (Lev. 16.2); they wore the Name on their foreheads (Exod. 28.36); and they were royal figures (Ps. 110.4). In John's vision, the Christians were the new royal priesthood, as Peter also said (1 Pet. 2.9). This has important impli- cations for reconstructing the origin of Christian worship, since the high priests did not function in a synagogue.

The Temple Scroll, the most magnificent of the Dead Sea Scrolls, also describes the new temple. It is not possible to say when this text was composed, but the best preserved copy dates from the time of King Herod, who virtually rebuilt the temple. The Temple Scroll sets out the plan for the ideal temple — an implied criticism of Herod's structure — and it was much bigger than anything ever built in Jerusalem. The part that gives the measurements is fragmented, but seems to describe a structure big enough to be the holy city itself, which may be what the visionary had in mind. The outer courtyard was a square of 1600 cubits, about 800 metres. The building of this temple was not linked to the Messiah in any surviving part of the Temple Scroll, but the hope for a huge temple, as depicted in 1 Enoch and Revelation, was shared by many people.

A Jewish text used and preserved by the early Christians links the new Jerusalem to the coming of the Messiah. The book has various names but appears in the Apocrypha as 2 Esdras.[2] Written about 100 CE, it is a series of visions addressing the questions of the Jewish community devastated by the destruction of their city and temple in 70 CE. Ezra the seer was told by the archangel Uriel that the hidden city would soon appear. Then the Messiah would be revealed with his entourage, and they would reign for 400 years (2 Esdras 7.26–28). The sequence in 2 Esdras is similar to the Book of Revelation, which may be why only Christians preserved it. When Jesus stood before the high priest accused of threatening to destroy the temple and rebuild it, he was accused of being the Messiah. Conversely, since the Christians proclaimed that Jesus was the Messiah, they would have expected a new temple, exactly as appears in the Book of Revelation, where the servants of God and the Lamb stand before the throne, see the face of God and the Lamb, and worship him (Rev. 22.3–4). This is the earliest picture of Christian worship — in the holy of holies of the new temple, which is the Kingdom.

Jesus warned the temple authorities that their days were numbered. As he was standing in the temple court, the chief priests and scribes and elders came to question him, and he told them a parable (Mark 11.27 — 12.9). The temple teachers would have recognized immediately that this was a version of Isaiah's parable about the fate of the temple (Isa. 5.1–7). A man planted a vineyard, the prophet said, put a hedge round it and dug a wine press. He built a tower, and

---

[2] It is also known as 3 Esdras in the Slavonic Bible and 4 Ezra in the Latin Vulgate.

then let it to tenants. The LORD expected to gather fine grapes, but when he found only sour fruit, he decided to destroy his vineyard. Isaiah explained the parable: the LORD had looked for justice and righteousness from his vineyard, but had seen only bloodshed and a cry of despair (Isa. 5.7). To understand the reaction of the temple authorities — 'they tried to arrest him ... for they perceived that he had told the parable against them' (Mark 12.12) — we need to see how that parable was interpreted at the time, how people in the synagogues would have 'heard' those words.

The Targums are Aramaic translations and interpretations of the Hebrew Scriptures, originally an oral paraphrase in the synagogue for people who no longer understood Hebrew. The Isaiah Targum understood the tower of the vineyard to be the temple and its altar: 'I built my sanctuary among them and gave them my altar to make atonement for their sins' (Tg. Isa. 5.2). The tenants of the tower, in Jesus' version of the parable, were the current temple authorities, and he warned them that they would lose possession. They would kill the heir and cast him out of the vineyard, and then the owner of the vineyard would destroy the tenants and give the vineyard to others (Mark 12.9). The Christians who read these words of Jesus had no doubt that they were the new tenants of the vineyard, the new people of the temple.

When the temple and the city were destroyed by the Romans in 70 CE, the Christians rejoiced at the death of a great harlot 'drunk with the blood of the saints and the blood of the martyrs of Jesus' (Rev. 17.6; 19.1–3). The saints in heaven rejoiced and prepared for the heavenly city, the true temple, to descend from heaven. Later interpretation of the Book of Revelation identified the wicked city as Rome, but in the original vision 'the great city which is allegorically called Sodom and Egypt, where their LORD was crucified' (Rev. 11.8) can only be Jerusalem. The Book of Revelation records the fulfilment of Jesus' prophecy that the temple would be destroyed, and Christians would have expected the fulfilment of the rest of that prophecy: that the Son of man would return. Josephus described an extraordinary incident during the final siege of Jerusalem, when the Romans were bombarding the city and huge white stones were being hurled over the walls. As the stone hurtled towards the city, the watchmen cried: 'The son is coming!' (*War* 5.272).

Now 'son', *ben*, and stone, *'eben*, sound very similar in Hebrew, and some have suggested that the watchmen were warning of a stone. Josephus was a native speaker of Hebrew and he is unlikely to have made that mistake. Writing 'stone' when they had said 'son' would have been understandable, but 'son' instead of 'stone' is unlikely. He continued: 'Those in the line of fire promptly made way and lay down ...' and so the stone passed over them. When the Romans painted the stones black, so that they were less easy to see, they hit their targets. A stone appearing could have been the first of the supernatural phenomena that heralded the return of the Messiah: before the portent in heaven of the woman clothed with the sun, there was heavy hail (Rev. 11.19); when the great city fell, 'great hailstones ... dropped on men from heaven' (Rev. 16.21). Hailstones were an ancient sign of the LORD appearing: 'Out of the brightness before him, there broke through his clouds hailstones and coals of fire' (Ps. 18.12, 13). The men who shouted 'the Son is coming' were expecting the Messiah to return as the city fell and the temple was destroyed.

But the Messiah did not return, and the literal destruction of the temple prompted a new understanding of the return of the Messiah. This was the moment in Christian history when they learned that the LORD came to them as they worshipped: 'Maranatha' and 'seeing the LORD' became the main element in their services. John did see the LORD return in his vision of the mighty angel wrapped in a cloud and wreathed with a rainbow, the fiery angel whose face was like the sun.[3] The rainbow around him was the sign of the LORD: Ezekiel had seen the likeness of the glory of the LORD wreathed in a rainbow (Ezek. 1.28), and John had seen the rainbow around the throne (Rev. 4.3). The Church was expecting the LORD to return in a cloud, just as he had departed (Acts 1.9–11), but John learned he would return in another way.

The fiery angel first gave John three revelations of new teaching: the message of the seven thunders that could not be written down (Rev. 10.4); the message that the mysteries of the prophets were about to be fulfilled (Rev. 10.7); and the little scroll which he had to eat, that is, to keep as secret teaching (Rev. 10.8–11). Origen, in *Against Celsus* 6.6, linked John's vision of the scroll to Ezekiel's:

---

[3] The fiery angel appears elsewhere in the Old Testament, each time to warn Jerusalem of impending disaster: Ezekiel had seen him, warning of the fate of the wicked city (Ezek. 8.2; 9.9–10); Daniel had seen him, revealing what would happen to the people in the future (Dan.10.5–6, 14). The early Christians recognized this unnamed angel in Daniel as the LORD, e.g. Hippolytus, (died 235 CE) when he expounded Daniel 10.6: 'Here it is not [Gabriel], but he sees the LORD, not yet indeed as perfect man, but with the appearance and form of man ...' (*On Daniel*, 24).

Our prophets did know of greater things than any in the Scriptures, which they did not commit to writing. Ezekiel, for example, received a scroll written within and without ... but at the command of the Logos he swallowed the book in order that its contents might not be written down and so made known to unworthy persons. John is also recorded to have seen and done similar things ... And it is related of Jesus, who is greater than these, that he conversed with his disciples in private, and especially in their secret retreats, concerning the gospel of God; but the words which he uttered have not been preserved because it appeared to the evangelists that they could not be adequately conveyed to the multitude in writing or speech.

These were the secrets of the high priesthood. John's vision was set in the temple, and he was remembered as a high priest. A letter from Polycrates, Bishop of Ephesus, to Victor, Bishop of Rome, written about 190 CE, lists the leaders of the Church who were buried in Ephesus, one of whom was John, 'who became the priest wearing the *petalon*' (quoted in Eusebius, *Church History* 3.31), that is, he became a high priest, since *petalon* was the Greek name for the golden seal that the high priest wore on his forehead (Exod. 28.26). What this meant in a Christian context we can only guess, but this title shows the Christians saw themselves as the temple community. John, the high priest, received in the temple a special revelation from the LORD, perhaps the mystery to be kept for the LORD and the sons of his house.[4] Origen, too, knew that special teaching was entrusted only to the Great High Priest and his sons.[5] What we have already seen about the secret teaching suggests that it concerned the temple and the liturgy,[6] and how the LORD came to his temple.

There were no chapter divisions in the original Book of Revelation, and so the following section — the command to measure the temple — was a part of the revelation from the mighty angel. Josephus says the Jews had a prophecy about the destruction of Jerusalem: when the temple area was square again, the city and temple would fall (*War* 6.311). This is not in the Hebrew Scriptures today, but the Dead Sea Scrolls show there were other holy texts at that time, and that the ones we know today sometimes had different wording. John's measuring the temple was an acted prophecy that the temple and city would fall, confirmation that the mighty angel was the expected sign of the Son of man that preceded the destruction of the temple (Mark 13.26–7).[7] After the measuring of the temple and the associated portents, the

---

[4] See above, pp. 2–3.
[5] See above, pp. 6–7.
[6] See above, p. 18.
[7] See my book *The Revelation of Jesus Christ*, Edinburgh: T&T Clark, 2000, pp. 187–190.

last trumpet was heard, and the Kingdom of the LORD and his Christ
was established on earth (Rev. 11.15–18). The secret teaching from
the mighty angel — whatever it was — was the inspiration for John's
Gospel, which he was commanded to write as the prophecy 'for many
people and nations and tongues and languages' (Rev.10.11, my translation). It involved new teaching about the destruction of the temple
and the return of the LORD.

Let me now quote from the Preface of B. F. Westcott's great
commentary on the Fourth Gospel, written before it had become
fashionable to date the Book of Revelation in the last decade of the
first century (rather than 60s CE Palestine and the turmoil of the
war against Rome), and to attribute the Fourth Gospel to another
John. Westcott showed how the Gospel grew from John's experience
of the fall of Jerusalem: 'The crisis of the fall of Jerusalem explains
the relation of the Apocalypse to the Gospel. In the Apocalypse,
that "coming" of Christ was expected and painted in figures: in the
Gospel the "coming" is interpreted. Under this aspect, the Gospel
is the spiritual interpretation of the Apocalypse'; 'The most striking
contrast lies in the treatment of the doctrine of Christ's Coming in
the two books. This is the main subject of the Apocalypse, while it
falls into the background in the Gospel and in the Epistles of John.
In the Apocalypse, the thought is of an outward coming for the open
judgement of men: in the Gospel of a judgement which is spiritual
and self executing ... In the former, the victory and the transformation are from without, by might, and in the future: in the latter,
the victory and the transformation are from within, by a spiritual
influence, and the "future" is present and eternal'.[8]

This was the message of the mighty angel. In the Fourth Gospel,
this experience appears as the Holy Spirit bringing to remembrance
what Jesus had taught (John 14.26); in other words, inspiration
enabling John to write his Gospel in the light of that experience.
Where the Gospel speaks of 'remembering' something, this is the
reinterpretation. When Jesus said 'Destroy this temple and in three
days I will raise it up' (John 2.19), those who heard him would have
taken the saying literally, as doubtless did John. It was the Messianic
claim to destroy and replace the temple. 'But he spoke of the temple
of his body. When therefore he was raised from the dead, his disciples

---

[8] B. F. Westcott *The Gospel according to St John*, London: John Murray, 1903, pp. lxxxv,
lxxxvii.

remembered that he had said this' (John 2.21–2).[9] If raising up the new temple was the resurrection, then everything they believed about the new temple would have been applied to the risen LORD himself, and to the Christian community which was the body of Christ (1 Cor. 12.27). Paul's description of the many parts of the body (1 Cor. 12.4–26) was the same idea as the living stones of the temple, and so it followed that 'Where two or three are gathered in my name, there am I in the midst of them' (Matt. 18.20). The resurrection *was* the return of the LORD, who came to the Church when they were gathered together. The LORD returned in the liturgy, and, as we shall see, the altar was identified with the tomb from which the LORD rose, and the consecration of the elements was the resurrection of the sacrificed LORD. It was the words of the epiclesis, the words invoking the divine presence at the Eucharist, that Basil said were the secret tradition not found in the New Testament.[10]

THE SECOND TEMPLE

The Messiah was expected to destroy the existing temple and build another. This implies two things: that there was something seriously wrong with the second temple; and that the messianic hope was rooted in another, earlier temple. Sometimes this was expressed as the comparison of two women: the Lady, who had been the genius of the city and the symbol of the temple, replaced by an alien woman, a harlot. The temple as a woman was an important symbol, and in Christianity was linked to Mary. John described the temple/city of his time as the great harlot (Rev. 17.1), dressed in the vestments of the high priesthood — purple and scarlet, gold jewels and pearls — and she had a name on her forehead: 'Babylon the great, mother of harlots and of earth's abominations' (Rev. 17.5), a parody of the Name worn on the forehead by the high priest (Exod. 28.36). The harlot would be burned, a punishment reserved for harlots of the house of Aaron, the high priestly family (Lev. 21.9). There is little doubt who she was. And as she burned, the saints in heaven rejoiced and sang praises to God (Rev. 19.1–3).

The second temple, built by the exiles from Babylon who began to return about 530 BCE, was controversial from the outset, and the

---

[9] John also corrected the belief that Jesus had said that John would live to see him return (John 21.21–3).

[10] See below pp. 142ff.

problem was who the chosen people were, who were eligible to enter the temple. The community in exile had consolidated and developed the definition of the chosen people, and all those ancient worshippers of the LORD, who had not been of the ruling class and therefore not deported, found themselves excluded. The accounts of the period are incomplete and confused. There was plenty to hide, but the final chapters of Isaiah give a glimpse of the gulf that opened up in post-exilic Judah. 'Foreigners' and 'eunuchs' were not allowed into the second temple, excluded under newly promulgated laws (Deut. 23.1–6), yet the temple was able to accept money for rebuilding from a foreign king (Ezra 6.6–12). The prophet spoke for the excluded: foreigners and eunuchs who joined themselves to the LORD, to love the LORD, keep the Sabbath and hold fast to the covenant: 'these will I bring to my holy mountain, and make them joyful in my house of prayer; their burnt offerings and their sacrifices will be accepted on my altar, for my house shall be called a house of prayer for all peoples' (Isa. 56.7). These were also Jesus' words when he cleansed the temple (Mark 11.17).

Isaiah was scathing in his attack on the second temple: it was no better than a harlot (Isa. 57.7–8); the priests and their sacrifices there were no better than idolatrous cults: 'The man who kills a bull is no better than one who kills a man, the one who sacrifices a lamb like one who breaks a dog's neck; the person who offers a cereal offering is like someone offering pig's blood, and the one who makes a memorial offering of incense is like someone who blesses an idol' (Isa. 66.3). The bull sacrifice was the special offering of the high priest, dogs and pigs were unclean animals, and idolatry was absolutely forbidden. The context of all this invective was: 'What is the house which you would build for me, and what is the place of my rest?' (Isa. 66.1). The second temple, with its new purity regulations, was no better than the idol temples of neighbouring cultures. Some priests had been excluded, but the detail is lost; Isaiah prophesied that one day they would be recognized and restored to their [temple] heritage: 'You shall be called the priests of the LORD ... Instead of your shame, you shall have a double portion ... For I the LORD love justice, I hate robbery and wrong' (Isa. 61.6–8). The prophet gave a dire warning to the excluders: 'You shall leave your name to my chosen for a curse, and the LORD God will slay you; but his servants he will call by a different name' (Isa. 65.15). If we knew that name, the history of the period could be reconstructed with more confidence. At the heart of these chapters of protest are the words with which

Jesus opened his ministry in the synagogue in Nazareth: 'The Spirit of the Lord GOD is upon me, because the LORD has anointed me ... to bring good tiding to the afflicted ...' (Isa. 61.1). Jesus claimed to fulfil those words, implying that exclusion from worshipping in the temple was fundamental to his ministry. His followers, by implication, were the restored priesthood.

A society divided over this issue was the setting in which the books of the Old Testament were edited and transmitted after the exile. The conflict is apparent. Ezra and the leaders of the return redefined Israel, and so many who had worshipped the LORD were excluded. The old priestly class, however, wanted to keep the wider definition of Israel, and this conflict can be seen in the differences between Deuteronomy and the priestly texts in Leviticus and Numbers. 'Repatriates from Babylon, who sympathised with the exclusionary religious policy of the governors such as Ezra and Nehemiah and those priests who were on their side, would have been very hostile to the open, liberal political stance of the priestly editors.'[11] The priestly laws make special provision for the *ger*, the stranger, who was neither a full member of the community nor a foreigner. Mary Douglas, reading the evidence with an anthropologist's eye, concluded: 'The *ger* was one of the other descendants of Jacob, not descended from Judah, nor from Levi or Benjamin, but those other remnants of the twelve tribes who had been defeated and scattered by invaders and who still lived in Canaan during and after the exile in Babylon ... The stranger in the Bible has a double sign, he is an exile, and yet he is also obliged to keep the ritual laws and entitled to religious consolations, the rituals of atonement.'[12] Jesus spoke of the priority of the lost sheep of the house of Israel (Matt. 10.6; 15.24), and these 'strangers' may be the lost sheep. The issue of inclusion and exclusion, and on what terms, was the first major problem that faced the Church.

Those who had not been in exile in Babylon found themselves in exile in their own land. Jeremiah's prophecy of seventy years in exile (Jer. 25.11; 29.10) was interpreted as seventy times seven (Dan. 9.24), and this fuelled the hopes that after the 490 years, sometimes called ten jubilees, the regime of the second temple would be removed. This date fell about 66–68 CE. According to the Melchizedek text

[11] M. Douglas *Jacob's Tears. The Priestly Work of Reconciliation*. Oxford: Oxford University Press, 2004, p. 59.

[12] M. Douglas 'The Stranger in the Bible', Archives de Sociologie Europeanne, XXXV (1994) 283–96, p. 286.

found at Qumran, the original great high priest Melchizedek would re-appear at the beginning of the tenth jubilee (i.e. 17–19 CE), rescue his people and make the great atonement. The Testament of Levi, a pre-Christian text reworked by Christian hands, describes the seventy weeks in which the sons of Levi (that is, the second temple priests) would wander astray, profane the priesthood and defile the sacrificial altars (T. Levi 16.1). The last of these priests would be idolaters, adulterers, money lovers, arrogant, lawless, voluptuaries, pederasts and men who practise bestiality. The temple would be destroyed as divine judgement upon them, and then a new priest would arise who would open again the gates of Paradise and enable the saints to eat (again) from the tree of life, the promise made by Jesus in Revelation 2.7 (T. Levi 17.11; 18.1, 10). The Christian claim is unmistakeable: the corruption of the priesthood had brought the downfall of the temple, and Jesus was the new high priest. The corruptions of the second temple priests, as listed in the Testament of Levi, are the lifestyles excluded from the heavenly city described in the Book of Revelation (Rev. 21.8, 27; 22.15). Jesus' words: 'Blessed are the pure in heart for they shall see God' (Matt. 5.8) were his comment on the purity of the priesthood, those who claimed the right to enter the holy of holies and look upon God.

The era of the second temple was the age of wrath, according to the conservative priestly community whose writings were found at Qumran (Damascus Document, CD I). They were a faithful remnant to whom God had revealed 'the hidden things in which all Israel had gone astray' (CD III). The liturgical calendar was wrong, and the Sabbaths and glorious feasts had not been observed correctly. The Melchizedek text (11Q Melch) mentions 'teachers who had been hidden and kept secret' and the inheritance of Melchizedek.[13] The Assumption of Moses,[14] another text from the end of the second temple period, gives an overview of the return from exile and observes: 'Some parts of the tribes will arise and come to their appointed place and they will strongly build its walls. The two tribes will remain *steadfast in their former faith*, sorrowful and sighing, because they will not be able to offer sacrifices to the LORD of their fathers' (Ass. Mos. 4.7–8). This former faith, superseded after the exile, was

---

[13] Thus in F. Garcia-Martinez, ed., *Discoveries in the Judaean Desert* XXIII, Oxford: Oxford University Press, 1998, p 229. G. Vermes, *The Complete Dead Sea Scrolls in English*, London: Penguin, 1997, renders this part of the line 'he will assign them to the sons of heaven'.

[14] Also known as the Testament of Moses.

the faith of the first temple, and the evidence is consistent that the priests of the second temple had very different ways. They were an apostate generation whose works were evil (1 Enoch 93.9). *The Christians claimed for Jesus the older priesthood of Melchizedek.*

The returned exiles emphasized that the second temple resumed the ways of the first. The original temple vessels that had been looted by the Babylonians (Jer. 52.17–23) were returned with the first group of settlers (Ezra 1.7–11). Basins, bowls and censers are listed, but there is no mention of the major items: the menorah, the ark, the golden altar. These are not mentioned in the list of loot taken to Babylon, which raises interesting questions: did these items not exist in the first temple, or had they already been removed? Later Jewish tradition hoped that five items from the first temple would be restored in the temple of the Messiah: the fire, the ark, the menorah, the Spirit and the cherubim (Numbers Rabbah XV.10). Since Origen knew that these temple furnishings symbolized the most sacred teachings of the temple, their removal could have been to protect them, or it could have been a way of saying that the teachings of the second temple were very different from those of the first, that *the faith of the first temple would be restored by the Messiah.* Another tradition was that the anointing oil had been hidden away in the time of King Josiah, at the same time as the ark and its contents — the jar of manna and Aaron's priestly staff that had borne almonds (Num. 17.8–10; Babylonian Talmud Horayoth 12a). King Josiah is associated with a purge of the temple in 623 BCE, presented by the writer of 2 Kings as a great reform (2 Kgs 23.4–14), but remembered by others as the time when the great apostasy began, when the priests lost their vision and forsook Wisdom, not long before the temple was burned (1 Enoch 93.8). The real destruction of the temple, then, took place before it was looted by the Babylonians, and it was the original temple, represented by the temple furnishings, that the Messiah would restore.

Of the five items, the cherubim and ark formed the throne of the LORD, and the menorah represented the tree of life. Ezekiel had seen the cherub throne leave the temple (Ezek.10.1–22), and the removal and destruction of the 'asherah' was almost certainly when the menorah left the temple (2 Kgs 23.6). All three — ark, throne and tree of life — reappear in the Book of Revelation: the cherub throne is seen (Rev. 4.2–11),[15] the ark appears (Rev. 11.19), and the servants

---

[15] Described as the throne of the living creatures, but a comparison of Ezekiel's two accounts in Ezek. 1 and 10 shows that the living creatures were remembered as the cherubim.

of God and the Lamb worship before the throne with the tree of life (Rev. 22.1–5). The setting of the worship in the Book of Revelation — which we assume is Christian worship — is the first temple, with the missing items restored.

All these items were kept in the holy of holies, except the menorah, which was in the outer part of the second temple (and so too of the tabernacle, which was described by people who knew the second temple and allowed their memories of the temple to influence accounts of the tabernacle). Now there had been a menorah in the second temple, famously depicted among the Roman loot on the Arch of Titus, but there must have been something about that menorah that was not acceptable, or why would a tradition have persisted that the menorah was missing from the second temple and would be restored in the time of the Messiah? It is possible that the second temple menorah had a different form, or that it was not correctly positioned in the temple. The restored Tree of Life in Revelation stood in the holy of holies by the throne, and not in the outer hall, and a menorah still stands in the holy of holies of an Orthodox church today. It is possible that the missing items — the fire, the ark and its contents, the menorah, the Spirit and the cherubim — together symbolized the secrets of the holy of holies, and the time of their disappearance suggests that they represented the difference between the world and worship of the first and second temples.

The Christian temple

From the very beginning, the Christians saw themselves as the temple of the Messiah, the new temple that was also the restored temple. Stephen was arrested and accused of speaking 'words against this holy place and the law, for we have heard him say that this Jesus of Nazareth will destroy this place and change the customs which Moses delivered to us' (Acts 6.13–14). In his speech before the high priest, Stephen recounted the story of the tabernacle and the temple, and alluded to Solomon's prayer: did God dwell in an earthly house? (1 Kgs 8.27). He quoted Isaiah 66.1 'Heaven is my throne and the earth is my footstool; what is the house which you would build for me ...?' His hearers would have recognized the rest of the passage: it was a condemnation of the second temple priesthood.

James, the first bishop of the Jerusalem church, was martyred about 62 CE. His death was seen, even by Jews, as the immediate cause of the destruction of Jerusalem and the temple. Josephus wrote: 'These things happened to the Jews in requital for the death of James the Righteous, who was brother of Jesus known as the Christ, for though he was the most righteous of men, the Jews put him to death' (quoted in Eusebius, *Church History* 2.23).[16] As late as the fourth century CE, people still believed that it was James' presence that had protected the city: 'At that time most of the apostles and disciples, including James himself, were still alive, and by remaining in the city, furnished the place with an impregnable defence' (Eusebius, *Church History* 3.7). When the last defence of the city had gone, a Jewish prophet, Jesus ben Ananias, appeared and began to utter oracles of woe for seven years, until he died in the siege of Jerusalem (Josephus, *War* 6.300–9).

The issue of the true temple and priesthood led to the first Christian martyrdom, and the martyrdom of James led to the destruction of the temple. The debate that continued for centuries was: What is the true temple? Was it literally the building in Jerusalem, or was it the spiritual temple prescribed in 1 Peter: 'Like living stones, be yourselves built into a spiritual house, to be a holy priesthood' (1 Pet. 2.5). The Christians in Ephesus were part of 'a holy temple in the LORD' (Eph. 2.21), and Jesus had told the Samaritan woman that in future, true worship would be neither in Jerusalem nor in Samaria, but 'in spirit and in truth' (John 4.21, 24). The risen LORD promised that the the faithful Christian would be a pillar in the temple (Rev. 3.12). Clement, bishop of Rome at the end of the first century, wrote to the church at Corinth and emphasized that the liturgy of the Church should be as well ordered as the services in the temple: high priest, priests, Levites and laymen all had their roles assigned (1 Clem. 41). The temple was used as the model for the Church community; it would have been natural to erect a church building like the temple, but there is little evidence for any early Christian building.[17]

The temple was completely destroyed when Jerusalem was taken by the Romans, and the Christians saw this as proof that Jesus' prophecy had been fulfilled. Josephus, an eye-witness of the events, said nothing remained: 'Caesar ordered the whole city and the temple to be razed to the ground, leaving only the loftiest of the towers ... and the portion of the wall enclosing the city on the west — the latter

---

[16] The present text of Josephus does not have this section, but Origen knew it.

[17] 'Although there is no definite trace of the followers of Jesus in the Holy Land from about 70 until 270 CE, literary sources suggest the presence of several forms of Jewish Christianity' (E. Meyers, *Biblical Archaeologist*, 51 (1988), p. 71).

as an encampment for the garrison that was to remain' (*War* 7.1).
'Hapless old men sit beside the ashes of the shrine' (*War* 7.377). As
to rebuilding the actual temple in Jerusalem, Christian hopes were
divided. Barnabas scorned the Jews' efforts to rebuild the temple
after the destruction of 70 CE: they were mistaken to set their hopes
on a building. There could only be a temple 'where God himself tells
us that he is building it and perfecting it', and it would not be made
with hands: 'This temple of the LORD shall be built gloriously, and
listen to the way in which this can be done ... When we were granted
remission of our sins, and came to put our hopes in his Name, we were
made new men, created all over again from the beginning ... This is
what the building up of a spiritual temple to the LORD means' (Barn.
16). Some members of Jesus' family were arrested and questioned a
few years after the destruction of the temple, in the time of Domitian,
who feared talk of the Kingdom. They were released when they said
that the Kingdom was 'not of this world or anywhere on earth, but
angelic and in heaven ...' (Eusebius, *Church History* 3.20).

Justin, on the other hand, born in Palestine twenty years after
Jerusalem had been destroyed, looked for the Kingdom to be established and Jerusalem literally restored. He assured Trypho, the Jew
with whom he was debating: 'I and every other completely orthodox
Christian feel certain that there will be a resurrection of the flesh,
followed by a thousand years in the rebuilt, embellished and enlarged
city of Jerusalem, as announced by the prophets Ezekiel, Isaiah and
the others' (*Trypho* 80). Ezekiel had given detailed instructions for
building a new temple, and so we assume that Justin was looking
for a literal rebuilding. Tertullian, writing early in the third century
in North Africa, hoped for a Kingdom on earth, but envisaged the
new Jerusalem coming down from heaven rather than being built
on earth (*Against Marcion* 3.24). Nepos, a bishop in Egypt in the mid
third century, understood the prophecies of the Book of Revelation
literally, and 'taught that the promises made to the saints in holy
scripture would be fulfilled more in accordance with Jewish ideas
...' (Eusebius, *Church History* 7.24). Jerome (died 420 CE) despaired
at such literalism in reading the Book of Revelation: 'If we accept it
literally, that is Judaising, but if spiritually, as it is written, we seem to
disagree with many of the beliefs of the ancients' (Jerome, *On Isaiah*,
Book 18).

The Jews cherished the hope that the temple would be rebuilt.
The Syriac Apocalypse of Baruch (known as 2 Baruch) is a book of
prophecies set in the sixth century BCE, after the destruction of the

first temple, but in fact written about 100 CE, after the destruction of the second temple. 'Baruch' prophesied that the second temple would be destroyed as the first had been: 'That building [the restored temple] will not remain; but it will again be uprooted after some time and will remain desolate for a time. After that it is necessary that it will be renewed in glory and that it will be perfected into eternity' (2 Bar. 32.3–4). The Jews were encouraged to believe that the temple would soon be restored, and then stand for ever. Barnabas implies that there were plans to rebuild the temple after 70 CE, but this could not have been possible after the second war against Rome in 135 CE, because Hadrian then banished all Jews from their homeland. Some must have returned as pilgrims, because a Christian visitor to Jerusalem in 333 CE saw a great stone which was revered by the Jews — the foundation stone that had been under the holy of holies: at the temple site 'stand two statues of Hadrian, and not far from them, a pierced stone, which the Jews come and anoint every year. They mourn and rend their garments and then depart' (The Pilgrim of Bordeaux, 333 CE)[18]. It is not possible to date other texts such as: 'I go up with weeping and I come down with weeping' (Lamentations Rabbah I.52).

These literal expectations were part of the long-established millennial hope: the new temple of the Messiah, according to 1 Enoch, would be a real building: new columns, new beams, everything bigger and better than the old temple, even though Barnabas quoted a similar Enoch text to argue for a spiritual temple. The Temple Scroll found at Qumran envisaged a new temple building, far bigger even than Herod's, but the community who preserved this text also saw themselves as the spiritual (true) temple while the unclean temple was still standing. Their Council was a holy house;[19] that is, a holy of holies for Israel (The Community Rule 1 QS VIII). Being a spiritual temple did not mean that they did not hope for a great temple building too. John saw no temple in his vision of the heavenly city, presumably because the whole city was the holy of holies, and there was no special place for the presence of the LORD (Rev. 21. 22–7). The Jewish Christian group known as the Ebionites hoped for the restoration of the temple and used to pray facing

---

[18] Text in J. W. Wilkinson, *Jerusalem Pilgrims Before the Crusades*, Warminster: Aris and Philips, 2002.

[19] The same words are used for the holy of holies in the fragment of the Leviticus Targum 4Q156.2

Jerusalem, in accordance with Solomon's prayer that his people should pray towards the temple (1 Kgs 8.30). Epiphanius was scathing about them: they forbad prayer towards the east and then insisted on praying towards the very temple whose sacrificial system they had rejected (*Panarion* 19.3.5).

The earliest recorded Christian pilgrim who went to see the sacred places was Alexander, a bishop from Cappodocia, who visited Jerusalem in about 212 CE 'to see the historic sites' (Eusebius, *Church History* 6.11). He remained there as bishop. In the *Onomasticon*, one of his early writings, Eusebius listed and located all the biblical places, and so he knew the land well before the great changes under Constantine. The new Roman city of Aelia had been built on the site of Jerusalem, but Christians continued to use the old name and remember the holy places. Eusebius tells the story of a Christian arrested during Diocletian's persecution and brought before the magistrate in Caesarea. He said he came from Jerusalem, but the magistrate did not recognize the name, and had to be told where it was (*Martyrs of Palestine* 11.9). There were Christian pilgrims in Bethlehem, 'today so famous that men still hasten from the ends of the earth to see it' (*Proof of the Gospel* 1.1). Expounding the prophecy in Zechariah 14, that the LORD would stand on Zion, and pilgrims come from all over the world to the temple (Zech 14.16), he said: 'Believers in Christ all congregate from all parts of the world, not, as of old time, because of the glory of Jerusalem, nor that they may worship in the ancient temple in Jerusalem, but they rest there that they may learn both about the city being taken and devastated as the prophets foretold, and that they may worship at the Mount of Olives opposite the city, whither the glory of the LORD migrated when it left the fallen city' (*Proof* 6.18).

Eusebius emphasized the importance for Christians of the temple ruins: 'Only from that date of our Saviour Jesus Christ's coming among men have the objects of Jewish reverence — the hill called Zion and Jerusalem, and the buildings there, that is to say the temple, the holy of holies, the altar and whatever else was there dedicated to the glory of God — been utterly removed or shaken', and this was fulfilment of prophecy. The site of the temple was desolate: 'It is sad for the eyes to see stones from the temple itself and from the ancient sanctuary and holy place, used for the building of idol temples and of theatres ...' (*Proof* 8.3). Eusebius said the actual temple site was ploughland: 'I have seen bulls ploughing there, and the sacred site sown with seed.' Was this just an over literal application of the prophecy in Micah 3.12: 'Zion shall be ploughed as a field', or was the site literally returned to open soil? If the latter, then the temple site Eusebius knew cannot have been on the 'Temple Mount' we know today.

During the centuries of persecution, temple imagery had been used to describe the Church community and to frame the liturgies, but little is known about Christian buildings before the great expansion in the time of Constantine. It is also difficult to distinguish the actual buildings from their spiritual interpretation, since the original tabernacle and temple were symbolic structures, erected as the result of visions. Moses had been instructed to build the tabernacle and its furnishings 'according to all he had been shown on Sinai' (Exod. 25. 9, 40) and David had received from the LORD the plan for the temple and its furnishings (1 Chron. 28.19). Methodius, who died a martyr in 311 CE, explained in his *Symposium* the relationship between the tabernacle and the Church, but he seems to mean the Church as a community: 'The Hebrews were ordered to construct the tabernacle as an imitation of the Church, so that they might have a picture which would, through its physical objects, prophesy things which were divine ... Therefore the tabernacle was a symbol of the Church and the Church is a symbol of the heavens ...' The two altars represented the women of the community: the brass altar was the widows and the golden altar the virgins (Methodius, *Symposium* 5.7–8).

When Christianity emerged from the last and fiercest of the early persecutions, new church buildings appeared. Eusebius said there had been many fine church buildings before Diocletian's persecution, and used temple imagery to describe them. Pride and sloth among Christians, however, had brought divine punishment. He compared the destruction of the buildings to the destruction of the temple: 'The LORD in his anger ... profaned to the ground, through the destruction of the churches, his sanctuary ...' (Eusebius, *Church History* 8.1). He continued: 'I saw with my own eyes the places of worship thrown down from top to bottom, the inspired holy Scriptures committed to the flames in the middle of the public squares' (History 8.2). The destruction had begun after the Imperial Council at Nicomedia in 302 CE, which resolved to suppress Christianity throughout the empire. The local cathedral was the first to be destroyed. There were many martyrs, Methodius being one of them. After Diocletian abdicated in 305 CE, the persecution continued under Galerius and Maximian until the Edict of Milan, issued by Constantine and Licinius in 313 CE, established religious freedom throughout the empire. The Christians were the main beneficiaries, and their confiscated property and buildings, such as remained, had to be returned to them.[20]

In their new-found freedom, the Christians built many churches, and described them with temple imagery. Eusebius records the speech he delivered in 323 CE to Paulinus, Bishop of Tyre, who had had the supreme honour of building God's house on earth and re-establishing it for Christ. He compared him to Bezalel who had built the tabernacle, to Solomon who had built the original temple, and to Zerubbabel who had built the second temple (*History* 10.4). Texts from the Psalms about entering the house of the LORD were applied to the new churches, but Eusebius also included the older belief that the Christian community was the living temple. Jesus Christ was the chief cornerstone, who had been rejected by the builders 'not only of that old building which no longer exists, but also of the building that still stands and consists of most of mankind'. In contrast was the 'temple built of yourselves, a living temple of the living God, the greatest truly majestic sanctuary'. He went on to speak of the temple of the universe, which the temple in Jerusalem had represented. The cathedral at Tyre was described as a temple: there were fountains in the courtyard before the temple, and the place of the altar was called the holy of holies. Its doors were in the east end, and its sanctuary in the west, exactly as in the second temple. Praying towards the east cannot have been a universally recognized Christian custom.

When Helena, the mother of the Emperor Constantine, travelled to the Holy Land in 326 CE, she was taken to the site of Jesus' tomb, which had been buried under a pagan temple. This was excavated, and the cave was found, together with three crosses, one of which was recognized as the cross of Jesus because a woman was miraculously healed.[21] Uncovering the cave was itself regarded as a resurrection: 'Stage by stage the underground site was exposed … and the cave, the holy of holies, took on the appearance of a representation of the Saviour's return to life … New Jerusalem was built at the very testimony to the Saviour, facing the famous Jerusalem of old, which after the bloody murder of the LORD had been overthrown in utter devastation' (Eusebius, *Life of Constantine*, 3.33). The great church

---

[20] Diocletian's mausoleum in Split was consecrated as St Domnius' cathedral in the seventh century.

[21] Eusebius does not mention finding the cross, but Cyril of Jerusalem writing some twenty years later, knew that relics of the cross were already spread throughout the world (*Catecheses* 10.19).

built at the site of the crucifixion and resurrection was 'an enormous house of prayer, a temple holy to the saving sign' (Eusebius, *In Praise of Constantine* 9.16).

The Church of the Resurrection was intended as a new temple, with its holy of holies in the west and its doors facing east. '[Constantine] first of all decked out the sacred cave ... On the side opposite the cave, which looked toward the rising sun, was connected the royal temple, an extraordinary structure of immense height, and very extensive in length and breadth ... (*Life of Constantine* 3.33). Its proportions were those of the temple, with the inner shrine over the tomb corresponding to the holy of holies. Just as the holy of holies had been one third the length of the temple (1 Kgs 6.16–17), so too the new holy of holies was one third the length of the church.[22] The new temple was dedicated in 335 CE, on 13 September, just as Solomon had dedicated his temple at the great autumn festival (1 Kgs 8.2, 65). Egeria, who visited the holy places in 381–6 CE, was one of the many pilgrims who came to see the sites and learn that this was the new temple. She noted in her diary, and so must have been told, that the annual commemoration of the Church of the Resurrection was just like Solomon's dedication of the temple (*Egeria's Travels* 48.2). About fifty years later, Sozomen described the dedication: 'The temple called 'The Great Witness', built in the place of the skull at Jerusalem, was completed about the thirtieth year of Constantine ... When the bishops arrived at Jerusalem, the temple was consecrated as were numerous ornaments and gifts ... Since that time, the anniversary of the consecration has been celebrated with great pomp by the church at Jerusalem, the festival lasting eight days and the people are baptised ...' (Sozomen, *Church History* 2.26, cf. Solomon's dedication 1 Kgs 8.65–6).

Constantine's new temple was not a replacement for the temple destroyed by the Romans. The Christians saw themselves as restoring the original temple, the temple of the Messiah, and so Constantine's temple was presented as the original temple. Ambrose (died 397 CE), bishop of Milan, would later assure his people 'that the sacraments of Christians are older than those of the Jews' (*On the Sacraments* 1.4). As early as Eusebius, who watched the Church of the Resurrection being built, there were allusions to Solomon. 'Wicked men — or rather, the whole tribe of demons through them' had tried to conceal the tomb of Christ (*Life of Constantine* 326). The popular legend was that

---

[22] J. Wilkinson *Egeria's Travels*, 3rd edn, Warminster: Aris and Phillips, 1999, p. 62.

Solomon had been hampered in his building by demons, and had controlled them with a magic ring.[23] Egeria was shown this ring as one of the relics in the new temple, and she also saw the horn of oil used for anointing the kings, which had disappeared from Solomon's temple in the time of Josiah (*Egeria's Travels* 37.3). A pilgrim's guide to the holy places, written about 500 CE, knew even more links to Solomon's temple.[24] There were twelve silver capitals on the marble pillars, where Solomon had sealed the demons, as well as the horn and the ring Egeria had seen. This was also the place where Adam had been formed from the dust, and where Abraham had prepared Isaac for sacrifice. In Jewish tradition, these had happened on the temple Mount: according to the Palestinian Targum, Adam had been created from the dust of the place of the sanctuary,'[25] and Isaac was offered on Mount Moriah, where the temple had been built (Gen. 22.2; 2 Chron. 3.1).

The shrine built over the tomb [the *edicule* or 'little house') was depicted on pilgrim souvenirs in the same way as the holy of holies on Jewish coins from the second war against Rome, 132–5 CE: a building with four pillars which housed the ark. Since the Jewish coins are far older than the pilgrim flasks, this must have been a conscious imitation: the *edicule* was the new holy of holies and the tomb was the ark.[26] Jewish and Christian pilgrim souvenirs were identical. In the view of an art historian: 'Both Christian and Jewish vessels ... were made in the same workshop, at the same time, but appealed to a different public, to different pilgrims ... the Holy Sepulchre Church came to be in Christian symbolism what the temple was in Jewish symbolism ...'[27] Two Christian women, who visited the tomb shortly after Egeria, described it as the holy of holies: 'The Jews formerly venerated the holy of holies ... Does not the tomb of the LORD seem more worthy of veneration?'[28] The equivalence of tomb and holy of holies passed into the liturgy written shortly after the great church

[23] The story is told in The Testament of Solomon, in J. H. Charlesworth (ed.), *Old Testament Pseudepigrapha*, London: Darton Longman and Todd, 1983, vol. 1.

[24] The Brevarius, text in Wilkinson, *Jerusalem Pilgrims*.

[25] Tg. Pseudo-Jonathan Gen. 2.7.

[26] See B. Kuhnel, *From the Earthly to the Heavenly Jerusalem, Representations of the Holy City in Christian Art of the First Millennium*, Freiburg, 1987, esp. p. 82.

[27] B. Kuhnel 'Jewish Symbolism of the Temple and the Tabernacle and Christian Symbolism of the Holy Sepulchre and the Heavenly Tabernacle', *Journal of Jewish Art*, 12–13 (1986–7), pp. 147–68, p. 152.

[28] Letter of Paul and Eustochia, in Jerome, *Letters* 46.

was built: the tomb being described as the place of the throne in Paradise and the source of the river of life. 'Truly thy tomb, O Christ, has been shown to be brighter than any royal chamber, as bringing life, and more beautiful than Paradise. It is the fountain of our resurrection' (Liturgy of St John Chrysostom, 347–407 CE). Centuries later, when he was explaining the symbolism of the liturgy, Germanus of Constantinople wrote: 'The altar corresponds to the holy tomb of Christ ... The chancel barriers indicate the place of prayer: outside is for the people and the inside, the holy of holies, is accessible only to the priests. The barriers, like those of the holy sepulchre, are made of bronze ...' (Germanus, *On the Divine Liturgy*, 6, 8).

Contemporary church leaders discouraged such pilgrimage. John Chrysostom, expounding Hebrews 12.18, said: 'Wonderful indeed were the things in the temple, the Holy of Holies ... The new covenant, however, was not given with any of these things' (*On Hebrews*, Homily 32). Gregory, bishop of Nyssa in Cappodocia, who died in 395 CE, explained that Christians had been called to a higher heritage in heaven, and so '[The LORD] has not counted the trip to Jerusalem among good deeds, nor did he include such a thing in the beatitudes.' He argued that women could not go on such a journey without a protector, and that the inns on the way were dreadful places: 'If the grace of God was greater in the places of Jerusalem, there would be less sin among those who live there.' The faith was neither increased nor decreased by pilgrimage: Christians believed in the incarnation without visiting Bethlehem, in the resurrection without visiting the tomb, and in the ascension without going to the Mount of Olives. So what was the point of pilgrimage? (Gregory, *Letter* 2).

The destruction of the temple continued to be cited as proof that Jesus was the Messiah. Athanasius (the great bishop of Alexandria who died in 373 CE) in his treatise *On the Incarnation* alluded to the enigmatic prophecy in Daniel, that after seventy weeks of years, the Most Holy One would be anointed, and that both vision and prophecy would be 'sealed' or fulfilled. Transgression and sin would be put away, and everlasting righteousness 'brought in' (Dan. 9.24). Athanasius wrote: 'Since that time, all prophecy has been sealed, and city and temple taken ... How can they ... deny Christ who has brought all this about? ... There is no longer any king or prophet, nor Jerusalem nor sacrifice nor visions among them; yet the whole earth is filled with the knowledge of God, and the Gentiles, forsaking atheism, are now taking refuge in the God of Abraham through the Word, our LORD Jesus Christ' (*On the Incarnation* 40).

When Athanasius' contemporary, the Emperor Julian (who reigned only two years and died in 363 CE) sought to restore the old Roman religion and prevent the further spread of Christianity, he encouraged the Jews to rebuild the temple, as proof against the claims of the Christians. Earthquakes and storms forced them to abandon the project which was started in May 363 CE. John Chrysostom, a boy in Antioch at the time, may well have heard reports from the Jewish community in his city, because he later wrote: 'They were just about to start building when suddenly fire leaped forth from the foundations and consumed not only a great number of the workmen but even the stone piled up there to support the structure' (*Against the Judaising Christians* 16). A poem by Ephrem reveals how contemporary Christians viewed the rebuilding project:

> '[The Most High] ordered gales to blow, he beckoned earthquakes and they came,
> lightning too and it caused turmoil; (he bade) the air and it turned murky,
> the walls, and they were overthrown, the gates and they opened themselves,
> fire came forth and consumed the scribes,
> who had read in Daniel that she would lie waste for ever;
> and because they had read without understanding, they were mightily struck and so learnt.[29]

A recently discovered letter in Syriac, attributed to Cyril (bishop of Jerusalem 349–87 CE)[30] seems to be a first-hand account: 'At the digging of the foundations of Jerusalem, which had been ruined because of the killing of the LORD, the land shook considerably, and there were great tremors in the towns round about ... There were strong winds and storms, with the result that they were unable to lay the Temple's foundation that day.' The Christians prayed, and processed around the city, and saw the doors of the synagogue open of their own accord and fire burst forth: 'We felt compelled to write to you the truth of these matters, that everything that is written about Jerusalem should be established in truth, no stone shall be left in it that shall not be upturned'; 'This year the pagan Julian died, and it was he who had especially incited the Jews to rebuild the Temple ...'[31]

---

[29] Ephrem, *Hymns against Julian* IV, in S. P. Brock, 'A Letter attributed to Cyril of Jerusalem on the Rebuilding of the Temple', *Bulletin of the School of Oriental and African Studies* 40(1977), p. 283.

[30] The letter was being attributed to Cyril in the sixth century, even if it was not written by him.

[31] Brock, 'A Letter', pp. 267–86.

One of the great mysteries of Constantinople may have been another temple. Construction work in 1960 uncovered some huge marble blocks, with parts of an inscription. It was recognized as the inscription on the Church of St Polyeuktos,[32] which had been built by Anicia Juliana, a royal lady. 'She alone did violence to Time and surpassed the wisdom of renowned Solomon by raising a habitation for God whose glittering and elaborate beauty the ages cannot celebrate.' The poem described a church with many columns of fine marble and a golden dome. It was completed in 527 CE; almost nothing remains, but archaeologists have identified pillars looted from the church in Venice and in Barcelona.[33] The dimensions of the church show that it was a temple: 100 royal cubits square. In his vision of the restored temple, Ezekiel saw a structure 100 cubits square (Ezek. 41.13–14), and this eventually became, in temple tradition, the ideal of a 100 cubit cube, although the Mishnah shows there were disputes as to how the measurements were to be taken.[34] When Herod the Great rebuilt the temple in 20 BCE, it was 100 cubits long and the façade was 100 cubits wide and high.[35] The walls of Solomon's temple had been decorated with cherubim, palm trees and open flowers (1 Kgs 6.29), the pillars with chequerwork capitals, pomegranates and lilies (1 Kgs 7.17–19). Even the remaining fragments of St Polyeuktos show that the pillars resembled trees or were topped with chequerwork capitals. Stylized lilies have also been found. An archaeologist who worked on the site concluded that, given 'the coincidence of measurements corroborated by coincidence of decoration', it was a temple.[36]

Sixth-century texts show that temple tradition, in all its aspects, was still important for Christian understanding of their church buildings. The building of the cathedral in Edessa began in 313 CE under Constantine, was badly damaged by floods in 525 CE, and was restored with funds from Justinian. A hymn composed to mark the completed restoration is the earliest evidence for the cosmic symbolism of a church building. The Jerusalem temple had been a microcosm of the creation, with the six days of creation in Genesis 1

---

[32] The text was preserved in full in *The Greek Anthology*, tr. W. R. Paton, London and New York: Loeb, vol. 1, 1916.

[33] Beside San Marco, known as the 'pilastri acritani' because it was thought they had been looted from Acre, and in the Barcelona Archaeological Museum.

[34] Mishnah Middoth 4.6.

[35] Josephus *Antiquities* 15.390; *War* 5.207.

[36] J. M. Harrison, *A New Temple for Byzantium*, Austin: University of Texas Press, 1989, p. 137.

corresponding to the stages by which the tabernacle (and later, the temple) had been erected.[37] The holy of holies and the outer hall had represented the invisible and the visible, heaven and earth, with the presence of God concealed at the heart of creation. This way of thinking about the temple was still current in the sixth century, as can be seen in the writings of Cosmas, an Egyptian Christian. Moses, he said, had seen the six days of creation in a vision on Sinai, and this is what he replicated in the tabernacle.[38] It was not new: Philo had explained that the divine temple of the creator had to represent the universal temple that was the creation (*Questions on Exodus* 2.85), and Christian writers such as Origen early in the third century CE (*On Exodus*, Homily 9) and Gregory of Nyssa in the mid fourth century CE (*Life of Moses* 2.170–88) show that the idea was well established in Christianity.

Even though the shape of the cathedral in Edessa differed from the Jerusalem temple — the dome was a novel form — the hymn writer compared the church to the tabernacle: 'Bezalel constructed the tabernacle for us with the model he learned from Moses, and Amidonius and Asaph and Addai built a glorious temple for you in Urha (Edessa).' Thus the hymn writer could say of the cathedral in Edessa: 'Clearly portrayed in it are the mysteries of both your Essence and your Dispensation', the Essence being God in the holy of holies, and Dispensation being the works of God visible in the creation. 'Exalted are the mysteries of this temple, in which heaven and earth symbolise the most exalted Trinity and our Saviour's Dispensation'; 'It is a wonder that its smallness is like the wide world ...' There were temple features too: cherubim on the altar, just as there had been cherubim over the ark; the throne of Christ in the sanctuary surrounded by places for the priests, just as there had been the throne of the LORD in the holy of holies, surrounded by the angel hosts.[39]

Justinian, who had seen the church of St Polyeuktos completed at the very beginning of his reign, had the opportunity to build a great church himself when the Church of the Holy Wisdom was destroyed by fire in 532 CE. His new church was consecrated in 537 CE, and, unlike the cathedral in Edessa which was destroyed in 1031 CE, the

---

[37] See my book *The Great High Priest*, London: T&T Clark, 2003, pp. 15–25.

[38] Cosmas, *Topography*, 2.35.

[39] Translation in K. McVey, 'The Domed Church as Microcosm: Literary Roots of an Architectural Symbol', *Dumbarton Oaks Papers* 37, 1983.

great Church of Constantinople still stands. Its form and dimensions can be studied. Ezekiel had a vision of the true temple, as it should be restored, revealed to him by an angel. He was told to recount everything to the 'house of Israel' so that they would be ashamed of all their sins. The exact form, measurements, laws and ordinances of the temple were important (Ezek. 43.10–11). Since the Christians aspired to restore the true temple, this may explain some of the measurements and features of the great church in Constantinople. Assuming that the information missing from accounts of the temple was supplemented by detail from the tabernacle, it is possible to explain why there were twenty pillars in both the north and south aisles of the great church: there were twenty pillars to the north and twenty to the south of the tabernacle court (Exod. 27.9–11). There were nine doors, and therefore ten 'pillars' between them at the western end of the great church, just as there were ten pillars at the western end of the tabernacle court (Exod. 27.12). The central area between the four piers is a square of side 100 feet, representing the size of the ideal temple. Tradition says that when he entered the church, Justinian said 'Solomon, I have surpassed you.' This was a temple.

The greatest of all the Christian temples was the New Church, the Nea, built in Jerusalem by Justinian and consecrated on 20 November 543 CE. The church was dedicated to Mary, the Holy Mother of God. The church was described, albeit briefly, by Procopius,[40] the court historian, and everything he says shows that the Nea was intended to be the new temple, beyond compare, built on the highest of the hills. It was built on the western hill of the city, on a site with no known Christian associations, on the south-eastern slope of the hill at that time called Zion. In the time of Solomon, however, Zion had been the eastern hill of Jerusalem, and Solomon's temple had been built on Zion. This explains the site, and also the enormous size of the structure, which was far too big for the site, and so the area under the apse was built over a vaulted cistern. Remains of the church have been excavated, and its dimensions are known: it was 200 cubits long and 100 cubits wide. This is exactly the size for the restored temple revealed by the angel to Ezekiel: the building was to be 100 cubits square, with a courtyard also 100 cubits square. Two huge columns stood before the entrance to the church, 'exceptionally large and probably second to no column in the whole world.'[41] There were no

---

[40] Procopius, *Buildings*, Book V.
[41] Procopius, *Buildings*, V. vi.

pillars like this in Herod's temple, but the mysterious pillars named Jachin and Boaz had stood before the entrance to Solomon's temple (1 Kgs 7.15-22). The cistern under the apse suggests that there could even have been water flowing in and from this temple, just as Ezekiel saw in his vision of the new temple in the new Jerusalem (Ezek. 47.1).

Shortly before the Nea was completed, in 543 CE, Justinian's general, Belisarius, had recovered the temple treasures from the Vandals who had taken them to Carthage when they had sacked Rome. The menorah and the table for the shewbread had been in a temple in Rome since the time of Titus, when the temple treasure had been taken in triumph from the ruins of Jerusalem. When they were brought to Constantinople, Justinian was warned by a Jew that they should be sent back to Jerusalem where they belonged, and so he sent them to 'the temples', *hiera*, of the Christians in Jerusalem. There is no record of where they were kept; the Nea is the most likely place. If Justinian was restoring the original temple, he would have restored also the tree of life, the symbol of Wisdom, that had been removed during Josiah's purge in 623 BCE.[42] This was one of the five things to be restored in the true temple (the ark, the fire, the spirit, the cherubim and the menorah). It also became a symbol of Mary, the Mother of God, which may account for the Orthodox Church celebrating the Entry of the Mother of God into the temple on 21 November, the day after the consecration of the Nea.[43]

The Christians believed that they were the true heirs to the temple. The unanswered questions were: should the restored temple be a spiritual temple, or a building that reproduced Ezekiel's ideal temple? And should the temple be in Jerusalem?

---

[42] Removing the 'asherah', the tree symbol, is described in 2 Kgs 23.6.

[43] A full account of the Nea can be found in my article 'The New Church' in *Sourozh*, February 2006.

Chapter 4

LORD *AND CHRIST*

No one can say 'Jesus is LORD' except by the Holy Spirit.

1 Corinthians 12.3

In the Book of Revelation there are many pictures of worship: the twenty-four elders worshipped the One on the throne (Rev. 4.10); every creature in heaven and on earth and under the earth and in the sea joined with heaven to worship the Lamb on the throne (Rev. 5.11–14); the multitude which no one could number joined with the angels, the elders and the living creatures to worship God and the Lamb (Rev. 7.9–12). Worship is the setting and pattern for the whole book. When John first saw the vision of the risen LORD as the Man among the lamps, he fell at his feet as though dead (Rev. 1.17), just as Ezekiel had fallen on his face before the vision of the glory of the LORD in human form (Ezek. 1.28), and Daniel had fallen on his face when he heard the words of the man clothed in linen, whom the early Christians identified as the LORD (Dan. 10.9).[1] Daniel was told: 'Fear not' (Dan. 10.12). Enoch fell prostrate when he saw the Glory, but the LORD said to him: 'Do not fear, Enoch, righteous man ... come near to me and hear my voice' (1 Enoch 15.1). There is something similar in 2 Enoch. When Enoch saw the fiery and glorious face of the LORD he fell before him, but the LORD called: 'Do not fear! Stand up, and stand before my face for ever' (2 Enoch 22.5). When John fell down at the feet of the angel who showed him the visions, however, he was forbidden to worship an angel: 'You must not do that. I am a fellow servant with you and your brethren the prophets, and with those who keep the words of this book. Worship God' (Rev. 22.9 with a similar verse at Rev. 19.10).

There was an important difference between the LORD and the angels, as is clear in the opening verses of Hebrews. The Son receives

---

[1] See above, p. 50n.

73

worship — 'Let all God's angels worship him' (Heb. 1.6) — but
the angels do not receive worship, because the Son has become so
much better than the angels 'as he hath by inheritance obtained
a more excellent name than they' (Heb. 1.4, Authorized Version).
The angels, on the other hand, are fellow servants with 'those who
hold the testimony of Jesus' (Rev. 19.10), showing that *the faithful
Christians were themselves angels*. The Name that Jesus had 'by inheritance obtained' was the sacred Name Yahweh,[2] which explains why
Christians worshipped Jesus: 'Therefore God has highly exalted him
and bestowed on him the name which is above every name, that at
the name of Jesus every knee should bow, in heaven and on earth and
under the earth, and every tongue confess that Jesus Christ is LORD,
to the glory of God the Father' (Phil. 2.9–11). The name above every
name is Yahweh, and the allusion is to Isaiah 45.23: 'To me every
knee shall bow, every tongue shall swear', originally said of Yahweh,
but here of Jesus. The hymn proclaims that Jesus has been given the
Name, and so all creation acknowledges that Jesus Christ is Yahweh.

The Greek text has *Kyrios Iesous Christos,* and some ancient versions
of the New Testament at this point have simply *Kyrios Iesous,* 'Jesus is
the LORD', just as in 1 Corinthians 12.3, where it is the acclamation in
Christian worship and usually translated 'Jesus is LORD.' Paul wrote to
the church in Rome: 'If you confess with your lips that Jesus is LORD,
(*Kyrios*) and believe in your heart that God raised him from the dead,
you will be saved' (Rom. 10.9). For any Greek-speaking Jew, however,
Kyrios was the usual way to render the name Yahweh. It meant 'LORD'
in vernacular Greek, but in the Scripture it represented Yahweh. In
the Greek Old Testament, where the LORD speaks to Moses at the
burning bush and reveals his Name, the Hebrew form Yahweh is
always rendered *Kyrios.* Thus: 'Say this to the people of Israel, "*Kyrios,*
the God of your fathers, the God of Abraham ... "' (Exod. 3.15); 'And
God said to Moses, "I am *Kyrios.* I appeared to Abraham, to Isaac,
and to Jacob, as God Almighty, but by my name *Kyrios* I did not make
myself known to them"' (Exod. 6. 2–3). In Genesis, 'Yahweh Elohim',
the LORD God, becomes '*Kyrios* the God' (Gen. 2.4). The earliest
Christian proclamation of faith was Jesus is *Kyrios,* Jesus is Yahweh.[3]
Peter's exhortation was: 'In your hearts reverence Christ as LORD'
(1 Pet. 3.15). At the Name that Jesus was given, every knee in heaven

[2] Not, as some hymns imply, the name 'Jesus'.
[3] For detail, see my book *The Great Angel. A Study of Israel's Second God,* London:
SPCK, 1992, pp. 218–9.

and earth and under the earth bowed in worship, and acknowledged that Jesus was Yahweh. *The unity and message of the Bible would be restored if the form 'Lord' were used throughout, showing that it represents the sacred Name in both Old and New Testaments.*

The earliest account of Christian worship in a non-Christian source is found in one of the letters of Pliny the Younger (*Letter* 10), written in 112 CE, when he was governor of Bithynia. He was reporting to the Emperor Trajan on his dealings with the Christians and outlined their customs: that they met before daylight on one day of the week and bound themselves with an oath. Since the word used is *sacramentum*, the Christians may well have been telling him about their sacrament, which is the more usual meaning of *sacramentum*. They also sang *carmen Christo quasi deo*, a hymn to Christ as a God. This hymn may have been an original composition, or it may have been one of the Psalms, but the Roman governor understood that this was worship of Christ. The temple tradition had been to invoke, to thank and to praise the Lord with music, which in the Greek became 'praising *Kyrios*, the God of Israel' (1 Chron. 16.4). The Psalmist had declared: 'I will sing and make melody to the Lord' (Ps. 27.6); 'Sing to him, sing praises to him' (Ps. 105.2); 'I will awake the dawn! I will give thanks to thee O Lord among the peoples, I will sing praises to thee among the nations' (Ps. 108.2–3)[4]. Justin shows that Christians thought the Psalms referred to Jesus: 'Say among the nations, the Lord reigns from the tree'[5] was seen as a prophecy of the crucifixion (*Trypho* 73, quoting Ps. 96.10). Using the Psalms as hymns to the Lord, meaning Jesus, or as prophecies of his life, was a determining factor in the development of Christian belief and worship. To say the Psalms were re-read, that is, *re-interpreted,* by the Church, is to make a distorting assumption. If the Christians declared 'Jesus is Yahweh', then they would have read the Psalms in their original sense, as praise to Yahweh, the God of Israel.

It is therefore quite natural that Matthew, the most Jewish of the Gospel writers, should often say that people worshipped Jesus. The wise men fell down and worshipped (Matt. 2.11); the leper worshipped Jesus (Matt. 8.2); the disciples worshipped Jesus after the miracle of walking on the water (Matt. 14.33); the Canaanite woman worshipped as she asked Jesus to cure her daughter (Matt. 15.25); the

---

[4] It would be interesting to know if these temple musicians or the early Christians, followed the Essene practice of praying before daybreak facing east.

[5] Reading the longer version of the text known in the early Church.

disciples worshipped the risen LORD (Matt. 28.9,17). The Greek verb used is *proskunein*, which usually means to worship or do obeisance, but it can also mean to give a respectful greeting to a superior. Thus Matthew also wrote of the man in debt who 'worshipped' his master and asked for forgiveness (Matt. 18.26). The problem is: which is the more likely meaning of the verb in those other instances, where people 'worship' Jesus?

The Jews amongst whom Jesus lived were prepared to die rather than allow the Emperor Caligula to have a statue of himself put in the temple. 'He wished to be considered a god' wrote Josephus, 'and he sent Petronius (in 40 CE) with an army to Jerusalem to install in the sanctuary statues of himself' (*Jewish War* 2.184–5). He met fierce resistance, and a crowd warned him that 'if he wished to set up these statues, he must first sacrifice the entire Jewish nation' (*Jewish War* 2.197). Caligula died, and so the matter could rest, but this episode shows how the Jews felt about worshipping a human being. This is one part of the context in which Matthew's Gospel must be read, the part which raises the question: is it likely that such Jewish people would have worshipped Jesus? The other part of the context, however, is the claim, unique to Christians, that Jesus was Yahweh, and so the only one who could be worshipped.

Yahweh was represented in the temple by the high priest, who wore the four letters of the Name on his forehead (Exod. 28.36). In about 300 BCE, a Greek writer described the high priest as an angel whom his people worshipped, *proskunein*. 'The high priest … is an angel to them of God's commandments' and when he spoke, the Jews 'immediately fall to the ground and worship the high priest as he explains the commandments to them.'[6] This was not just a Gentile visitor describing what he saw in his own terms and getting it wrong. The prophet Malachi, who cannot be dated, but seems to address the situation in the fifth century BCE, described priests as angels of the LORD, and condemned them for neglecting their calling: 'The lips of a priest should guard knowledge, and men should seek instruction from his mouth, for he is the angel/messenger of the LORD of Hosts (Mal. 2.7). Philo, the exact contemporary of Jesus, thought of the high priest as an angel. When he read Leviticus 16.17, which describes Aaron going into the holy of holies alone, 'no man in the tent of meeting', he understood it to mean that the high priest was not a man when he was in the holy place: he was an angel (Philo, *On*

---

[6] Hecataeus, quoted in Diodorus Siculus XL 3.5–6.

Dreams II.189, 231). This is probably how we should understand the Jewish description of Simon the high priest, written in Jerusalem in about 200 BCE. When he emerged from the holy of holies he was like the morning star, like the sun shining on the temple; his very presence made the court of the temple glorious. When he had poured the libation, the trumpets sounded and 'all the people together ... fell to the ground upon their faces to worship (*proskunein*) their LORD (*Kyrios*) ...' (ben Sira 50.17). The most natural way to read this is that they were worshipping the high priest, or rather, Yahweh whom he represented.

In the New Testament there are doxologies ascribed to Christ: '... our LORD and Saviour Jesus Christ. To him be the glory both now and to the day of eternity' (2 Pet. 3.18); 'to him who loves us and has freed us from our sins by his blood ... to him be glory and dominion for ever and ever' (Rev. 1.5–6).[7] There are benedictions: 'May our God and Father himself, and our LORD Jesus, direct our way to you; and may the LORD make you increase and abound in love ...' (1 Thess. 3.11–12; also 2 Thess. 3.5 and 3.16). The disciples prayed to Jesus before choosing someone to replace Judas (Acts 1.24). The dying Stephen prayed: 'LORD do not hold this sin against them' (Acts 7.60). The leaders of the church in Antioch worshipped the LORD and fasted before sending Paul and Barnabas on their mission (Acts 13.2). Presumably 'the LORD' here is Jesus. Paul had prayed to the LORD three times about his 'thorn in the flesh' (2 Cor. 12.8).

Jesus was also described as 'Yahweh'. John the Baptist had preached 'Prepare the way of Yahweh' (Matt. 3.3; Luke 3.4 quoting Isa. 40.3). He sent to ask Jesus if he was indeed the one who was to come (Luke 7.18–23), and Jesus implied that he was. Jesus was called 'Saviour' and 'Redeemer', titles of Yahweh in the Old Testament. The Psalmist prayed: 'Yahweh save me' (Pss. 3.7; 6.4; 7.1; 22.21; 31.2; 44.6; 54.1; 55.16; 59.2; 69.1; 71.2; 119.94). Isaiah constantly proclaimed that Yahweh was Israel's Saviour and King: 'For I am the LORD your God, the Holy One of Israel, your Saviour' (Isa. 43.3); 'I am the LORD your Saviour and Redeemer, the Mighty One of Jacob' (Isa. 49.26; also Isa. 33.22; 43.11–12; 60.16; 63.8). Jesus was recognized as that Saviour: his name meant Saviour (Matt. 1.21–3), he was proclaimed at birth as a Saviour (Luke 2.11), he was mocked as Christ the Saviour (Luke 23.39), recognized as Saviour by the Samaritan woman (John 4.42), and Peter proclaimed him as Saviour (Acts 5.31), as did Paul (Acts

---

[7] There are other examples, but less clear: Rom. 9.5; Heb. 13.20–1; 2 Tim. 4.18.

13.23). Jesus could be described as 'Our God and Saviour Jesus Christ' and immediately afterwards as 'Our LORD and Saviour Jesus Christ' (2 Pet. 1.1 and 11). Jesus was also called the 'Redeemer': Zechariah sang of the LORD God of Israel who had 'visited and redeemed his people' (Luke 1.68), and the disciples on the road to Emmaus said that they had hoped that Jesus would be the one to redeem Israel (Luke 24.21). When the risen LORD spoke to John in his vision, he said: 'I am the first and the last and the living one; I died, and behold I am alive for ever more' (Rev. 1.17–18). These had been the words of Yahweh: 'Thus says the LORD, the King of Israel, and his Redeemer, the LORD of Hosts: "I am the first and I am the last ... "' (Isa. 44.6). In their use of Scripture, the early Christian freely applied to Jesus the roles, titles and words of Yahweh.

SEARCHING THE SCRIPTURES[8]

When the Christians read the Old Testament, they read it as a record of the work and words of Yahweh, the LORD, the pre-incarnate Jesus. Paul, who had been most zealous for the traditions of his people, applied Yahweh texts to Jesus. 'All who call on the name of the LORD shall be saved' (Joel 2.32) was quoted by Paul when he was showing that the gospel was for all people. 'If you confess with your lips that Jesus is LORD ... Everyone who calls upon the name of the LORD will be saved' (Rom. 10. 9, 13). Jesus was Yahweh, and those who called on him, as Joel had said, would be saved: 'I have been found by those who did not seek me. I have shown myself to those who did not ask for me' were the words of Yahweh through Isaiah (Isa. 65.1), but used by Paul of Christ (Rom. 10.20). 'When he ascended on high he led a host of captives ...' had originally described Yahweh appearing in his holy place, conquering his enemies and then ascending to his sanctuary on the holy mountain (Ps. 68.18). In the Letter to the Ephesians, the verse described Jesus' ascension (Eph. 4.8).

When Paul read the Old Testament, he understood that Yahweh was Christ. In the story of the Exodus and desert wanderings, the Rock that gave them water (Exod. 17.6; Num. 20.11) was Christ (1 Cor. 10.1–4). Some ancient manuscripts of the New Testament even have Jesus saving the Israelites from Egypt: '... saved a people out of the land of Egypt' (Jude 5) is found as '*God* saved', 'the LORD saved'

---

[8] For detail of this, see my book *The Great Angel*, London: SPCK, 1992, pp. 190–231.

and '*Jesus* saved'.[9] Hebrews, like John, (John 1.3), presented Jesus as the agent of creation (Heb. 1.2) and said that Moses considered the abuse suffered for the Christ greater wealth than the treasures of Egypt (Heb. 11.26). John was emphatic that the One who appeared in the Old Testament was not God the Father but Jesus, before his incarnation: 'Not that anyone has seen the Father except him who is from God; he has seen the Father' (John 6.46); the Jews had never heard the Father's voice nor seen his form (John 5.37). The Yahweh of the Scriptures was Jesus: 'You search the Scriptures ... and it is they that bear witness to me' (John 5.39). Moses wrote of him (John 5.46); Abraham had seen him (John 8.56), perhaps a reference to the LORD appearing to Abraham at Mamre (Gen. 18.1).

This is what the Church continued to believe. In the time of Constantine, a great basilica was built at Mamre, to commemorate the place where the LORD, meaning Jesus, had appeared to Abraham. Sozomen, the church historian from Palestine who was writing in the fifth century, was quite clear about this: 'It is recorded that here [Mamre] the Son of God appeared to Abraham, with two angels ... He who, for the salvation of mankind, was born of a Virgin, there manifested himself to a godly man.' What the Old Testament records as the appearance of Yahweh to Abraham is here clearly understood as a story about Jesus. The Emperor Constantine ordered 'the erection of a church worthy of so ancient and so holy a place' (Sozomen, *History* 2.4).

The Old Testament was read as the record of two deities: God Most High and his Son Yahweh. Philo emphasized this, and since he was chosen to represent the Jewish community in Alexandria before the Emperor Caligula in 40 CE, he and his beliefs must have been acceptable. When he was expounding the verse 'I am the God of Bethel' (Gen. 31.13), that is, the God who appeared to Jacob, he said: 'For just as those who are unable to see the sun itself see the gleam of the parhelion and take it for the sun, and take the halo round the moon for that luminary itself, so some regard the Image of God, the Angel His Logos, as His very Self' (*On Dreams* I.239). Philo implies there that some had mistakenly identified the Logos as God Most High. We do not know how Philo understood monotheism, but he did recognize the Great Angel who could be called God.

The one text in the Hebrew Scriptures that spells out this relationship of God Most High and the sons of God has been altered

---

[9] 'Jesus saved' is found in the fourth century Vaticanus text and the fifth century Alexandrinus text.

in transmission, and, until the Dead Sea Scrolls were found, this vital piece of evidence was missing. The Song of Moses describes how God Most High divided up the nations of the world and assigned them to their guardian angels, who were known as the sons of God. In the Hebrew text from which the Old Testament is usually translated, however, 'sons of God' appears as 'sons of Israel', and so the verse reads: 'When the Most High gave to the nations their inheritance, when he separated the sons of men, he fixed the bounds of the peoples according to the number of the sons of Israel' (Deut. 32.8). The Greek translation had 'according to the number of the angels of God', suggesting that it had been translated from a different version of the Hebrew, and so it was interesting to find the form 'sons of God' instead of 'sons of Israel' in the Qumran Hebrew text. When God Most High assigned the nations to the sons of God, he gave Jacob into the care of Yahweh. This implies that *Yahweh was the Son of God Most High.*

In a dialogue between Peter and Simon Magus (probably fictional, but showing what people believed to be the case) Peter explained the role of these guardian angels, the sons of God:

> For every nation has an angel to whom God has committed the government of that nation; and when one of these appears, although he be thought and called God by those over whom he presides, yet being asked he does not give such a testimony to himself. For the Most High God, who alone holds the power of all things, has divided the nations of the earth into seventy two parts and over these he has appointed angels as princes. But to the one among the archangels who is the greatest, was committed the government of those who, before all others, received the worship and knowledge of the Most High. (*Clementine Recognitions* II.42)

Eusebius, writing early in the fourth century, understood this verse in the same way: 'In these words (Moses) names first God Most High, the Supreme God of the universe, and then as Lord, His Word, Whom we call Lord in the second degree after the God of the universe' (Eusebius, *Proof of the Gospel* IV.9). This is how Paul could emphasize, when rejecting the many gods of the Roman world, that for Christians there was One God, the Father, *and* One Lord, Jesus Christ (1 Cor. 8.6).

For the Church, the appearances of Yahweh or the Angel of Yahweh in the Old Testament were appearances of the pre-existent Christ. Justin, who came from Palestine, wrote *The Dialogue with Trypho*,[10] a

---

[10] This may be a record of an actual debate or a fictional piece.

debate with a learned Jew which shows how matters stood between Jews and Christians in the middle of the second century. Justin believed that the Angel had been present on Sinai, had filled the tabernacle and the temple with his glory, and had brought judgement on Sodom: 'Then neither Abraham nor Isaac nor Jacob nor any other man ever saw the Father and Ineffable LORD of all things and of Christ Himself; but (they saw) Him who according to his will, is both God his Son, and his Angel from ministering to his will (*Trypho* 127). Justin's contemporaries were using prayers very like those used in synagogues, and the Apostolic Constitutions preserve prayers with allusions to the Old Testament where 'Christ' has replaced 'Yahweh': 'Having placed our father Jacob in Mesopotamia, having shown him the Christ, through him you spoke, saying, 'Look I am with you ...' (Ap. Con. 7.33); 'For you, O God Almighty, through Christ, planted a paradise in Eden ...' (Ap. Con. 8.12); 'You showed [to Abraham] your Christ' (Ap. Con. 8.12).

At the end of the second century, Irenaeus of Lyons, the self-proclaimed guardian of orthodoxy, read the Old Testament in the same way. Of Jacob's dream at Bethel, when he saw the LORD above (or by) the ladder, and heard him say 'I am Yahweh, the God of Abraham your father ...' (Gen. 28.13), Irenaeus said: 'All visions of this kind signify the Son of God in his speaking with men and his being with them. For it is not the Father of all, who is not seen by the world ... who would stand circumscribed in space and speak with Abraham, but the Word of God who is always with mankind' (Irenaeus, *Proof of the Gospel* 45). In the middle of the third century in Rome, Novatian wrote *On the Trinity*. He explained that Hosea 1.7 'I will deliver them by Yahweh their God' was God the Father promising to send help through Yahweh (*On the Trinity* XII). This second God was Christ who came down to Babel, appeared to Abraham, spoke to Hagar, and destroyed Sodom. 'We are led to understand that it was not the Father, who has never been seen, that was here seen, but the Son, who repeatedly descended to this earth and was seen' (*On the Trinity* XVIII).

Origen, writing a generation later, explained that the prophets had been taught by the pre-incarnate Jesus: 'The saints before the bodily advent of Jesus had an advantage over most believers in their insight into the mysteries of divinity, since the Word of God was their teacher before he became flesh ...' He described the throne visions of Isaiah and Ezekiel, and continued: 'Those who were made perfect in earlier generations knew not less than the apostles did of what Christ revealed to them, since the same Teacher was with them who revealed to the apostles the unspeakable mysteries of godliness (Origen, *Commentary on John* 6.2).

Eusebius shows what part this understanding of the Old Testament played in Christian discourse in the early fourth century. In both *The Preparation of the Gospel* and *The Proof of the Gospel* he assumes and demonstrates that it was Yahweh, the God of the Jews, who appeared in human form and was finally manifested in Jesus. He began *The Proof of the Gospel* by setting out his case: 'Remember how Moses called the Being who appeared to the patriarchs and often delivered to them the oracles written down in Scripture, sometimes God and LORD, and sometimes the Angel of the LORD.' He clearly implies that this was not the Omnipotent God, but a secondary Being, 'rightly called the God and LORD of holy men, but the Angel [i.e. messenger] of the Most High His Father' (*Proof* I.5). The Second person could be called the Great Angel, the King, the High Priest and the Anointed One, and Eusebius' discussion of the two divine Beings in the Hebrew Scriptures was very similar to contemporary debate among Jewish scholars, as we shall see. The Psalmist, he said, had addressed the Second Person. In Psalm 91, where Eusebius read the Hebrew accurately, it says: 'You O Yahweh are my refuge, You have made Elyon your dwelling place' (Ps. 91.9), clearly distinguishing Yahweh from Elyon, that is, the LORD from God Most High.

The Second Person was the Anointed One, who was a heavenly reality with an earthly counterpart. The Jews did believe in incarnate angels, as can be seen from *The Prayer of Joseph*, a Jewish text of 1,100 lines that is lost apart from fragments preserved in Christian texts.[11] The longest is preserved in Origen's *Commentary on John*, cited in his discussion of how John the Baptist could have been both human and an angel: 'To render more credible the belief concerning John the Baptist ... an angel who took a body in order to bear witness to the light' (*On John* 2.31). He described *The Prayer of Joseph* as 'an apocryphal book presently in use among the Hebrews' in which the human Jacob was also 'Israel, an angel of God and a ruling Spirit ... a man seeing God ... the chief captain among the sons of God ... the first minister before the face of God.' One of the explanations given for the name Israel was 'the man who sees God', and this became an

---

[11] Three fragments preserving nine sentences in all, in Origen's *Commentary on John*, 2.31, in the *Philocalia* 33.15, in Eusebius *Preparation* 6.11 and in Procopius *Commentary on Genesis* 29.

important part of early Christian discourse and debate with the Jews. The one who saw God, by definition, became an angel.

One of the Coptic texts discovered at Nag Hammadi in 1945 records a similar belief, but this time the Great Angel is Jesus. *On the Origin of the World* (CG II.5) describes the world of the holy of holies, with the ranks of angels and the chariot throne of the cherubim. There are seventy-two gods there, who have charge of the seventy-two nations of the world: they must be the 'sons of God' who are found in the Qumran text of Deuteronomy 32.8. The text is not entirely clear, but there is 'a first born called Israel, that is, the man who sees God, who has also another name Jesus the Christ, who is like the Saviour who is above the eighth, sits at his right upon an excellent throne. But on his left the Virgin of the Holy Spirit sits upon a throne praising him ...' (CG II.5.105).

Eusebius knew that the Second Person in his human form was the anointed High Priest, and here we return to the mysteries of the holy of holies. Discussing the command to build the tabernacle to represent what Moses had seen on Sinai (Exod. 25. 8,40), he wrote: 'And Moses himself, having first been thought worthy to view the divine realities in secret, and the mysteries concerning the first and only Anointed High Priest of God, which were celebrated before him in his theophanies, is ordered to establish figures and symbols on earth of what he had seen in his mind in visions' (*Proof* IV.15). In this section of the *Proof,* Eusebius sets out at length Old Testament evidence for the Second Person and his identity. He discusses the correct translation of the difficult Hebrew of Psalm 45.6–7: 'Your divine throne endures for ever and ever' or 'Your throne is a throne of God ...' or 'Thy throne, O God ...', followed by 'Therefore God, your God has anointed you, ...', and concludes that it refers to God Most High anointing the LORD. 'So that the Anointer, being the supreme God, is far above the Anointed, he being God in a different sense. And this would be clear to anyone who knew Hebrew ... Therefore in these words you have it clearly stated that God was anointed and became Christ ... And this is He who was the Beloved of the Father and his Offspring and the eternal Priest and the being called the Sharer of the Father's throne. Therefore the prophetic word ... referring to the Highest Power of God, the King of Kings and LORD of LORDS, calls him the Christ and the Anointed' (*Proof* IV.15); 'Among the Hebrews [the high priests] were called Christs who long ago symbolically represented a copy of the first Christ' (*Proof* IV.10). This is what Origen had said, one hundred years earlier: 'To the Son we present [our petitions] and beseech him, as the propitiation for our sins and our High Priest, to offer our desires and sacrifices and prayers to the Most High' (*Celsus* 8.13).

Origen also knew the Son as an Angel, 'not simply an angel, but the Angel of Great Counsel' (*Celsus* 5.53), and Eusebius knew that this was no innovation on the part of the Christians. The anointed heavenly figure, he said, was 'the captain of the angels, and when he leads them he is called the Angel of Great Counsel' (*Proof* IV.10). Eusebius knew that the Hebrews believed this angel to be the Messiah (*Preparation* VII.14–5). Justin, in the mid second century raised this matter in his *Dialogue with Trypho*. This Angel of Great Counsel appears in the Greek text of Isaiah 9.6. Where the Hebrew gives four names for the angel child who was to rule on the throne of David — Wonderful Counsellor, Mighty God, Everlasting Father, Prince of Peace — the Greek summarizes all four as 'the Angel of Great Counsel.

There is no doubt that Jesus was recognized and proclaimed as Yahweh, the LORD, the Son of God Most High. The prayers of the Christians and their way of reading the Old Testament are consistent in their witness. According to Eusebius, the Hebrews had believed that the Angel of Great Counsel was the Messiah; the difference between Jews and Christians was that the Jews did not accept that Jesus had been the Messiah, that the Angel had already come. This implies that belief in the Second Person was not unique to Christians; the problem was the identity of the Second Person.

THE TWO POWERS

Worshipping one God and one LORD means that there were two divine figures in heaven to receive this worship. Who were these figures? This is a very complex issue, not least because there is so little evidence for anything. Absence of evidence is not evidence of absence, especially when other factors such as later evidence makes one identification of the figures more likely than another.

A collection of temple tradition known as '3 Enoch' was compiled by Jews in Babylon by the sixth century CE, although much of it clearly has roots in second temple Palestine.[12] It is attributed to Rabbi

---

[12] For a concise discussion of the date, see P. Alexander in J. Charlesworth, ed., *The Old Testament Pseudepigrapha*, London: Darton Longman and Todd, 1983, vol. 1, pp. 225–9.

Ishmael, who died in 132 CE and is described as a high priest who had visions in the holy of holies (Babylonian Talmud Berakoth 7a). These texts were all written long after the time of Rabbi Ishmael, but they show how the high priesthood and its tradition were remembered. Rabbi Ishmael ascended to heaven and there talked with Metatron, the Great Angel who had, in his earthly life, been Enoch. Metatron (whose name probably means 'the throne sharer') had been taught the secrets of heaven, and was robed, crowned and enthroned in great splendour. He was called the Servant of the LORD (3 Enoch 10.3), identified as the Angel of the LORD — 'my name is in him' (Exod. 23.21) — and all the powers of heaven fell prostrate before him (3 Enoch 14.5). This is exactly what Paul described in Philippians 2: Christ Jesus the Servant on whom God bestowed the Name which is above every name 'that at the name of Jesus every knee should bow, in heaven and on earth and under the earth, and every tongue confess that Jesus Christ is the LORD ...' (Phil. 2.9–10).

It is unlikely in the extreme that Jewish temple mystics would have developed this as a new idea after the advent of Christianity, and after these claims had been made for Jesus, so we can only assume that the human enthroned as the Great Angel was a pre-Christian belief. This is confirmed by an obvious addition to 3 Enoch. Rabbi Elisha ben Abuya entered heaven and saw Metatron enthroned in splendour among the angels. He exclaimed: 'There are indeed two powers in heaven', and for this he was banished. A divine voice said: 'Come back to me, apostate sons, apart from Aḥer' — the name by which the heretical rabbi was known. The great angel Metatron was then removed from his throne, lest there be further misconceptions about him (3 Enoch 16.1–5). Since Elisha ben Abuya lived in Palestine immediately after the destruction of the temple in 70 CE, whatever controversy is represented by this episode was set in the early years of Christianity.

A homily incorporating rabbinic teaching from this period shows conflict over Christian claims, not just the 'two powers' but even the Trinity: 'In regard to the appearances of God, R. Hija bar Abba said: If the son of a harlot[13] should say to you "They are two Gods" quote God as saying in reply "I am the One of the sea and I am the One of Sinai" ... R. Levi taught at Sinai the Holy One, blessed be He, appeared to them with many faces, with a threatening face, with a severe face, with an angry face, with a joyous face, with a laughing face, with a friendly

---

[13] A designation for Jesus.

face. How so? In regard to God's many faces, Rabbi Hija bar Abba taught: should the son of a harlot say to you " There are two Gods", reply to him that Scripture does not say "the Gods have spoken … face to face", but "the LORD [i.e. singular] has spoken to you face to face"' (Deut. 5.4).[14] Rabbi Hija bar Abba was a Babylonian scholar who settled in Palestine and was active as a teacher at the end of the third century CE. 'The faces of God' is interpreting the Hebrew word for 'presence', *panim*, which is plural and literally means 'faces'. The Greek equivalent, *prosopa*, became the 'persons' of the Trinity in later Christian discourse. We can guess what prompted this rabbinic pronouncement about the many faces at that period.

The debate over the 'two powers' was to occupy the finest Jewish minds for many generations.[15] The debate was almost entirely confined to rabbis in Palestine, and a key factor was the interpretation of Scripture. The 'two powers' heretics were not named, nor was their teaching recorded, but it is clear from the arguments ranged against them that they did not think of two opposing powers in heaven — they were not dualists — but rather they believed in a far God and a near God. One of the key texts was Daniel 7, the vision of the human figure going with clouds and being enthroned in heaven. There seem to be two thrones (Dan. 7.9) and two divine beings: the Ancient of Days and the one who is enthroned. This was an important text for Christians, since Jesus quoted it at his trial, in response to the high priest's question: 'Are you the Messiah, the Son of the Blessed?' (Mark 14.61–2). The human figure in this passage was understood *by the high priest* to be the Messiah, the Son of God. Then there were the conflicting appearances in the Exodus narrative: at the Exodus the LORD was a man of war, and so assumed to be young (Exod. 15.3), whereas on Sinai he was the lawgiver and so assumed to be old; and as the tribes left Sinai, they were entrusted to an angel in whom was the Name (Exod. 23.21). 'Although the answers to the heretics were worked out by the academies, the question must have been raised in relation to Bible reading and by groups who were interested in hearing the Jewish Bible expounded.'[16]

During the early years of Christianity there were other debates about the identity of the Divine in the Hebrew Scriptures, for example the significance of the two names: Yahweh, the LORD, and

---

[14] In Pesikta Rabbati 21.

[15] For a full discussion, see A. F. Segal *Two Powers in Heaven*, Leiden: Brill, 1978.

[16] Segal p. 154.

Elohim, God. The two powers in the rabbinic debate were the older figure and the young warrior. The warrior at the sea was named the LORD, Yahweh, and the lawgiver on Sinai was named 'the God of Israel', Elohim. Did these two names, then, imply two figures? No, it was argued, because there are places where both names occur together, as in 'I am the LORD your God ...' (Exod. 20.2). It was decided that the two names signified different aspects of the one God of Israel: Yahweh was justice, the ruling Power, and Elohim was mercy, the creative Power.

Philo knew this distinction, but he applied it to the two Powers of the Second God. Since he was contemporary with the origin of Christianity he is an important witness. Philo said that the cherubim over the ark were symbols of the two primary Powers of God: 'the creative and the kingly, of which one is called God, *theos*, and the other, the kingly one, is called LORD, *kyrios*.' (*Questions on Genesis* 1.57). Explaining them, he wrote: '[God] means to show that the most senior Powers of the One Who Is, the beneficent and the punitive, are equal ...' (*Who is the Heir?* 166).[17] The form 'the LORD God' indicated a double invocation: Abraham 'uttered a double invocation to the Powers of the Father, the creative and the kingly ...' (*Questions on Genesis* IV. 37). Hence Thomas's exclamation when he met the risen LORD: 'My LORD and my God!' (John 20.28).

Philo was careful to state that neither of these powers was the High God, the God whose name was not known. The third commandment — 'You shall not take the Name of the LORD your God in vain' (Exod. 20.7) — he said, 'concerned the name of the LORD, not that name, the knowledge of which has never even reached the world of mere becoming — He that Is cannot be named in words — but the name which is given to his Powers' (*Who is the Heir?* 170). 'For nothing mortal can be made in the likeness of the Most High One and Father of the universe, but only in that of the Second God, who is his Logos ... since the pre-Logos God is superior to every rational creature' (*Questions on Genesis* II.62).

A. F. Segal, a Jewish scholar, suggested that the evidence of Philo and the rabbis could be set in sequence: 'A second manifestation of God can be shown in Hellenistic mystical and apocalyptic Judaism

---

[17] In later usage, the roles were reversed; the LORD indicated the creative power and God the kingly, and it has been suggested that this occurred after the Bar Kochbar war, 135 CE, see A. Marmorstein, 'Philo and the Names of God', *Jewish Quarterly Review* 22 (1931), pp. 295–306, p. 301.

as early as the beginning of the Common Era (e.g. Philo). Extreme varieties of this kind of speculation came to be opposed by the rabbis. By the mid second century, R. Akiba, or his admiring successors in his name, were using the doctrine of God's aspects of mercy and justice to counter the heresy.[18] This form of words implies that Philo was not representative, even though he was chosen by the Jewish community of Alexandria to lead their embassy to the Emperor Caligula in 40 CE, and 'extreme varieties' of this speculation were Christianity.

Belief in a 'Second Person' may, however, have been more widespread than some scholars allow, and it is not possible to speak of Jewish 'orthodoxy' in the time of Christian origins. Nor is it wise to assume that later 'rabbinic' Judaism developed as the dominant and only 'legitimate' flowering of the Hebrew heritage. The evidence, especially after the inclusion of the Dead Sea Scrolls in the picture of first century Palestine, is that the religious scene was rather different from what earlier generations of scholars had imagined: 'The idea that already during the Second temple period Rabbinic Judaism was normative or mainstream Judaism belongs to the history of scholarly research.'[19] The development of the Hebrew text of the Scriptures in the early years of the Church, again using the evidence of the Scrolls, shows a clear pattern: readings that could support the Christian claims did not become part of the official text. Different versions of key texts found at Qumran show that Justin's accusation to Trypho — 'Your scholars have been changing the text of Scripture' — was justified (*Trypho* 71). The passage implying that Yahweh was one of the sons of God Most High (Deut. 32.8–9), an important Christian proof text, has a different form in the Hebrew text used today, and another line quoted to identify Jesus as the Firstborn, the LORD (Heb. 1.6), is not in the current Hebrew text of Deuteronomy 32.43. Both these texts, as quoted by the Christians, have been found at Qumran in pre-Christian Hebrew texts. It cannot be assumed that the 'Christian' forms were variants.[20]

Another aspect of the 'two powers' problem is the 'binitarian' character of early Christian worship, described as 'the accommodation of Christ as an additional figure along with God (the Father) within a strong concern to maintain a monotheistic religious commitment

[18] Segal, *Two Powers* p. 54.
[19] G. Boccaccini, *Roots of Rabbinic Judaism*, Grand Rapids: Eerdmans, 2002, p. xiii.
[20] See my book *The Great High Priest*, London: T&T Clark, 2003, pp. 294–315.

...'[21] Paul, in his early letters to the Thessalonians used a singular verb when writing, apparently, of two: 'May our God and Father himself, and our LORD Jesus direct (singular) our way to you' (1 Thess. 3.11, and also 2 Thess. 2.16–17). Paul also recognized that one God and Father, and one LORD, Jesus Christ, were different from the many so-called gods of other nations (1 Cor. 8.5–6). Two were named, and yet not considered a plurality. There are two 'problems' here: the two Gods in a Jewish context, and using a singular verb for the 'plural' subject.

The two Gods are not, in fact, a problem, since the Hebrew Scriptures were widely understood in this way, as we have seen. Father and Son were not unknown in the Hebrew tradition. Jesus was proclaimed as Yahweh, and so worshipping him as Yahweh was to be expected. Failure to recognize this fundamental has created many problems and produced unnecessary complications. Thus we read: 'The adoption/adaptation of OT cultic expression to Jesus is probably to be seen as indicating that these early Christians intended a direct association and analogy between their devotion to Jesus and the OT cultic devotion to Yahweh.'[22] It was more than analogy. The Christians called on the Name of the LORD just as their fathers had done in the ancient temple, and they meant the same LORD. To say: 'Jesus' cultic presence and power clearly operate here in the manner we otherwise associate with a god. Moreover, there is simply no parallel for this in any other group of the period with comparable connections to the biblical/Jewish monotheistic scruple about involving figures other than the God of Israel in cultic devotion'[23] makes an erroneous assumption. *The Christians were not involving a figure other than the God of Israel in their worship. They worshipped Yahweh incarnate.*

The other problem — a singular verb to express the unity of two Gods — is the key to understanding both 'monotheism' and 'incarnation', since there can be no division within the divine state. Separation and distinction are characteristic only of the material, visible world, and of the demonic. The account of creation in Genesis 1 has the recurring theme of 'separation' and 'according to their kinds' when describing the visible material world, but the very beginning, described as Day One, was different — a state beyond

---

[21] L. Hurtado, 'The Binitarian shape of early Christian Worship', in *The Jewish Roots of Christological Monotheism*, ed. C. C. Newman, J. R. Davila and G. S. Lewis; Leiden: Brill, 1999, pp. 187–213, p. 191.

[22] Hurtado, 'Binitarian shape', p. 199.

[23] Hurtado 'Binitarian shape', p. 199.

time and matter which could not be divided. It was represented in the temple by the holy of holies behind the veil, and the lore of Day One was part of the secrets entrusted to the high priesthood. It is not surprising that this teaching is not recorded in Scripture for public reading, but some of it can be reconstructed from other sources.[24] Day One was understood as the state when the Holy One was one with his universe,[25] the state of the angels, as we shall see.[26] All the angels were a unity but perceived in separation only when they entered the material creation. A restoration of the unity seems to be the future hope that Paul describes, enigmatically: 'And when all things shall be subjected unto [the Son], then shall the Son also himself be subject unto him that put all things under him, that *God may be all in all*' (1 Cor. 15.28, AV). Jesus said that this unity was the sign and proof of divinity: '... that they may be one even as we are one, I in them and Thou in me, that they may become perfectly one ...' (John 17.11, 22, 23). Elsewhere He explained to the Jews: 'I and the Father are one' (John 10.30). Here, 'one' is neuter, i.e. one thing.

Unity within the divine included the understanding that the divine could be *perceived* in manifold form, and in human form. The Hebrew text of Genesis 18 described how the Lord appeared to Abraham at Mamre (Gen. 18.1), but in the next verse it was three men (that is, three angels) appearing to Abraham. Josephus, however, reading this Hebrew text in the first century CE, retold the story as the appearance of three angels, with no mention of the Lord (*Ant.* 1.11).[27] The first Christians lived among people who believed that the one Lord could be present in three — or presumably any number — of his angels. Those angels were a unity, and this was proof of their identity and origin: 'That they may be one even as we are one, I in them and Thou in me, so that they may become perfectly One, *so that the world may know that Thou hast sent me* ...' (John 17.22–3).

The divine unity extended, as with Jesus' disciples, to those humans who became a part of it, and were transformed by that experience into angels. Jesus, teaching about the heavenly state, said: 'They cannot die any more, because they are equal to angels, and are sons of God, being sons of the resurrection' (Luke 20.36). In other words, the

---

[24] See my book *The Great High Priest*, London: T&T Clark, 2003, pp. 146–87.

[25] Genesis Rabbah III.8, teaching attributed to R. Judan and R. Johannan, first century CE.

[26] See below p. 232ff.

[27] The traditional Jewish exposition named the three as Michael, Gabriel and Raphael — no mention of the Lord (Genesis Rabbah L.2).

resurrected, those who live the life of eternity, are called angels and sons of God. They are part of the unity. In the Book of Revelation, a singular verb frequently occurs after dual subjects, and indicates *theosis*, that a human has become divine and part of the unity. In Revelation 5 the Lamb takes the scroll and then, in the midst of the throne and the living creatures, he is worshipped by every creature in heaven and earth, under the earth and in the sea (Rev. 5.13). The praise is 'to him who sits upon the throne and to the Lamb' (Rev. 5.13). The multitude in white robes cry out 'To our God who sits upon the throne and to the Lamb!', and they worship God, with no mention, apparently, of the Lamb (Rev. 7.10–11). There is the throne of God and the Lamb, followed by 'his servants shall worship him, they shall see his face and his name shall be on their foreheads' (Rev. 22.3–4). All these are singular forms: whom did they worship, whose face did they see, whose name did they bear? The faithful would be 'priests of God and of Christ, and reign with him [with whom?] for a thousand years' (Rev. 20.6). The voices in heaven proclaimed 'the Kingdom of our LORD and of his Christ, and he shall reign for ever and ever' (Rev. 11.15). Who would reign? The earliest scribes were aware of this problem, and sometimes there are two versions of the text, singular and plural: 'Fall on us and hide us from the face of him who is seated on the throne, and from the wrath of the Lamb; for the great day of their/his wrath has come'(Rev. 6. 16–17). The fourth century Sinai text has 'their' wrath; the fifth century Alexandrian text has 'his' wrath.

The pairing is either God-and-the-Lamb or God-and-the-Christ. In each case they are one, because in each case it is a human figure who has become divine. In the convention of visionary texts, an animal represents a human being and a 'man' an angel. The Lamb is, therefore, a human being taken up to the throne and, as he is enthroned, he becomes divine, united with 'him who sits upon the throne'. The Lamb is worshipped *after* he has stood in the midst of the throne (Rev. 5.6). When Solomon was made king, there was an exactly similar sequence; it must have been the ancient temple ritual. Solomon sat on the throne of the LORD as king (1 Chron. 29.23), 'and all the assembly blessed the LORD, the God of their fathers, and worshipped the LORD and the king' (1 Chron. 29.20, translating literally). At his enthronement, the human king became the LORD. Whether this was imagined as the incarnation of the LORD, or as the adoption of the king as the divine son is not known. Perhaps such questions — the stuff of later theological controversies — were never asked. It was *theosis*, becoming divine, and incarnation.

In ancient temple texts we glimpse the *theosis* — the ritual that inspired John's vision of the Lamb — but the process is not explained. 'I will tell you of the decree of the LORD: he said to me, "You are my son, today I have begotten you"' (Ps. 2.7). The kings and rulers of the earth take counsel 'against the LORD and his anointed', which, in the light of Solomon's enthronement, we know were deemed to be one: 'the-LORD-and-his-anointed' would then have sat on the throne of the LORD. This is exactly what we have in Revelation 11.15: 'The kingdom of our LORD and of his Christ', in other words, the-LORD-and-his-anointed. Another enthronement psalm once described this process of *theosis,* but the Hebrew text of Psalm 110.3 is now opaque. Reconstructing from the Greek, it seems that the king was begotten in the glory of the holy ones; that is, among the angels in the holy of holies. 'Dew', later a symbol of resurrection, was part of the mysterious process. His birth as a divine son was his resurrection. The human had become a priest like Melchizedek. And then the angels sang: 'Unto us a child is born', celebrating the one who was to reign on the throne of David, and be called 'Wonderful Counsellor, Mighty God, Everlasting Father, Prince of Peace', or 'the Angel of Great Counsel' (Isa. 9.6).

Returned to its temple context, and interpreted within temple norms, early Christian worship was binitarian because all temple worship was binitarian. The human king was the presence or face of the LORD, Immanuel, and so Christian devotion to Jesus the Anointed One as Yahweh the LORD was no innovation. Far from there being no parallel to this Christian practice in Hebrew tradition, it was in fact the restoration of the original temple cult.

THE ETERNAL HIGH PRIEST

Yahweh was represented in the temple by the high priest. The temple itself represented the whole creation, visible and invisible, the great hall being the material world and the holy of holies the invisible creation. Philo explained: 'The highest, and in the truest sense the holy, temple of God is, as we must believe, the whole universe, having for its sanctuary the most sacred part of all existence, even heaven, for its votive ornaments the stars, and for its priests the angels (*Special Laws,* 1.66). Since the angels were priests in the temple of creation, the priests in the Jerusalem temple represented the angels, as we shall see. The high priest was the chief of the priests and also the chief of the angels, the LORD of the hosts: 'For there are, as is evident, two temples of God: one of them this universe, in which there is also as High Priest His First-born, the divine Logos and the other the rational soul, whose Priest is the real man' (*On Dreams* I.215). The high priest was the only person permitted to enter the holy of holies, and so he was the link between the visible and invisible worlds, between earth and heaven.

The holy of holies had originally housed the great cherub throne of the LORD and the ark of the covenant (1 Chron. 28.18), but in the second temple, the holy of holies was empty. When Pompey took Jerusalem in 63 BCE, he entered the temple and saw the furnishings: 'Pompey ... penetrated to the sanctuary, entry to which was permitted to none but the high priest, and beheld what it contained: the candelabrum and lamps, the table, the vessels for libation and censers, all of solid gold ...' (Josephus, *War* 1.152). There was no mention of the cherub throne or the ark and the mercy seat, and so we can only assume that the holy of holies was empty. All visionary texts that are set in the 'furnished' holy of holies must be remembering the original temple as well as looking forward to the restored temple in the time of the Messiah.

Those who remembered the furnishings of the holy of holies presumably remembered other aspects of the older cult. Philo says several things about the Logos High Priest and his earthly counterpart, for example: 'The High Priest is not a man but a Divine Logos ... his father being God who is likewise Father of all, and his mother Wisdom, through whom the universe came into existence. Moreover, his head has been anointed with oil, and by this I mean that his ruling faculty is illumined with a brilliant light, in such wise that he is deemed worthy to "put on the garments"' (*On Flight* 108–110). God the Father is familiar, but who is Wisdom the Mother?[28] It is inconsistent to suggest that God the Father is God Most High and Wisdom is only a late personification, influenced by Hellenistic ideas. The theological system that knew of the heavenly High Priest also knew of his Mother, and this system was the framework for Christianity.

The veil of the temple represented matter, that which screened the divine presence from the material world. It corresponded to the firmament created on the second day, and was woven in *hošeb* work[29] from four colours: red, blue, purple and white (Exod. 26.31), which Josephus said represented the four elements. Earth was the white —

---

[28] See below p. 236
[29] Usually translated 'skilled work'.

because linen grew in the earth, air was the blue, fire was the red, and purple was water, since purple dye came from a seashell (*Antiquities* 3.183). The explanations for the white and the blue are somewhat fanciful — perhaps Josephus was looking for a rational explanation for a system already established. It is remarkable that detailed specifications were given for the fabric, but no explanation of why it should be woven in that way. 'In fact, every one of these objects is intended to recall and represent the universe' (*Antiquities* 3.180). The veil separated the changing world from the unchanging, and separated mortality and corruption from eternal life and incorruption: 'the changeable parts of the world which … undergo changes of direction, and the heavenly (state) which is without transient events and is unchanging' (Philo, *Questions on Exodus* 2.91).

The fabric of the veil was also used for the outer vestment of the high priest, but threaded through with gold (Exod. 28.5–6). This vestment therefore represented modified matter. The high priest only wore this coloured vestment when he was in 'the world'; when he was in heaven, in the holy of holies, he wore the linen garb of the angels. Thus he had two roles: divine and human. The coloured vestment worn over the white linen indicated the angel robed in transformed matter: incarnation. Aaron's robe had depicted the whole creation: 'Upon his long robe (*poderes*) the whole world was depicted … and thy majesty on the diadem on his head' (Wisdom of Solomon 18. 24). Philo and Josephus agree that the corresponding vestment of the Logos High Priest was the whole creation: 'Now the garments which the supreme Logos of Him that IS puts on as raiment are the world, (*kosmos*), for he arrays himself in earth and air and water and fire and all that comes forth from these' (Philo, *On Flight* 110). 'His upper garment denotes universal nature, which it pleased God to make of four elements, being further interwoven with gold, I imagine, in token of the all pervading sunlight' (Josephus, *Antiquities* 3.184). Since gold symbolized the divine — all vessels within the temple were made of gold — this unique mixture of linen, wool[30] and metal probably represented the interweaving of divine and human.

The mixing of seeds or animals or fibres was forbidden and rendered them 'holy' (Deut. 22.9–11), the characteristic of the material world being that everything was separated according to its kind (e.g. Gen. 1.12). The mingled fabric of the veil marked the border between earth and heaven, and the golden thread of the

---

[30] Mixed fibres were forbidden to anyone but the high priest, Deut. 22.11.

vestment symbolized the mingling of human and divine. This imagery of veil and incarnation was widely known. The writer to the Hebrews, expounding the role of the high priest, equates *without explanation* the veil of the holy of holies and the flesh of Jesus: '... the new and living way he opened for us through the curtain, that is, through his flesh ...' (Heb. 10.20). The Infancy Gospel of James — not in the New Testament but widely known and used in the ancient churches — tells the story of Mary's birth and childhood, and describes how she was weaving the new veil of the temple whilst she was pregnant. That is why the Annunciation ikon shows her spinning scarlet wool when Gabriel comes to her.

When the Hebrew Scriptures say that the LORD appeared, there is rarely any description. The LORD appeared to Abraham, but we are given no details of what Abraham saw (Gen. 17.1; 18.1); Isaiah saw the LORD enthroned, but there are no details apart from the robe that filled the temple (Isa. 6.1–5); Ezekiel saw the likeness of the Glory of the LORD, a fiery human figure on a sapphire throne (Ezek. 1.26–28); Daniel saw a fiery man, clothed in linen, whom the early Christians identified as the LORD (Dan. 10.5–6).[31] When John saw the LORD in his vision, however, he saw a high priest. The fiery human form standing in the midst of the seven lamps was the LORD with the menorah, clad in a long linen robe and girded with gold. The long linen robe, *poderes*, is often used in the Greek Old Testament to describe the high priest's vestments although, curiously, it seems to describe different items. It could be the long fringed garment (Lxx Exod. 28.4), or it could be the ephod (Lxx Exod. 25.6). The Greek of Ezekiel used *poderes* for the linen garment worn by the chief angel in the vision of judgement on Jerusalem. The Greek text here is rather different from the Hebrew, which says that the man had an inkpot at his side. Now the Hebrew word for an 'inkpot' is very like the word for 'rainbow', and the words for 'scribe' and 'sapphire' are also similar. The Hebrew text has a scribe and his pot, but the Greek has a rainbow of sapphire worn as a girdle (Ezek. 9.2). Whatever the original, the Greek translator saw here a figure like the one in Ezekiel's vision of the throne, a human figure with brightness round his loins, 'brightness like a rainbow' (Ezek. 1.27–8). The *poderes* was also the 'rich garment' that Zechariah received from the angel when he was made high priest (Zech. 3.4). What makes it certain that the figure of John's vision was the high priest is the golden girdle: all the

---

[31] See above, p. 50n.

priests wore multi-coloured girdles — red, blue, purple and white — but only the high priest had a girdle woven with gold (*Antiquities* 3.158–9).

The fullest description of a heavenly High Priest is found in the Apocalypse of Abraham, which tells how Abraham ascended to heaven during the sacrifice described in Genesis 15. The text mentions the fall of Jerusalem in 70 CE, and there are allusions to its content in the *Clementine Recognitions* 1.33, so the Apocalypse of Abraham could have been known in the early years of Christianity. In Genesis 15, 'the Lord Yahweh' appeared to Abraham and promised him many descendants. Now 'the Lord Yahweh' (literally Adonai Yahweh) is an unusual form, and it became, in the Apocalypse of Abraham, Yahweh-el, a mighty angel. In the *Recognitions*, the figure is described as an angel and as the True Prophet. The text is not entirely clear, but it seems that the lower part of his body was like sapphire and his hair was white like snow. He wore the high priestly turban that looked like a rainbow (*kidaris*, Exod. 39.28, Zech. 3.5) and purple robes, and he carried a golden staff or sceptre. The heavenly figure had human form, and he came to consecrate and strengthen Abraham. He said he had to keep the warring heavenly powers separate — a curious role, but one that Philo ascribed to the Logos: 'the Divine Logos stations himself to keep the elements apart ...' (*On Planting* 10). Yahweh-el had been appointed as the guardian angel of Abraham and his descendants (Ap. Abr. 10.16), and he appeared as the High Priest.

This heavenly High Priest appeared immediately after Abraham had met Melchizedek, another mysterious high priest figure. Jesus was identified as Melchizedek — 'another priest in the likeness of Melchizedek' (Heb. 7.15) — and a remarkable text found among the Dead Sea Scrolls seems to use Old Testament 'Yahweh' texts of Melchizedek, just as the New Testament used them of Jesus. The Melchizedek text (11Q Melch) describes Melchi-zedek, the righteous king, writing the 'name' as two words, just as it appears in Psalm 110.4. It was his title, and he was expected to appear (again) during the first seven years of the tenth jubilee. Since we know that the ten jubilees in question were to end about 66 CE, he was expected to appear between 17 and 24 CE, the time when Jesus began his ministry.[32] Melchizedek

---

[32] Jesus was born about 6 BCE, since Herod died in 4 BCE, when Jesus was a small child. Jesus was baptized when he was about 30 years old, so his public ministry began at the time when Melchizedek was expected. See my book *The Great High Priest*, London: T&T Clark, 2003, pp. 34–41.

would bring the final Jubilee, the good news of the Jubilee release, *d'ror*, that was proclaimed on the Day of Atonement (Lev. 25.8–12). In the Old Testament, the agent of the Jubilee had been the Servant, who was to release prisoners (Isa. 42.5) and bring back the scattered people of Israel (Isa. 49.5, 9). The greatest Jubilee text was Isaiah 61.1–3, the passage Jesus read in the synagogue at Nazareth and claimed to fulfil. 'The Spirit of the Lord Yahweh[33] is upon me, because Yahweh has anointed me, ... to proclaim liberty (*d'ror*) to the captives ...' (Isa. 61.1). It was *the Lord Yahweh* who appeared to Abraham and became the high priestly angel in the Apocalypse of Abraham.

The Qumran Melchizedek text is woven around these texts and others.[34] 'The year of Yahweh's favour' (Isa. 61.2) became the year of Melchizedek's favour; 'God has taken his place in the divine council' (Ps. 82.1) became Melchizedek taking his place; 'Your God reigns' (Isa. 52.7) seems to apply to Melchizedek too, but the text is fragmented. Philo knew Melchizedek as a Logos High Priest (*Allegorical Interpretation* III.82), and elsewhere he described the Logos as the High Priest (*Migration of Abraham* 102). When the Christians declared that Jesus was Yahweh this implied he was a High Priest like Melchizedek. As Yahweh, Jesus was Son of God Most High, and so it could be said of him: '... resembling the Son of God, he continues a priest for ever' (Heb. 7.3), just as the Psalmist had declared of the royal high priest: 'In the glory of the holy one ... I have begotten you ... You are a priest for ever after the order of Melchizedek' (Ps. 110.3–4, my translation, reconstructing the obscure Hebrew from the Greek text). This was the context for Jesus' words in his dispute with the Jews about blasphemy: 'Do you say of Him whom the Father consecrated and sent into the world "You are blaspheming" because I said, "I am the Son of God"?' (John 10.36).

Melchizedek as Yahweh was a sensitive issue in the early years of Christianity. Melchizedek was priest of God Most High, and all the ancient versions and commentaries of Genesis are clear on this point. Only the Masoretic Hebrew text, which became the 'official text' after the advent of Christianity, has a different name for Melchizedek's God. Uniquely, he is Yahweh God Most High, conflating the two divine names and thus removing the possibility that Melchizedek was Yahweh, the priest of God Most High (Gen. 14.22).

---

[33] The designation in Gen. 15.

[34] In the order: Lev. 25.9, 13; Deut. 15.1–2; Isa. 51.1–3; Ps. 82.1, Ps. 7.7–8; Isa. 52.7; Dan. 9.25.

The Christians worshipped the LORD, the God of Israel. They knew — how we do not know — the ways of the original temple and restored them. They proclaimed Jesus as the great High Priest, the LORD, Melchizedek, the Son of God Most High, Immanuel, God with us.

Chapter 5

BAPTISM AND RESURRECTION

His name shall be on their foreheads.

Revelation 22.4

There is a glimpse of early Christian worship at the end of the Book of Revelation. The servants of God-and-the-Lamb stand before his throne and worship him. They see his face, and his Name is on their foreheads. From the throne flows the river of life, and the tree of life stands nearby. The LORD God is the light of his servants, and they reign for ever and ever (Rev. 22.1–5). This is a temple scene, or rather, a scene in the holy of holies which in the original temple had housed the throne of the LORD. Only the high priests were permitted to stand there and see the LORD, or so we assume from the prescription for Aaron in the tabernacle on the Day of Atonement. He was the only one permitted to pass within the veil and see the LORD appearing over the mercy seat (Lev. 16.2). It is likely that Isaiah's great vision of the LORD on his throne in the temple was a Day of Atonement vision, and that Isaiah was a high priest whose guilt was taken away by the fiery coal (Isa. 6.1–7). *The Christians worshipping in John's vision were all high priests.* This was the royal priesthood 'called out of darkness into his marvellous light' (1 Pet. 2.9). In Revelation many people had the Name on their foreheads. The 144,000 followers of the Lamb assembled on Zion had his Name and his Father's Name written on their foreheads (Rev. 14.1): presumably they were the same as the 144,000 sealed on their foreheads with the seal of the living God (Rev. 7.3). They must have been those faithful Christians to whom the risen LORD promised 'the name of my God and the name of the city of my God, ... and my own new name' (Rev. 3.12).[1]

---

[1] The name of the city comes from the way Ezek. 48.35 was read in Jesus' time: 'her name shall be the LORD'. See my book, *The Revelation of Jesus Christ*, Edinburgh: T&T Clark, 2000, pp. 108–9.

Those marked with the seal of the living God were protected from the fury of the four winds. The angel with the great seal commanded the four angels who controlled the winds to withhold their power, so there was time to save the chosen (Rev. 7.1–3). Ezekiel recorded a similar scene. Jerusalem was doomed to destruction because of 'the abominations committed in it' (Ezek. 9.4), and an angel appeared to mark the foreheads of all who had resisted the abominations. The LORD then commanded the six angels of judgement to pass through the city and spare only those who bore the mark (Ezek. 9.6). The word translated 'mark' is in fact *tau*, the last letter of the Hebrew alphabet, which in the time of Ezekiel was written as a diagonal cross. Since he was a priest of the first temple (Ezek.1.3), in his time *the cross had been the sign of the LORD's protection*. The angel John saw in the sunrise was also carrying the seal of the living God, to mark, presumably with a cross, the 144,000 to be saved.

These scenes suggest that the cross which sealed Christians at baptism was the Name, and this protected them from the imminent wrath. If they were the restored high priesthood with access to the holy of holies — 'Let us then with confidence draw near to the throne of grace ... since we have confidence to enter the sanctuary ...' (Heb. 4.16; 10.19) — the Name they wore would have been this baptismal cross. The ancient high priests had worn the Name on their foreheads to protect them when bearing iniquity (Exod. 28.38), which may be another aspect of the protection afforded by the Name. By the end of the fourth century, the original significance of the X as the Name was fading, and the X was said to represent the crucifixion — another example of temple customs being reinterpreted. As the priestly roots of baptism were lost, it was explained as dying and rising with Christ, and the elements of the ritual were reassigned: 'The water is instead of [i.e. represents] the burial, the oil instead of the holy spirit, the seal instead of the cross' (Apostolic Constitutions 3.17).

The oldest known forms of baptism in the Eastern church were modelled on Jesus' baptism. The Didache gives no detail apart from requiring the baptism to be 'in the name of the Father, the Son and the Holy Spirit', but by the early third century in Syria, the baptizing bishop was the one 'through whom you were sealed, and through whom you became the sons of light, and through whom the LORD in baptism, by the imposition of the hand of the bishop, bore witness to each one of you and uttered in his holy voice saying "You are my Son. I have this day begotten you.'"[2] In the West, Justin described baptism as being 'born again': 'This washing is called illumination, because they who learn these things are illuminated in their understanding.' (*Apology* 1.61). Tertullian spoke of 'that water of ours in which the sins of our original blindness are washed away, and we are set at liberty to life eternal' (*On Baptism* 1). The imagery associated with Christian initiation, both in the New Testament and in the early Church — the Name, spiritual birth that gave access to the Kingdom, enlightenment, putting on Christ, putting on a new nature, becoming a son of God, anointing with the Spirit — must all be kept in mind when attempting to reconstruct its origin and significance. *All baptism imagery was associated with the royal high priesthood.* 'Let us draw near (to the holy of holies) with a true heart ... with our hearts sprinkled clean from an evil conscience and our bodies washed with pure water' (Heb. 10.22). Whether or not new Christians were literally anointed and dressed in white garments, and whether they were illuminated with a new way of knowledge we cannot know, but the imagery indicates a temple and indeed a high priestly origin for baptism.

BAPTISM AS WASHING

Baptism, immersion, was a purification ritual required by the law of Moses, and it eventually became part of the initiation into Judaism. The question is: when did this happen? Was Jewish baptism adopted by Christians, or did Christian baptism have another meaning? One problem is that the Hebrew word *ṭᵉbilah* can mean either immersion for a proselyte or the ordinary ritual bath; another is the date of the texts. Some scholars say that the immersion of proselytes was a second temple practice, and that it must have existed in the time of John the Baptist in order to account for the Christians adopting baptism (!).[3] Baptism of proselytes, however, is not mentioned in the Old Testament, and the forced conversions to Judaism instituted by John Hyrcanus towards the end of the second century BCE, mention only circumcision and observance of the Jewish law (*Antiquities* 13.9; 13.11). Josephus does not mention baptism for proselytes, nor does

[2] R. H. Connolly, *Didascalia Apostolorum*, Oxford: Clarendon Press, 1929, ii. 32, p. 93.

[3] Thus L. Schiffman, *Who was Jew? Rabbibic and Halakhic Perspectives on the Jewish-Christian Schism*, Hoboken, New York: Ktav, 1985, p. 29.

Philo. The earliest certain reference to proselyte baptism is a saying attributed to Rabbi Joḥanan, a leader when Jerusalem fell in 70 CE. He taught that 'a man cannot become a proper proselyte unless he has been circumcised and has also performed ritual ablution'. The debate continued in the next generation: Rabbi Eliezer said that only circumcision was necessary; Rabbi Joshua that only the ritual ablution was necessary for a proselyte. It was eventually decided that both washing and circumcision were necessary (Babylonian Talmud Yebamoth 46a). None of this evidence shows that baptism was part of Jewish initiation in the time of Jesus, and so there is no proof that Christians adopted an existing Jewish custom for the initiation of converts.

Ritual washing — before eating, before and after touching the sacred texts, before worship and entering the temple — was part of daily life for an observant Jew. Jesus criticized the Pharisees for their scrupulous washing of hands and food vessels (Mark 7.3–8), when they were neglecting more important aspects of the Law. There were *mikwaoth*, deep baths in which unclean people and vessels had to be immersed for purging specific bodily or ritual impurities, for example washing any cloth that was spotted with blood from a sin offering (Lev. 6.27); washing any leprous item or person (Lev. 13.54; 14.8); washing after contact with bodily discharge (Lev. 15.5) or eating forbidden meat (Lev. 17.15). There were strict rules for the type of water that could be used in them: the best and most efficacious was running water (Mishnah Mikwaoth 1.8). There were dozens of *mikwaoth* around the temple, and there were immersion chambers within the temple courts too, for example next to the priests' lavatories under the temple (Mishnah Tamid 1.1). During the first war against Rome, the additional troops required to defend the temple were not allowed in unless they had been purified (Josephus *War* 4.205). Ritual washing could also be part of ascetic discipline. Josephus had spent some time in his youth as the disciple of a desert hermit named Banus, who bathed himself frequently in cold water 'to preserve his chastity' (*Life* 2), and he also knew that the Essenes bathed in cold water 'at the fifth hour' before entering the refectory to eat a simple meal (*War* 2.129). A ritual bath before meals is not mentioned in the Qumran texts, but there were several baths at Qumran, and washing is mentioned in other contexts. Hegesippus, a Christian of Jewish origin who lived in Palestine early in the second century CE, said there was a Jewish sect which he called the Hemerobaptists, those who baptized themselves every day (quoted in Eusebius, *Church History* 4.22). John the Baptist was remembered as one of them (*Clementine Homilies* 2.23).

Bathing or immersion was usually a ritual cleansing before participating in worship. Aaron had to bathe before entering the holy of holies on the Day of Atonement (Lev. 16.4), and the same ritual is prescribed for the priests in the second temple: 'No one may enter the temple Court for service, even though he is clean, until he has immersed himself. On [the Day of Atonement] the high priest five times immerses himself and ten times he sanctifies [his hands and feet]' (Mishnah Yoma 3.3). There was a special immersion pool for him in the temple (Mishnah Middoth 5.3). Other texts describe the same process: the priest had to bathe before entering the sanctuary, and to wash both before and after offering sacrifice (T. Levi 9.11; Jub. 21.16). The priests on temple duty washed each morning before beginning their duties; the watchman woke them saying: 'Let him who has immersed himself come and cast the lots' (Mishnah Tamid 1.2). Later, the duty priest had to sanctify his hands and feet with water before clearing ashes from the altar and lighting the fire (Mishnah Tamid 1.4).[4]

Washing was also seen as the outward sign of an inner purification. The Community Rule at Qumran prescribed purification by water: 'He shall be cleansed from all his sins by the Spirit of holiness uniting him to His truth, and his iniquity shall be expiated by the spirit of uprightness and humility. And when his flesh is sprinkled with purifying water and sanctified by cleansing water, it shall be made clean by the humble submission of his soul to all the precepts of God' (1QS III). The purpose of this cleansing was 'so that he may contemplate the light of life'. This is similar to Christian ideas, as can be seen from a later passage in the Rule: '[God] will cleanse him of all his wicked deeds with the Spirit of holiness; like purifying waters, He will shed on him the Spirit of truth ... for God has chosen them for an everlasting covenant, and all the glory of Adam shall be theirs' (1QS IV). The Rule distinguished between purification by atonement and cleansing by waters. Josephus, who knew the Essenes, suggested that John the Baptist's baptism was similar: 'The washing would be acceptable to him not for the remission of some sins, but for the purification of the body, supposing that the soul was thoroughly purified beforehand by righteousness' (*Antiquities* 18.117). This is what Paul meant when he said that John had preached 'a baptism of repentance to all the people of Israel' (Acts 13.24).

---

[4] Perhaps the reason why Peter, having been washed, needed only to have his feet washed (John 13.10).

Philo often mentioned the purification necessary before one could approach the mysteries, but for him, this symbolized also the spiritual purification necessary to perceive the divine Presence. He emphasized how the Israelites had washed themselves at Sinai before the LORD came onto the mountain: 'He who is about to receive the holy laws must first cleanse his soul and purge away the deep set stains'; 'they had cleansed themselves with ablutions and lustrations for three days' (*On the Decalogue* 10 and 45). He marvelled that a man could enter the temple after cleansing his body only, yet would attempt to pray and sacrifice with a soiled heart (*The Unchangeableness of God* 8). True washing meant leaving behind the attractions of the material world. Expounding the impurity laws, that nobody who had had contact with uncleanness could approach holy things (Lev. 22.6), he wrote: 'No one is absolutely free from pollution so as to celebrate the holy and reverend mysteries, by whom the splendours of this mortal life ... are still held in honour' (*On Dreams* 1.14).

Washing completely clean from sin was part of the future hope for Israel: 'On that day, there shall be a fountain opened for the house of David and the inhabitants of Jerusalem, to cleanse them from sin and uncleanness' (Zech. 13.1). It would be part of the restoration and renewal of Israel, when they would receive a new heart, and the gift of the Spirit: 'I will sprinkle clean water upon you, and you shall be clean from all your uncleannesses ... a new heart I will give you, and a new spirit I will put within you' (Ezek. 36.25–7). Rabbi Akiba[5] linked these lines in Ezekiel to the true cleansing of the Day of Atonement, and quoted also Jeremiah 17.13: 'O LORD the hope of Israel', where the Hebrew word for hope is also *mikweh* (Mishnah Yoma 8.9). The LORD himself was the cleanser/hope of Israel. This wordplay, characteristic of temple style, shows the original force of Jeremiah's words: 'O LORD the *mikweh* of Israel, all who forsake thee shall be put to shame ... for they have forsaken the LORD, the fountain of living water' (Jer. 17.13).

Since *mikweh* means literally 'the gathering', the great and original *mikweh* had been the waters that gathered together as the creation was brought into being. 'The gathering, *mikweh*, of the waters he called seas' (Gen. 1.10, translating literally). Life emerged from the gathered waters in Genesis, and so new life emerged from the *mikweh*. Tertullian was to write that just as water brought forth life at creation, 'in baptism it need be no wonder if waters already knew how to make

---

[5] A leader during the second war against Rome in 135 CE.

alive' (*On Baptism* 3). Now a symbolic 'sea' played an important role in the temple. The bronze sea was set in the courtyard so that the priests could wash their hands and feet before entering the tent or approaching the altar (Exod. 40.30–32;[6] 2 Chron. 4.6). There were also temple visions of a man rising from the 'sea' and going to heaven to be enthroned (Dan. 7.2, 13–14), presumably based on a ritual, or the memory of a ritual. Daniel was a second temple text reworked from older material, but there is another Jewish text from early in the second century CE which records the same scene and the interpretation current in the time of the early Church: 'A man came up out of the sea and flew with the clouds of heaven' up onto a great mountain. The interpretation given was that this man was the Son of the Most High, kept hidden for many ages, but destined to deliver the creation (2 Esdras 13.3, 26, 32). In other words, the Son of God was expected to rise up from the waters.

For Christians, baptism was not a regular cleansing ritual but marked the moment of initiation. The effects of baptism were described in various ways: as the forgiveness of sins and the gift of the Spirit (Acts 2.38); as spiritual birth that gave access to the Kingdom of God (John 3.5); as the washing of regeneration and renewal (Titus 3.5); as enlightenment (Heb. 6.5; 10.32); as sharing the death and resurrection of Christ (Rom. 6.4–5; Col. 3.1); as putting on a new nature (Col. 3.10); as becoming a son of God (Rom.8.14). The Christian passed from darkness to the Kingdom of the beloved Son (Col. 1.13); was called from darkness to light as the royal priesthood (1 Pet. 2.9); was renewed in his mind (Eph. 4.23). These different images do not necessarily imply that 'the process of becoming a Christian was interpreted and expressed in variety of ways', nor can we know if the images of anointing and clothing were actual baptismal practices or only imagery.[7] But why choose these images, if they were not a part of the rite itself, or part of what the rite represented? *The little that can be recovered about the initiation of the ancient royal high priests suggests that this was the origin of Christian baptism.*

Anointing and clothing does suggest making a priest. The description of consecrating Aaron and his sons in Exodus 29 and

---

[6] The descriptions of the great laver in Exod. 40 only appear in the Hebrew text. The Lxx, perhaps wondering how such a vast amount of water was available in the desert, did not have Exod. 40. vv. 7, 11, 30–32). The great 'sea' was a feature of the temple that had slipped back into descriptions of the earlier tabernacle.

[7] P. F. Bradshaw, *The Search for the Origins of Christian Worship*, London: SPCK, 1992, p. 46.

Leviticus 8 — putting blood on the right ear lobe, the right thumb and the big toe of the right foot — have little obvious similarity to Christian baptism, but there is another consecration ritual described in the Testament of Levi, a pre-Christian text that was only preserved by Christians. It mentions washing, but also anointing, feeding with bread and wine, vesting and crowning. Some of this corresponds to Exodus 29 and Leviticus 8, but much does not, showing that another rite was known at the end of the second temple period. There may be Christian additions to the Testament of Levi, but until we can be certain of what second temple Judaism and early Christianity believed and had in common — and this may be very different from what has formerly been assumed — the text must be read as it stands. Any Christian additions to an earlier text about priesthood will have served to emphasize the importance of the text for Christians who believed themselves to be the royal priesthood. The ritual in the Testament of Levi resembles the earliest Christian baptisms.

Levi, the patriarch of the priestly tribe describes his initiation; that is, what was believed about the role of a priest. The heavens opened and the angel of the LORD told Levi that he would be a son (of the Most High), a minister and priest in his presence (T. Levi 4.2). Later he saw the vision again, and this time there were seven angels vesting him as a priest. The first angel anointed him with holy oil and gave him a staff; the second washed him, gave him bread and wine and put on his glorious vestment; the third put on him a linen garment; the fourth gave him a purple sash; the fifth gave him an olive branch; the sixth put a wreath on his head; and the seventh gave him the priestly diadem and the incense (T. Levi 8.2–11). There is no sacrifice nor smearing with blood mentioned in the Testament (cf. Lev. 8.22–30), and Leviticus does not mention the wine, the staff and the olive branch. Bread and wine were associated with Melchizedek (Gen. 14.18), the eternal priest of the older priesthood in Jerusalem.

The Testament of Levi is clearly hostile to the corrupted priesthood of the second temple: Levi warns his descendants that for seventy weeks there will be corrupt and apostate priests (T. Levi 16.1). He tells of the progressive decline, from the glorious first priest to the men of the seventh jubilee who will be utterly wicked: idolaters, adulterers, money lovers, lawless, voluptuaries, pederasts, practising bestiality (T. Levi 17.11). Then there would be a new priest, over whom the heavens would open. He would be consecrated and receive the glory of the Most High. The Spirit would rest upon him in the water and he would have no successor. He would give the majesty of the LORD to those who were his sons, open again the gates of Paradise and permit the saints to eat from the tree of life (T. Levi 18.1–14). This is the vision of Revelation: the faithful are restored by the LORD to the tree of life (Rev. 2.7; 22.14), and the truly impure are excluded from the heavenly city, which John describes as a huge holy of holies (Rev. 21.1–17). The new priest in the Testament of Levi would give the majesty of the LORD to his sons, and the majesty was understood, at this time, to be represented by the Name on the diadem of the high priest (Wisdom of Solomon 18.24). The new priest, therefore, would give the Name to his 'sons', just as the faithful were marked on the forehead with the Name in baptism. It is likely — we can say no more — that the ritual described in the Testament of Levi was the origin of Christian baptismal practice: washing, clothing, anointing, feeding with bread and wine, becoming a son and wearing the Name. If this was a Jewish text untouched by a Christian editor, it throws remarkable light on the baptism of Jesus; if it was reworked by Christian hands, it shows that the baptism of Jesus was remembered as the moment when he became the High Priest with no successor — Melchizedek.

Often the New Testament accounts give no detail of how a baptism was performed. Paul regained his sight and was filled with the Spirit and then 'He was baptised' (Acts 9.18). This is all we are told of that great event in the story of the early Church: the baptism of Paul. Philip baptized the Ethiopian in some roadside water, once he had declared 'I believe that Jesus Christ is the Son of God' (Acts 8.36–7).[8] Peter had Cornelius and his companions baptized 'in the name of Jesus Christ' after they had received the Spirit and spoken in tongues (Acts 10.44–48). Lydia was baptized with her household (Acts 16.15) — we assume in the river since the meeting place was the riverside. Nothing is said of the words used or of any confession of faith. So too when the gaoler at Philippi was baptized together with his family in the middle of the night, and, we assume, in his gaol (Acts 16.33). Crispus, the ruler of the synagogue and his family, along with many people of Corinth were baptized, but there is no mention of the words or ritual used (Acts 18.8).

John the Baptist had baptized in the River Jordan 'with water for repentance' (Matt. 3.11), but no detail is given. Mark implies that Jesus was immersed[9] — 'When he came up out of the water ...'

---

[8] But some ancient versions omit this line.

[9] The Fourth Gospel does not say that John baptized Jesus, only that he saw the Spirit come upon him.

(Mark.1.10) — but the baptism given by John was different from Christian baptism. There were disciples of John in Ephesus who told Paul that they had never heard of the Holy Spirit, presumably meaning that they had not heard of the gift of the Spirit at baptism (Acts 19.1–6). Their master John spoke of the Spirit coming onto Jesus, and of Jesus himself baptizing with the Spirit (John 1.33), so it is unlikely they had never heard of the Spirit. John's disciples at Ephesus were baptized by Paul 'into the name of the LORD Jesus' and when he laid his hands on them, they received the Spirit and began to speak in tongues and prophesy. Elsewhere, Paul explained that all who received the Spirit were sons of God, fellow heirs with Christ (Rom. 8. 14–17).

The Didache has practical instructions for performing a baptism: 'After rehearsing all the preliminaries, immerse in running water [reminiscent of the rules for the *mikweh*] "in the Name of the Father and of the Son and of the Holy Spirit". If no running water is available, immerse in ordinary water. This should be cold if possible, otherwise warm. If neither is practicable, then sprinkle water three times on the head'. Both the baptizer and the one being baptized should fast before the baptism, and other supporters too (Did. 7). There is no theology here. No explanation. Scholars debate whether the Trinitarian formula could have been in the original text, but there is no evidence to decide the issue either way.

Justin, writing in the mid second century for a Gentile reader, mentioned the Trinitarian formula. People who had been convinced of the truth of Christian teaching, he wrote, prayed and fasted with others and were then 'brought to the water and regenerated'. This washing, he said, was called illumination 'because those who learn these things are illuminated in their understanding' (*Apology* 1.61, 65). He quoted John 3.5, that this was how one entered the Kingdom. He gave more detail when debating with Trypho the Jew, comparing baptism to circumcision, and claiming he had no need of circumcision once he had been baptized by the Holy Spirit, for baptism was spiritual circumcision, like that of Enoch (*Trypho* 29, 43). He contrasted the ritual purification practised by Jews and the true purification effected by baptism: 'The useless baptism of cisterns has nothing to do with the baptism of life,' he said (*Trypho* 14, 19), and alluded to words of Jeremiah like those quoted by his contemporary Rabbi Akiba: 'They have forsaken (the LORD), the fountain of living waters, and hewed out cisterns for themselves, broken cisterns that can hold no water' (Jer. 2.13; Akiba had quoted 17.13). He also alluded to Isaiah 1.16: 'Wash yourselves, make yourselves clean; remove the evil of your doings.'

Cleansing was clearly part of the meaning of baptism, and the accusation of superficial cleansing was part of a bitter debate. Jesus' words: 'Blessed are the pure in heart, for they shall see God' (Matt. 5.8), and the enigmatic words in John 3.25, that the disciples of the Baptist debated with 'a Jew' over purification, show that ritual bathing was being abused. When the cleansing was accompanied by anointing and clothing — whether literal or symbolic — it suggests initiation into the priesthood. Rebirth, entry to the Kingdom, that is, to the holy of holies, becoming a son of God and a member of the royal priesthood, and wearing the Name all suggest that Christian baptism was based on the initiation of the high priest. Washing Aaron and his sons was the first stage in their consecration (Lev. 8.6), before being anointed and clothed. An enigmatic passage in the Clementine literature seems to refer to the vision of the man from the sea described by Esdras, but here the reference is to Jesus: 'After Aaron who was a priest, another was taken out of the waters. I do not speak of Moses, but of Him who, in the waters of baptism, was called by God his Son' (*Clem. Rec.* 1.48).

Jewish ritual washing was frequently repeated; Christian baptism happened once; Qumran purification never included anointing because the Essenes considered oil a defilement (Josephus *War* 2. 123); and there is no pre-Christian precedent for baptizing in or into the Name. Christian baptism repeated the baptism of Jesus; whatever that represented was the rite of initiation into the Church. We shall examine these three aspects of baptism: the baptism of Jesus, baptism in/into the Name, and the anointing.

THE BAPTISM OF JESUS

The Gospels of Matthew, Mark and Luke agree that Jesus' public ministry began with his baptism in the Jordan. The heavens opened, the Spirit came upon him, and there was a voice from heaven saying that he was the Son. Then Jesus went into the desert and battled with Satan. This has long been recognized as an enthronement ritual. E. O. James, in his study of king-making, noted that the Gospel accounts 'contain most of the essential elements of the pattern': proclamation by John, then washing and anointing by the Spirit, with a divine manifestation in the form of a dove. Thus reborn, the king had a period of seclusion and trial, after which he merged victorious over the evil powers and began to establish his Kingdom.[10]

The Gospel accounts differ slightly: did Jesus alone see the heavens open and hear the voice, or did everyone around share the experience? For our purposes, these differences are not important. Only Matthew records John's reluctance to baptize Jesus (Matt. 3. 14). The Jewish community for whom Matthew wrote must have sensed this difficulty, knowing that John's baptism was the sign of repentance in preparation for the Kingdom, and repentance was deemed inappropriate for Jesus. The Fourth Gospel does not mention Jesus' baptism, the vision of the open heavens and the voice; it simply has John the Baptist testify that he saw the Spirit descend onto Jesus as a sign that he would baptize with the Spirit (John 1.33). The gift of the Spirit distinguished Christian baptism from the baptism of John.

A heavenly voice spoke to Jesus, but whose voice? According to Matthew and Mark, the voice said: 'Thou art my beloved Son; with thee I am well pleased' (Mark 1.11, and similar in Matt. 3.17). The earliest texts of Luke,[11] however, are different and afford a valuable clue to the original meaning of baptism: 'You are my Son; today I have begotten you' (Luke 3.22, quoting Ps. 2.7). This psalm describes the 'birth' of the Davidic king as the divine son, not his physical birth, but the moment when he was enthroned on Zion. The difficulty with this text is obvious: there must have been early Christians who thought of Jesus' baptism as the moment when he became the divine Son. He was born of the Spirit, and so born again/born from above — the Greek can mean either. Jesus explained this to Nicodemus: those born from above see the Kingdom, those born of water and Spirit enter the Kingdom (John 3.3–5). The Gospel of the Hebrews, now lost apart from quotations in early writers, said the voice was the Holy Spirit, and there is no reason not to understand the Gospel accounts in that way. 'And it came to pass when the LORD was come up out of the water, the whole fount of the Holy Spirit descended and rested upon him and said unto him: "My son, in all the prophets I was waiting for thee that thou shouldst come, and I might rest in thee. For thou art my rest, thou art my first begotten son, that reignest for ever."' This Gospel also described the Holy Spirit as Jesus' heavenly

---

[10] E. O. James, *Christian Myth and Ritual. A Historical Study*, London: John Murray, 1933, p. 100.

[11] The Western Bezae text, the Old Latin, Justin, Clement of Alexandria and Origen.

mother (quoted by Jerome, *Commentary on Isaiah* 11.2, 9). 'Spirit' is a feminine noun in Hebrew.

Paul, who had learned about his new faith from the Palestinian church, seems to know both these — the Spirit as the voice, and the baptism as Jesus' birth as the divine Son — and to be quoting an established statement of belief in Romans 1.3–4: '[God's] Son, descended from David according to the flesh, and designated Son of God in power according to the Spirit of holiness by his resurrection from the dead, Jesus Christ our LORD ...' The rather awkward 'Spirit of holiness' instead of Holy Spirit suggests a literal rendering of a Hebrew phrase; in other words, that this was something Paul had learned from the Palestinian church, rather than formulated himself. Those who used the Gospel of the Hebrews would have known that the voice at Jesus' baptism was the voice of the Holy Spirit, recognizing and empowering her Son. This early statement of belief is saying that when Jesus was named and empowered as Son of God, it was his resurrection. There are several indications that Jesus' baptism and experience of the open heaven *was* his resurrection. Early texts say that the post-resurrection period, when Jesus taught his disciples, was 550 days (Apocryphon of James), 545 days (The Ascension of Isaiah), or 18 months (Irenaeus, *Against Heresies* 1.3.2 and 1.30.14, describing the beliefs of the Valentinians). These could well represent the teaching ministry, the period after the baptism, when as we have seen, Jesus gave secret teaching to the disciples. Most remarkable and enigmatic of all is the line in the Gospel of Philip: 'Those who said that the LORD died first and then rose up are in error, for he rose up first and then he died. If one does not first attain the resurrection, will he not die?' (CG II.3 56). The resurrection preceded Good Friday, and Easter confirmed the resurrection for those who had been 'chosen beforehand' as witnesses (Acts 10.41, translating literally).

Resurrection could mean many things, but in temple tradition it meant ascent to the heavenly throne. Such ascents were part of the king-making ritual in ancient Jerusalem, but they are often obscured in translation. Two associated with King David will illustrate this point: 'I have set the crown upon one who is mighty/ I have exalted one chosen from the people/... with my holy oil I have anointed him' (Ps. 89.19–20); and 'The oracle of David, the son of Jesse/ the oracle of the man who was *raised on high*/ the anointed of the God of Jacob ...' (2 Sam. 23.1). Raising up in this context means both ascent to heaven and resurrection.[12] David was raised up and anointed; that is, made a Messiah. This means that 'resurrection' in this sense was part of what it meant to be the Messiah. In the New Testament, resurrection texts that imply bodily resuscitation, such as Isaiah 26.19: 'Thy dead shall live, their bodies shall rise'; or Ezekiel 37, the valley of the dry bones; or Daniel 12.2: 'Many of those who sleep in the dust of the earth shall awake', are not used of the resurrection of Jesus, nor do we consider the raising of Jairus' daughter or of Lazarus as resurrection in the same sense. We assume they lived ordinary lives, and then died. The most frequently cited resurrection proof texts are Psalm 2 and Psalm 110, both describing the ascent and enthronement of the king, and Isaiah 53, which describes the exaltation of the Servant.

When Hebrews compared the two priesthoods — Melchizedek's and Aaron's — the difference between them was resurrection. The unknown writer explained that the sons of Aaron were priests due to 'descent', but Melchizedek was a priest due to 'ascent'. He 'arises' — the word means resurrection — 'by the power of an indestructible life' (Heb. 7.16). The Aaronite priests die and have successors, but Melchizedek is priest for ever, because he is already resurrected (Heb. 7.23–4). He has become like the Son of God (Heb. 7.3). This is the pattern of Romans 1.4, becoming Son of God by resurrection. Jesus' resurrection was like Melchizedek's, the initiation into priesthood, and it seems that Christian baptism was similar.

What did the early Church understand by resurrection? John's Jesus explained to Nicodemus that to see the Kingdom one had to be born from above, or born again, and to enter the Kingdom one had to be born of water and Spirit. Birth in the flesh and birth in the Spirit were different processes (John 3.3–6). Paul contrasted 'according to the flesh', *kata sarka*, and 'according to the Spirit of holiness', *kata pneuma hagiosunes* as the twin sources of Jesus' sonship: human and divine (Rom. 1.3–4). Jesus' speaking of water and Spirit indicates baptism, and being born again was resurrection, starting life anew. In debate with the Sadducees, Jesus explained that 'sons of God', 'sons of the resurrection' and 'angels' were equivalent terms (Luke 20.36). It is in this context that we must understand Paul's words to the church at Colossae: 'If then you *have been raised* with Christ, seek the things which are above, where Christ is, seated at the right hand of

---

[12] The same word is used for raising for the dead in Job 14.12; Isa. 26.14, 19; Ps. 88.10. The Aramaic equivalent in found in Jesus' words to Jairus' daughter: 'Talitha *cumi*', Little girl, arise (Mark 5.41).

God' (Col. 1.1). The Christians at Colossae were already raised. John taught this too: 'We know that *we have passed* out of death into life' (1 John 3.14). Peter linked baptism to entering the royal priesthood: 'Having purified your souls ... You have been born anew ... to be a holy priesthood ... called out of darkness into his marvellous light' (1 Pet. 1.22, 23; 2.5, 9).

There is a remarkable text in 2 Enoch 22 which describes the transformation of Enoch into an angel; that is, his resurrection. Since Enoch was a high priest figure — he entered the holy of holies — this probably describes how he became a high priest. Enoch ascended to the highest heaven and stood before the throne. The LORD told the archangel Michael to remove Enoch's earthly clothing; that is, his mortal body, to anoint him with myrrh oil, 'dew', and then to clothe him in the garments of divine glory. As Enoch was anointed and clothed, he saw himself transformed into 'one of the glorious ones' (2 Enoch 22.4–10). The date of this text is uncertain, but texts found at Qumran show the belief that people could become angels: 'May you be as an angel of the Presence ... May you attend upon the service in the temple of the Kingdom'(The Blessings, 1QSb IV); 'Thou hast cleansed a spirit of great sin, that it may stand with the host of the holy ones, and that it may enter into community with the congregation of the sons of heaven' (1 QH XI); 'Thou hast purified a man of sin that he may be holy for thee ... that he may partake of the lot of the holy ones' (1QH XI); 'I am reckoned with the *'elohim* and my glory is with the sons of the King (4Q 491.11). Philo said the Therapeuts no longer lived the life of this world: 'Such is their longing for the deathless and blessed life that, thinking their mortal life already ended, they abandon their property to their sons, daughters or kinsfolk' (*On the Contemplative Life* 13).

These contemporaries of the first Christians believed that resurrection meant being taken up into the presence of God and becoming angels before their physical death, and The Odes of Solomon, early baptismal hymns, show that the Church had similar beliefs. Until more is known about early baptism, however, much in these texts will remain a mystery. They seem to show that resurrection meant being taken up into the presence of God. 'The LORD renewed me with his garment/ And possessed me by his light/... My eyes were enlightened,/ And my face received the dew/ and my soul was refreshed/ By the pleasant fragrance of the LORD (Ode 11.11, 14,15); 'I rested on the Spirit of the LORD/ And she lifted me up to heaven/... [She] brought me before the face of the LORD .../ And he anointed me with his perfection/ And I became one of those who are near him (Ode 36.1, 3, 6). This sense of transformation, *theosis*, can be detected in Luke's account of the transfiguration, which seems to record Jesus' own experience. 'As [Jesus] was praying, the appearance of his countenance was altered, and his raiment became dazzling white ... Now Peter and those who were with him were heavy with sleep, and when they wakened they saw his glory ...' (Luke 9.29, 32). If the disciples had been asleep, who saw Jesus' appearance change and his clothes become dazzling white? Did Jesus, like Enoch, experience his own transformation? However we try to explain this text, it is generally recognized as a resurrection appearance; some say it has been misplaced into the middle of the Gospel narrative, but it is more likely that this resurrection appearance was the disciples glimpsing the resurrected Messiah before his death, just as the Gospel of Philip attests. In the Fourth Gospel, when debating with the Jews, Jesus said he had become the Son, the High Priest: 'Do you say of him whom the Father consecrated and sent into the world "You are blaspheming" because I said "I am the Son of God"?' (John 10.36). Presumably the Jews would have recognized and accepted this argument.

There was a 'curious and remarkable connection,' wrote J. H. Bernard in his study of The Odes of Solomon[13], between the baptism of Jesus and his descent into hell. The triumph over the evil powers took place in the Jordan, and not just on the cross as taught by Paul (Col. 2.15). The Odes are probably from late second century Syria, but this same connection appears in the Letter of Barnabas, a second or third-generation text. Barnabas treats the waters of baptism and the cross together, and paraphrases an interesting catena of texts: First, that Israel has forsaken the fountain of life and chosen the cisterns (Jer. 2.13); then the mysterious prophecy to Cyrus: 'I will go before you ... breaking the doors of bronze and cutting the bars of iron. I will give you treasures that are mysterious, secret and unseen, so that you may know me for the LORD God' (Isa. 45.2–3 with allusions to Ps. 107.13–16); and then 'You shall dwell on high in a rocky place where there are springs of never failing water. Your eyes shall see the King in glory ...' (Isa. 33.16–17). Barnabas here associates baptism with the harrowing of hell and the vision of God enthroned (Barn. 11). Ode 24 is similar. It begins by describing the baptism of Jesus, with the dove fluttering over the head of the Messiah, and then declares: 'The

[13] J. H. Bernard *The Odes of Solomon*, Cambridge: University Press, 1912, p. 32.

chasms were submerged in the submersion[14] of the LORD ...' In Ode 22, where Christ seems to be the speaker, there is another allusion to baptism: 'He who caused me to descend from on high and to ascend from the region below ... overthrew by my hands the dragon with seven heads ...'

Hippolytus, writing in Rome early in the third century, also knew of the conflict in the Jordan and the significance of the open heaven. 'The waters saw him and were afraid' (Ps. 77.16) and 'What ails you, O sea, that you flee, and Jordan that you were driven back? (Ps. 114.5). The waters replied, 'We have seen the Creator of all things in the form of a servant.' The LORD approached John without any royal retinue, to elude the snares of the dragon. When the heavens opened, there was a reconciliation of heaven and earth, the angels rejoiced, the earth was healed and enemies were reconciled (*On the Holy Theophany* 2, 4, 6). Cyril of Jerusalem, writing about baptism in the mid fourth century, said that Jesus broke the heads of the dragon, and he went down and bound the strong one in the waters, so that we might have power to tread on serpents and scorpions (*Catecheses* 3.11, quoting Luke 10.19). Epiphany hymns sang of Christ opening the way to heaven at his baptism and crushing the head of the serpent, and ancient baptismal prayers spoke of breaking the head of the dragon in the waters, a reference to Psalm 74.14, but also to the curse on the serpent in Eden — that the child of Eve would bruise his head (Gen. 3.15)[15].

The open heavens, the birth of the divine son and the defeat of the ancient serpent all occur in the Book of Revelation, in the vision that follows the proclamation of the Kingdom on earth. The heavens open to reveal the woman clothed with the sun about to give birth to her Son, who is destined to rule with a rod of iron. This is Psalm 2, the birth of the divine Son who is set on Zion to rule the nations with a rod of iron. In Luke's original account of the baptism, Jesus heard the words of this psalm: 'You are my son. Today I have begotten you' (Ps. 2.7). In the vision, the dragon waits to devour the child, but he is snatched up to heaven and enthroned,[16] and then Michael and his angels defeat the dragon and drive him from heaven. This, briefly

---

[14] Thus J. H. Charlesworth, *The Odes of Solomon*, Oxford: Clarendon Press, 1973. Bernard has 'seal'.

[15] For detail, see my book, *The Risen Lord. The Jesus of History as the Christ of Faith*, Edinburgh: T&T Clark, 1996, pp. 37–41.

[16] For detail, see my book, *The Revelation of Jesus Christ*, Edinburgh: T&T Clark, 2000, pp. 200–202, 219–225.

and enigmatically, describes the birth of the Son of God. There is no hint elsewhere in the New Testament that defeating the dragon was linked to the birth of the Son, but the consistent association of the dragon with Jesus' baptism, and of his baptism with his birth from above, suggests that this was part of the original tradition. The other elements of the vision were realized in the baptism and desert experiences of Jesus. He was born from above, heard Psalm 2 and saw the Kingdom when the heavens opened and revealed the holy of holies. Then Jesus had visions in the desert that reflected Psalm 2: being set on a high place, and refusing to accept all the kingdoms of the world from the devil. The enigmatic 'He was with the wild beasts; and the angels ministered to him' (Mark 1.13) is likely to indicate a throne vision. The Hebrew for 'wild beasts', *hayyoth,* also means 'the living creatures' of the throne (e.g. Ezek. 1.5), and the serving angels suggests the vision of the Son enthroned amidst the living creatures, receiving the homage of the host of heaven (Rev. 5.6–14). Then Jesus returned from the desert and began to proclaim: 'The Kingdom of God is at hand' (Mark 1.15), or, in the words of Revelation: 'The Kingdom of the world has become the Kingdom of our LORD and of his Christ' (Rev. 11.15).

Origen knew that Jesus had seen the throne at his baptism. He noted that Ezekiel had received the vision of the chariot throne by the River Chebar in the thirtieth year. This he took to be Ezekiel's age, just as Jesus was thirty at his baptism (Ezek. 1.1 cf. Luke 3.23), the age at which priests began their duties (Num. 4.3). Both were by a river, and each saw the heavens opened (*On Ezekiel,* Homily 1.4–7). This resembles Levi's vision, when he too saw the heavens open, and an angel told him he would become a Son of the Most High, and a priest in his presence (T. Levi 4.2). Ezekiel's vision was on the fifth day of the fourth month, which, reckoned on the old temple calendar, was about the time of Epiphany, the feast of Jesus' baptism. Origen implies that what Ezekiel saw, Jesus saw: the chariot throne over the waters, and the Spirit of the Living One[17] (or the Spirit of life) beneath the throne of God (Ezek. 1.20.22). Origen was an expert on the text of the Old Testament, and so it is unlikely that he made this link between Ezekiel's vision and the baptism without good reason: the open heavens, the water and the throne were elements in becoming a priest.

Origen came from Alexandria but moved to Caesarea in Palestine. Teachers in all parts of the Christian world described a similar

---

[17] The Hebrew is singular despite some English translations.

phenomenon to the throne vision: fire on the water when Jesus was baptized. Justin, who was born in Palestine but moved to Rome, knew there had been fire in the Jordan as Jesus went into the water (*Trypho* 88). Hippolytus, writing in Rome a generation later, had John the Baptist say to Jesus, 'Baptise me with the fire of divinity' (*On the Holy Theophany* 4), which may be an allusion to the fire on the Jordan. Epiphanius was born in Palestine early in the fourth century and moved as a bishop to Cyprus. He knew the Gospel of the Ebionites, which he said resembled Matthew, and he quoted the passage about Jesus' baptism: 'Jesus also came and was baptised by John; and as he came up from the water, the heavens were opened, and he saw the Holy Spirit in the likeness of a dove ... And immediately there shone about the place a great light.'[18] Two of the old Latin texts of Matthew 3.15 also mention the light: 'When he was baptised, a great light shone from the water so that all who had come were afraid.'[19] Ephrem, a contemporary of Epiphanius but writing in Edessa, knew there was a bright light on the water and a voice from heaven (*Commentary on the Diatessaron* IV.5).

The link between the fire and the vision of the chariot throne is found in the stories told about Rabbi Johannan ben Zakkai and his disciples, throne mystics who were contemporaries of Jesus and the first generation. 'Rabbi Eleazar ben Arakh expounded until fire burned all around him. When Rabbi Johannan ben Zakkai saw that fire was burning all around round him, he descended from his ass, kissed him and said: "Rabbi Eleazar ben Arakh, happy is she who bore you."' The narrators of these stories said nothing about the throne vision they were expounding: it was forbidden to read this chapter of Ezekiel in public (Mishnah Megillah 4.10) and it was forbidden to read it with a disciple unless he already understood it 'of his own knowledge' (Mishnah Hagigah 2.1). Commenting on this, Halperin wrote: 'What they wanted to show was the wondrous greatness of the ancient sages. They did this by describing the vivid tokens by which God and the angels showed their regard for the way these men expounded the Scriptures.'[20] Presumably

---

[18] Epiphanius, *Panarion*, 30.

[19] Codex vercellensis, fourth or fifth century, has: 'et cum baptizaretur, lumen ingens circumfulsit ut timerent omnes qui advenerant'. Codex Sangermanensis, seventh century, has 'et com baptizaretur Jesus, lumen magnum fulgebat de aqua, ita ut timerent omnes qui congregati sunt'.

[20] D. J. Halperin, *The Faces of the Chariot. Early Jewish Responses to Ezekiel's Vision*, Tübingen:Mohr, 1988, pp. 13–15, quoting Jerusalem Talmud Hagigah 2.1; Babylonian Talmud Hagigah 14b.

the Jewish writers of the Gospels were showing the greatness of Jesus in the same way, and implying that he too was a throne mystic.

Halperin also speculated as to why there was a change of attitude towards the chariot throne mystics. By the time the Mishnah was compiled, about 200 CE, there was a cautious and even hostile attitude towards them and their teaching.[21] He suggested that the threat was from Gnosticism. This is unlikely. The books most concerned with the chariot throne were the apocalyptic texts and the Enoch literature, which had already been excluded from the canon of Hebrew Scripture and forbidden by Rabbi Akiba (early second century CE). Those who read them, he warned, would have no place in the world to come (Mishnah Sanhedrin 10.1). Those who studied things above and things below, the future and the past, were also cursed (Mishnah Ḥagigah 2.1). These forbidden texts were only preserved and studied by Christians, and so it is likely that Jewish aversion to the throne mystics was for the same reason: their teachings were important to the Christians, and their visions were shaping the Church's liturgy. Since the Kingdom was the state of the holy of holies, the place of the throne,[22] where faithful Christians with the Name on their foreheads worshipped the God-and-the-Lamb, the picture emerges of the baptized/born again/resurrected, experiencing at their baptism what Jesus had known in the Jordan.[23]

BAPTISM AND THE NAME.

The first Christians were baptized 'in the name of the Father, the Son and the Holy Spirit', according to the final words of Matthew's Gospel (Matt. 28.19). The Didache, the earliest source outside the New Testament, prescribes the same Trinitarian formula (Did. 7), and later says that only those baptized in the name of the LORD could participate in the Eucharist (Did. 9). The Didache therefore reckoned the Trinitarian formula and the simpler 'In the name of the LORD' as equivalents. There has been much debate about this: did the earliest baptisms really use the Trinitarian formula? There is no way of answering that question.

It may, however, be possible to discover something of the significance of the Name in baptism by examining the form of words: 'in

---

[21] Halperin, pp. 25–28.

[22] See my book, *The Hidden Tradition of the Kingdom of God*, London: SPCK, 2007.

[23] For detail, see my book, *The Risen Lord. The Jesus of History as the Christ of Faith*, Edinburgh: T&T Clark, 1996.

the name of' is used to translate Greek phrases meaning literally 'into the name of' and 'in the name of'. The question of baptizing *into* the name — changing the status of the person baptized — or baptizing *in* the name — apparently emphasizing the status of the person baptizing — is complicated by the problem that besets all attempts to reconstruct Christian origins: there are only Greek texts for evidence of a movement in Palestine whose members are unlikely to have had spoken Greek as their mother tongue or to have used it for worship and ritual. All evidence available only in translation could have lost something in the process. What underlies '*in* or *into* the name of ...' is fundamental to this enquiry.

'Into the Name', *'eis*, occurs in Matthew 28.19, in Acts 8.16, and in the Didache. Paul described baptism *into* Christ Jesus (Rom. 6.3), baptism *into* one body (1 Cor. 12.13), implying that baptism transferred the new Christian into Christ, into the body of the Church. The baptismal formula, understood in this way, implies transferring the new Christian *into* the Name. Other texts have 'in the name ...', *en,* as do some early texts of Matthew 28.19: 'baptising them *in* my name ...', which could imply that the name was borne by the baptizer and was the source of authority. Acts 10.48 has Peter command that Cornelius's household be baptized in, *en,* the name of Jesus Christ. 'In the name of the LORD' could have meant 'with the authority of the LORD', the Name indicating the status of the baptizer and not that of the baptized. The situation in Corinth implies that the 'name' of the baptizer determined the group one joined: 'Were you baptised *into* the name of Paul? (1 Cor. 1.13) implies that the 'status' of the baptizer conferred a new status on the one baptized. The one who acted '*in* the name' of the LORD, i.e. as the representative of the LORD, could transfer others '*into* the name' of the LORD.

Evidence for early practice is scarce. At first the apostles and evangelists baptized: Peter and the apostles in Jerusalem (Acts 2.41); Philip (Acts 8.38); Ananias (Acts 9.18); and church leaders in Corinth (1 Cor. 1.14). Ignatius, writing to the Church at Smyrna very early in the second century, emphasized that only the bishop or his representative could baptize: 'Where the bishop is to be seen, there let all his people be, just as wherever Jesus Christ is present, we have the catholic Church. Nor is it permissible to conduct baptisms or love feasts without the bishop ...' (Letter to Smyrna 8). Ignatius implies that the bishop represents Jesus Christ, and thus he is empowered to baptize, presumably *into* Christ. Tertullian too, writing about 200 CE, said: 'The supreme right of giving baptism belongs to the high priest, that is, to the bishop, and then to presbyters and deacons with the bishop's permission' (On Baptism 17).

The Palestinian setting of early Christianity means that Hebrew tradition is the most likely context for its practices, and Hebrew usage the most likely explanation of the Greek formulae found in the New Testament. '*In* the name of the Father, and of the Son and of the Holy Spirit' may be best explained by Psalm 118, which was much quoted by the Christians, especially in accounts of Holy Week. 'Hosanna! Blessed is he who comes *in the name of the* LORD*!*' (Ps. 118.26 in Matt. 21.9; 23.39; Mark 11.9–10; Luke 13.35; John 12.13). Here the Hebrew word for 'in' is the preposition *b*ᵉ, which has a wide range of meaning, and the Greek translation of the Psalm has *en*, 'in'. No single English word covers the whole range of meaning of the Hebrew *b*ᵉ, which may account for the variety of New Testament usage. The Hebrew *b*ᵉ can mean 'in' — *in* the town, *in* the house; it can mean 'into', as in 'the Assyrian will come *into* Egypt ...' (Isa. 19.23); it can mean 'as' as in 'I appeared to them *as* El Shaddai' (Exod. 6.3); it can mean 'with' as in '*with* bow and arrows' (Isa. 7.24). 'In the name of' also meant 'as the representative of', as in 'my words which he shall speak *in my name*' (Deut. 18.19). Three of these usages are possible for the early Christian baptismal context: baptizing with the Name, in the sense of marking with the Name; baptizing as the representative of the Name, or baptizing as the Name, these two latter being in effect the same.

When someone came *b*ᵉ *šem*, 'in/with the name of' Yahweh, it meant more than simply coming as a representative, because the Davidic king, as we shall see, 'was' the LORD.[24] One of his titles was Immanuel, 'God with us' (Isa. 8.8). Sometimes the Name meant the LORD himself: 'Behold, the Name of the LORD comes from far, burning with his anger and in thick rising smoke' (Isa. 30.27). Sometimes the Name was 'in' an angel, as when an angel guided Israel from Sinai: 'my Name is in/within him' (Exod. 23.21). In the Deuteronomic tradition of the Old Testament, the Name implied the presence of the LORD. He made his Name dwell in the temple (Deut. 12.5, 11). But the presence was also a way of describing the LORD himself. The promise to Moses: 'My presence will go with you' became, in the Greek, 'I myself will go with you' (Exod. 33.14). The LORD was known to be a pluriform presence: those who had his Name had his presence and were his presence.

In the later Jewish mystical texts that preserved ancient temple traditions, many angels have Yahweh as part of their name. In

---

[24] See below p. 160.

3 Enoch, a collection of Hebrew material,[25] there are sixteen great princes in heaven, with names such as Galliṣur-Yahweh, who reveals the secrets of Torah; Šoqedḥozi-Yahweh, who weighs men's merits in the presence of the Holy One; and Soperi'el-Yahweh, in charge of the books of the living and the dead (3 Enoch 18). These mighty angels were all believed to be aspects of Yahweh, who was present or perceived in each of them. When Josephus told the story of Yahweh appearing to Abraham at Mamre (Gen. 18), he did not mention Yahweh even though he had the same version of Genesis as we do. Josephus described three angels appearing to Abraham 'and they declared they were angels of God' (*Antiquities* 1.196). This shows that an educated Palestinian Jew in the first century CE, coming from a high priestly family, thought of Yahweh as present in his angels. Josephus would also have declared as the fundamental of his faith: 'The LORD our God (*'elohim*, a plural noun) is One LORD' (Deut. 6.4). The plurality of Yahweh was a Unity, but the plurality could be perceived and described as his angels. Coming 'with the Name of the LORD' meant coming as his presence, one of his presences. Giving the Name in baptism and being baptized *into* Christ were developments in the belief of the plurality of the presence.

The high priest wore the Name of the LORD, and so the LORD was present in him, but one detail of his regalia may afford a clue as to the meaning of the baptismal formula: 'to/into the name of the LORD'. On the front of his turban the high priest had to tie a golden plate (*ṣiṣ*, an almond flower), engraved like a sacred seal 'To Yahweh' (Exod. 28.36). The Hebrew is usually translated rather differently: 'You shall make a plate of pure gold, and engrave on it, like the engraving of a signet, "Holy to the LORD"' (thus the RSV), but writers in the first century CE knew that the seal bore nothing but the Name 'which only those whose ears and tongues are purified may hear or speak in the holy place and no other person nor in any other place at all. That Name has four letters ...' (*Moses* II. 114)[26]. Philo, who wrote this, was of a priestly family, as was Josephus who attributed to Ananus the high priest these words: 'I who wear the high priest's vestments am called by the most honourable of venerated names' (*War* 4.163). Both Philo and Josephus were contemporary with the first Christians,

---

[25] Thought to have been collected in Babylon in the fifth century CE, but preserving ancient tradition.

[26] Similarly in *Moses* II.132: 'Above the turban is the golden plate on which are graven four letters, indicating, we are told, the name of the Self Existent....'

and presumably thought in the same way about the Name. Aristeas, whose writing cannot be dated, also mentioned the Name: 'On his head he wore ... the royal diadem full of glory with the name of God inscribed in sacred letters on a plate of gold' (Aristeas 98). It was the name of the LORD, not a 'Holy to the LORD' that was worn on the forehead of the high priest.

The original prescription on Exodus 28.36 says that Moses had to engrave the golden *ṣiṣ* with the engravings of a holy seal belonging to the LORD. The seal was holy, and it bore the Name. 'To the LORD' was the usual way to engrave a seal. The ancient Hebrew seals and seal impressions that have been found show it was customary to inscribe them not simply with the name of the person, but with the form 'to X', that is, belonging to X.[27] When Isaiah wrote the symbolic tablet, bearing the strange name of his son, Maher-shalal-hash-baz, what he actually wrote was '*to* Maher-shalal-hash-baz' (Isa. 8.1). Isaiah was writing a huge seal. Exodus 28.36 describes exactly the form of an ancient Hebrew seal of the LORD: 'To the LORD', *lyhwh*. The high priest wore this seal — it is interesting that his ritual dress included a sacred seal — and the seal was deemed to be the majesty of the LORD, the presence. Aaron was able to protect his people from the plague because the majesty was on the diadem that he wore (Wisdom of Solomon 18.24). This curious seal formula 'to the LORD' might account for the other common usage in baptismal formulae: baptism 'into/to the name of the LORD', meant marking as the high priest had been marked. It must be significant that 'sealing' was one of the rituals of baptism, and that the angel of the dawn in Revelation 7.2 came with the seal of the living God. Initially, the angel marked only the twelve tribes of Israel, in other words, this was a pre-Christian hope that became part of Christianity.

In the first century CE there were two seals in the temple, kept in a casket (Mishnah Yoma 4.1): one inscribed 'to the LORD' and the other 'to Azazel', as prescribed in Leviticus 16.10. When the seals were drawn out of the casket as lots, they determined which of the two goats on the Day of Atonement was to be 'to/as Azazel', that is, to represent Azazel and be driven out into the wilderness bearing the sins of Israel, and which was to be 'to/as the LORD' and sacrificed as the atonement offering. *The sin offering bore the Name.* The high priest also wore the Name so that he could take upon himself any 'guilt'

[27] See G. I. Davies, *Ancient Hebrew Inscriptions*, Cambridge: Cambridge University Press, 1991, pp. 118–246.

in the people's offerings and thus make them pure and acceptable (Exod. 28.38). This was a dangerous task, and the high priest was warned that if he wore the Name 'lightly' he would not be protected from the guilt that he bore. 'You shall not wear the Name of the LORD your God lightly, for the LORD will not hold him guiltless who wears his name lightly' (Exod. 20.7, my literal translation of the familiar 'Thou shalt not take the Name of the LORD thy God in vain ...'). This may account for the severe punishment anticipated for those who lapsed after baptism (Heb. 6.4–6): they had worn the seal of the Name 'in vain'.

There were two stages in anointing a high priest: the oil was poured over his head, and then he was signed with the X of the Name, but this order was disputed. Other scholars said that he was signed first and then had the oil poured over him (Babylonian Talmud Horayoth 12a). There was agreement, however, that there had been two stages and that the holy oil had been hidden away in the time of King Josiah; in other words, that none of the second temple priests had been anointed. The account of Joshua being made high priest in the second temple confirms this: he was vested, but not anointed. He wore the glorious robes and could enter the holy of holies to stand among the angels, but he was not anointed (Zech. 3.1–7). Christian anointing, therefore, was restoring the rites of the older temple, and marking with the cross was restoring the ancient anointing of the high priest, which would have meant the royal high priest, the Melchizedek. Creating the Christians as this restored priesthood is a theme in Revelation: Jesus Christ had made them a kingdom, priests to his God and Father (Rev. 1.6); the Lamb had made a kingdom and priests to God (Rev. 5.10); and in the millennium Kingdom, they would reign with Christ for a thousand years (Rev. 20.6). They were 'a chosen race, a royal priesthood, a holy nation' (1 Pet. 2.9).

When the royal high priest was vested and anointed, he became an angel, a son of God. Those who had been baptized into (*eis*) Christ became sons of God, had put on the Anointed One — the vesting imagery — and were beyond any divisions known in their former life: there was neither Jew nor Greek, slave nor free, male nor female (Gal. 3.26–8). The person baptized became a high priest, or rather, *part of* the high priest, part of the LORD incarnate. This was old temple lore, and since the angels were a unity, this became the model for the Church. The imagery surfaces in the Fourth Gospel, for example in Jesus' debate with the Jews over the meaning of sonship (John 10.36). Consecration in the holy of holies before being sent 'into the world' was the anointing of the high priest, and Jesus could appeal here to a belief that the Jews would accept: the anointed one was a Son of God. The unity of all the anointed ones became an important theme in Christian teaching, and appears first in Jesus' prayer after the Last Supper (John 17), often described as his high priestly prayer: 'Keep them in thy Name, which thou hast given me, that they may be one, even as we are one' (John 17.11). The disciples were to be kept 'in the Name', and being in the Name made them a unity in the way that Jesus and the Father were a unity. This suggests that baptism 'into the Name' meant literally incorporation into the Name, becoming the body of the Anointed One. 'Putting on Christ' was drawn from the imagery of vesting, and so being baptized 'into the Name' implied that the new Christian became part of the Name, one of the *'elohim* that were the unity of the LORD.

The high priest had bound on the Name with a blue thread (Exod. 28.37), and this binding of the Name later symbolized union with the LORD. It could well have had this meaning from the beginning, but the Old Testament texts that prescribe the furnishings and rituals of the temple or tabernacle never explain them: they never say why the vestments had to be in that particular form, or the Name worn in that particular way. 'Binding oneself to the LORD', the verb *dbq*, cleaving to the LORD, was used in the Old Testament. In Deuteronomy it meant obeying the commandments, and was linked to binding on the *tefillin*: 'You shall bind them as a sign upon your hand ... be careful to do all this commandment which I command you to do, loving the LORD your God, walking in all his way, and cleaving to him ...' (Deut. 11.18, 22; Deut. 30.20 is similar). Other texts imply a more literal idea of union: a man cleaves to his wife and they become one flesh (Gen. 2.24): 'As a waistcloth clings to the loins of a man, so I made [them] cling to me, says the LORD' (Jer.13.11); 'My soul clings to thee' (Ps. 63.8). The related noun means 'solder' (Isa. 41.7). There were conflicting interpretations of 'to cleave': some followed Deuteronomy and said it meant simply doing good deeds, following the commandments closely; others took it more literally and said it meant a mystical union with the LORD. One of the latter was Rabbi Akiba, who emphasized: 'You who are cleaving to the LORD your God, literally cleaving' (Babylonian Talmud Sanhedrin 64a).[28] Since R. Akiba lived in the first half of the second century CE, this 'literally

---

[28] For the development of 'cleaving' *devekut*, in Jewish thought, see M. Idel, *Kabbalah. New Perspectives*, New Haven and London: Yale University Press, 1988, pp. 35–58.

cleaving' could have been known to the early Church. Union with the LORD was not unknown in Jewish circles, and binding on the Name symbolized the union. Later Jewish mystical texts, even though they cannot be dated with certainty, had their roots in the temple. In many places there are striking similarities to Christian belief, but it is unlikely that Jewish mystics would have borrowed from Christians if these teachings had been Christian innovations. More likely is a common pre-Christian source. A mystical ascent attributed to R. Akiba,[29] for example, revealed that the LORD *bound* himself even to a 'stranger', *ger*, provided that he was pure from idolatry, bloodshed and forbidden sexual practices. These were precisely the restrictions placed on Gentile converts to Christianity (Acts 15.39):[30] those who were to be baptized into the Name.

Marking with the Name was a protection for the high priests performing their duties and for those who would escape the judgement (Ezek. 9.3; Rev. 7.2–3). 'Touch not my anointed ones' (1 Chron. 16.22 = Ps. 105.15). A discourse attributed to Peter (but in fact evidence of what was later believed about the early period of the Church), shows that baptism was believed literally to protect from war and disaster. 'Evident proof of this great mystery [Christian baptism] is supplied in the fact that everyone who ... is baptised in his name shall be kept unhurt from the destruction of war which impends over the unbelieving nation and [Jerusalem] itself' (*Clementine Recognitions* 1.39). This suggests that there may have been more than spiritual concerns behind the question put to Peter and the apostles at Pentecost when the people had been convinced that the judgement was imminent: 'Brethren, what shall we do?' (Acts 2.37).

ANOINTING

Anointing was characteristic of Christian baptism, and showed it was more than a purification ritual. The very fact that followers of Jesus came to be called 'Christians', anointed ones, shows its importance. In the mid fourth century, Cyril of Jerusalem said of the newly baptized: 'You have been made Christs, by receiving the anti-type of the Holy Spirit' (*Catecheses* 21.1), and the Apostolic Constitutions in the Syrian Church were similar: 'Christians, or anointed, from

---

[29] The leading Jewish teacher in the time of the second war against Rome, 135 CE.

[30] The three Noachide laws used to represent all seven, see P. Schaefer, *The Hidden and Manifest God*, New York: State University of NY Press, 1992, p. 119.

Christ the Anointed ...' (3.15).[31] In the Gospel of Philip we find: 'the chrism is superior to baptism, for it is from the word chrism that we have been called Christians. And it is because of the chrism that the Christ has his name' (CG II.3.74). If baptism was initiation into the royal priesthood, this would explain why there was anointing as well as washing. The true anointing oil had been 'hidden away' at the end of the first temple period: 'At the time when the Holy Ark was hidden away, there was also hidden the anointing oil, the jar of manna, and Aaron's rod with its blossoms' (Babylonian Talmud Horayoth 21a), and so anointing would have been a clear sign of restoring the ancient royal priesthood. The Apostolic Constitutions at this point also associated anointing with the mysterious 'new name' that Isaiah promised to the restored Jerusalem and to the true servants of the LORD (Isa. 62.2; 65.15). If this was a memory in context, and not just the insertion of a suitable text, then Christian anointing was linked directly to the restoration of Jerusalem: the city rebuilt in sixth century BCE had been rejected as impure by many who looked for the restoration of another priesthood (Isa. 61.5–9).

The significance of anointing derives from the original meaning of the oil: it had been the symbol of *theosis*, of becoming divine. The anointed called God their Father (Ps. 89.20–26), and Eusebius, explaining Psalm 45.6–7, said the original Christ had been the Second God: 'The Anointer, being the supreme God, is far above the Anointed, he being God in a different sense ... Therefore in these words you have it stated clearly that God was anointed and became the Christ.' The high priest was 'the figure and symbol on earth' of the Second God, the heavenly High Priest (*Proof* IV.15). The high priest was anointed with special oil, *šemen hamišhah*, Greek *elaion* (Exod. 29.7), prepared to a formula that could not be used outside the temple (Exod. 30.25, 33). Its predominant perfume was myrrh, but it was always called simply *šemen*, oil. There was no special name for the anointing oil, other than holy oil or anointing oil. Oil was the sacrament of Wisdom, as can be seen from the different ways that Josiah's purge of the temple was described: the oil had been hidden, and Wisdom had been rejected, which meant the priests lost their spiritual vision (1 Enoch 93.8). The oil gave vision. After she had been rejected, Wisdom called to her rebellious children and warned

---

[31] Although the writer is careful to add: 'not because those who are now baptised are ordained priests ... but are a royal priesthood and a holy nation, the Church of God.'

what would follow if they did not return. Wisdom — her name has a plural form here, a sign of divinity — promised to pour out her Spirit[32] on her people (Prov. 1.20–23). The restoration of anointing meant the return of Wisdom and her children.[33]

How Wisdom related to the Holy Spirit is not clear. The Jews in Egypt thought Wisdom was the Holy Spirit: 'Who has learned thy counsel unless thou hast given them Wisdom, and sent thy Holy Spirit from on high?' (Wisdom of Solomon 9.17). Wisdom and the Spirit were both names for the mother of the anointed one who was the high priest and the Logos. Philo used complex imagery, but when he wrote of God as the Father and Wisdom as the Mother of the Logos High Priest, we assume that the underlying images were familiar to his readers. The high priest was anointed with oil, and thus his mind was 'illuminated with a brilliant light' (*On Flight*, 109–110). The Gospel of the Hebrews, used by Jerome and so still available early in the fifth century, said it was the Holy Spirit who spoke to Jesus in the Jordan and acknowledged him as her son, and that Jesus referred to the Holy Spirit as his Mother.[34] Jerome quoted this when expounding Isaiah 11.1–9, which describes the manifold nature of the Spirit of the LORD that would rest on the Davidic king: 'The spirit of wisdom and understanding, the spirit of counsel and might, the spirit of knowledge and the fear of the LORD.' These were spiritual gifts that altered one's way of knowing, and so the effect of anointing was Wisdom. Isaiah's text continues: 'His *perfume* shall be the fear of the LORD' (Isa. 11.3 translating literally). The anointed one gave forth the fragrance of the oil, because Wisdom 'was' in the oil. Ben Sira, writing in Jerusalem at the beginning of the second century BCE, described her as serving in the holy tabernacle — she was a high priest — and 'giving forth the aroma of spices' — cassia, camel's thorn and myrrh (ben Sira 24. 10.15). Paul wrote of the fragrance of the knowledge of Christ, spread by his followers (2 Cor. 2.14–16).

Wisdom was represented by the tree of life, and she gave resurrection. A poem in Proverbs shows that she gave her disciples true riches, long life and honour, and that her ways were pleasantness and peace. '[Wisdom] is a tree of life to those who lay hold of her ...' (Prov. 3.18). The human pair had chosen the forbidden tree

---

[32] The Hebrew is 'spirit' despite some English versions.
[33] See below p. 215.
[34] Quoted in M. R. James, *The Apocryphal New Testament*, Oxford: Clarendon Press, (1924) 1980, p. 5.

and so had rejected the tree of life and the Wisdom it represented. Rejecting the tree and losing Eden were yet other ways of describing the changes in the time of Josiah. The Enoch tradition remembered that the perfumed tree had been taken to the south, and stood by the throne of God. After the judgement, it would be taken north and planted again by the temple, to be food for the chosen ones (1 Enoch 25.3–5). All of these images and hopes were part of early Christianity: the risen LORD restored access to the tree of life, and the faithful could eat from it (Rev. 2.7); and John saw the new high priests standing before the throne and the tree of life which had returned to the temple (Rev. 22.1–5). Baptism was a return to Eden. Tertullian wrote: 'In this way is man being restored to God, to the likeness of him who had aforetime been in God's image' (*On Baptism* 5).

The anointing oil was extracted from the perfumed wood of the tree of life, and the temple oil was compounded to imitate its perfume. In the *Clementine Recognitions* 'Peter' explained: 'The Son of God, the beginning of all things, became Man. Him first God anointed with oil which was taken from the wood of the tree of life ... In the present life, Aaron the first high priest was anointed with a composition of chrism which was made after the pattern of the spiritual ointment ... If then this temporal grace, compounded by men, had such efficacy, consider how potent was that ointment extracted by God from a branch of the tree of life' (*Clem. Rec.* 1.45–6). Origen reported a claim of the Ophite Gnostics: 'I have been anointed with the white chrism which flows from the tree of life' (*Celsus* 6.27). The Adam legends told how Seth tried to beg some of the precious oil for his dying father Adam, but Michael said that the oil would not be restored until the last days, when all flesh would be raised up and healed.[35] The oil that had formerly raised up, that is, resurrected, the ancient kings and high priests, would be available for all. The oil as the means of resurrection appears also in the Gospel of Philip: 'The tree of life is in the midst of Paradise, and from the olive tree[36] comes chrism, and from chrism comes resurrection.' 'People who say they will die first and then arise are mistaken. If they do not first receive resurrection while they are alive, once they have died they will receive nothing.

---

[35] There are versions of this story in The Life of Adam and Eve, 36–42, and The Apocalypse of Moses 9–13.

[36] This implies that the tree of life was an olive — but the tree of life had many forms.

Just so it is said of baptism: Great is baptism. For if one receives it, one will live' (CG II.3.73).

There were several different ways of anointing: before baptism and/or after baptism, anointing the head only, anointing the whole body, marking with the seal. East and West differed not only in practice but also in the meaning they gave to the anointing. This was because the emphasis in baptism shifted from identifying with Jesus' baptism and what it represented to identifying with his death and resurrection. It would have been natural for Christian baptism to re-enact Jesus' own baptism, and so earliest surviving evidence from third century Syria probably does reflect the original practice: sealing, becoming sons of light, and reliving the Jordan. The bishop was the one 'through whom the LORD in baptism, by the imposition of the hand of the bishop, bore witness to each one and uttered in his holy voice saying "You are my Son. I have this day begotten you."'[37] The oldest sources of both Syriac and Armenian origin use the terms 'oil', 'oil of anointing' and 'holy oil',[38] which correspond to temple usage.[39] Further, this anointing was called the 'sign/mark' *rušma*, exactly as Ezekiel described the angel marking the chosen.[40] Sometimes there were two pre-baptism anointings: the head and the whole body,[41] but this too corresponds to memories of temple practice and the double anointing of the high priest: the whole head and then signing with the X. 'How were the kings anointed? In the shape of a wreath. And the priests? In the shape of a X.' One [rabbi] reported that the oil was poured on his head first and afterwards between his eyelids. Another reported that the oil was first applied between his eyelids and then was poured on his head. (Babylonian Talmud Horayoth 12a).

In the East, the original practice had been to anoint before baptism, whereas Jesus had been anointed with the Spirit when he came up out of the water. Investigation of the original practice and meaning of anointing, however, has been hampered in some recent scholarship by determination to find evidence in early sources for the Anglican custom of confirmation, in the practice of post-baptismal anointing. Ratcliff, for example, originally disregarded the evidence

[37] R. H. Connolly, *Didascalia Apostolorum*, Oxford: Clarendon Press, 1929, ii. 32, p. 93.

[38] Rather than *myron*.

[39] See G. Winkler, 'The Original Meaning of the Pre-baptismal Anointing and its Implications' *Worship* 52.1 (1978), pp. 24–45.

[40] Ezek. 9.4 Peshitta has *rušma*, for the Hebrew tau, the letter shaped like a cross.

[41] S. Brock, 'The Syrian Baptismal Rites', *Concilium* 122 (1979), pp. 98–104, p. 98.

of pre-baptismal anointing in the 'remote and isolated church of eastern Syria', but later recognized that the old Eastern custom with regard to baptismal anointing 'differed markedly' from that of the West, [42] even though, as now seems likely, the east Syrians had kept the original rite and its meaning. This is the problem: there was a great variety of customs, but the common themes indicate their roots. *Both East and West compared anointing with the Old Testament anointing of the kings and of the high priests.* The Didascalia, in early third century Syria, prescribed: 'As of old the priests and kings were anointed in Israel, you must in like manner, with the imposition of the hand, anoint the head of those who receive baptism' (Didascalia XVI). Tertullian, writing in North Africa a generation earlier, said the new Christian was anointed, just as Moses had anointed Aaron: 'That is why the high priest is called a Christ' (*On Baptism* 7). Cyril of Jerusalem knew the same tradition: Moses made Aaron high priest, anointing him after he had bathed (Lev. 8.6–10); Solomon was anointed after he had bathed in the Gihon (1 Kgs 1.39) (*Catecheses* 21.6). At an early stage in the West pre-baptismal anointing was exorcism, perhaps reflecting Jesus' conquest of the dragon in the waters, but this was not used in parts of the East until the fourth century, when it became a purification to prepare the catechumen for baptism.

The clearest descriptions of pre-baptismal anointing are in the Acts of Thomas, an early third-century text describing the missionary work of Thomas in India. The five accounts of anointing at baptism suggest, from their emphasis, that this was the more important part of the rite. King Gundaphorus was anointed and chrismed as he stood in the water, and the voice of the LORD was heard. Thomas prayed: 'Come, holy name of the Messiah that is above every name, Come power of the Most High, Come, gift of the Most High, Come, compassionate mother ... Come, Holy Spirit and cleanse their reins and their hearts ...' Then a mysterious figure appeared holding a lighted torch, and at dawn, they celebrated the Eucharist (A.T. 27). On another occasion, after exorcizing a woman, Thomas went to a river where he sealed her in the name of the Father, the Son and the Holy Spirit. A table was then prepared for a Eucharist, and Thomas prayed over the bread as he had prayed over the oil: '... Come, O perfect compassion ... Come, she that knoweth the mysteries of him that is chosen ... Come, the hidden Mother ...' (A.T. 49). The woman Mygdonia

[42] E. R. Ratcliff, *Liturgical Studies*, pp. 125 and 135, reprinting articles written in 1946 and 1965 respectively.

was anointed ('sealed'), baptized and clothed, and then received the Eucharist as bread and water. Later her sisters were received in the same way, although the cup was described as 'the blood' and so perhaps was wine rather than water (A.T. 121, 157–8). The family of Siphor were anointed, baptized and clothed, and then received bread as the Eucharist (A.T. 132–3).[43]

There are many problems with the Acts of Thomas: different readings in the Greek and Syriac texts, for example, and the possibility that inconsistencies reflect practice at different periods, but the overall picture is clear. Thomas's Christians were anointed before baptism, and the power of the Most High invoked with the oil was not simply 'the Holy Spirit'. She was 'the compassionate mother, the revealer of the hidden mysteries' (A.T. 27); 'she that knows the mysteries of the chosen one' (A.T. 50); 'the revealer of hidden treasures' (A.T. 121). This sequence — oil, water, bread (and wine) — corresponds to the consecration of the high priest in the Testament of Levi 8.4–10, a text that promises that the consecrated one will tell forth the mysteries of God (T. Levi 2.10). This must be the context of John's words: 'You have been anointed by the Holy One and you know all things ... The anointing which you received from him abides in you and you have no need that any one should teach you' (1 John 2.20,27). If John was writing about baptismal anointing — and what else could it have been? — the oil conferring Wisdom must have been part of the earliest belief, and so Jerome's linking Isaiah 11.1–9 and the baptism of Jesus was not an innovation. The manifold gifts of wisdom were given to the ancient kings and priests, and to Jesus in the Jordan. This was remembered by 'Clement': '[Jesus] instituted baptism by water among them in which they might be absolved from all their sins on the invocation of his name ... being purified not by the blood of beasts but by the Wisdom of God' (*Clementine Recognitions* 1.39).[44]

There is little early evidence for anointing and its meaning in the West. Justin did not mention oil, but said that the new Christian was

---

[43] Other examples of pre-baptism anointing with similar patterns can be found in R. H. Connolly, *The Liturgical Homilies of Narsai*, Cambridge: Cambridge University Press, 1909, pp. xlii–xlix.

[44] Jacob of Serugh, who died in 521 CE, said little about pre-baptismal anointing. It corresponded to the circumcision of the old covenant, he said, the mark of ownership. Baptism, too, was a sign of ownership: it protected the Christian and made him a brother of Jesus, so he could say the 'Our Father'. See S. Brock, 'Baptismal Themes in the Writings of Jacob of Serugh' in *Symposium Syriacum* 1976, Orientalia Christiana Analecta 205 (1978), p. 338.

enlightened and reborn with baptism (*Apology* 1.61, 65). Both illumination and rebirth could imply anointing, although emerging from
the waters could also imply being a new creation. The other evidence
is in Hippolytus, who described three anointings; one before baptism,
which sealed the catechumen after s/he had renounced the works of
Satan; the second after baptism, with the oil of thanksgiving, when
the elder said: 'I anoint you with holy oil in the name of Jesus Christ',
and the third when the bishop anointed each new Christian on the
head and sealed her/him on the forehead (*Apostolic Tradition* 21).
A derivation from this text, used in Egypt, mentions only one post-
baptismal anointing, when the elder put oil on the forehead, mouth
and breast, the whole body, head and face, in the name of the Father,
the Son and the Holy Spirit (*Canons of Hippolytus* 19).

Bishop Serapion, in mid fourth century Egypt, prayed over the
oil of exorcism: 'That it may heal away from their soul, body, spirit,
every mark of sin and lawlessness or satanic fault ... that being
recreated through this anointing, and being cleansed through the
washing and being renewed in the spirit, they shall ... have victory
over all the opposing energies and deceits of this world ... bound
up and united with the flock of our LORD and Saviour.' With the
post-baptismal anointing there was the prayer for the Holy Spirit,
and then the seal to keep the new Christian secure. Tertullian, about
200 CE, is the only other source of information from North Africa,
and he knew only post-baptismal anointing. The water made one
clean to receive the Spirit (*On Baptism* 6), because the presence of
Jesus in the Jordan had consecrated all baptismal waters: 'The nature
of waters, having received holiness from the holy, itself conceived
power to make holy' (*On Baptism* 4). This had been known a century
earlier by Ignatius of Antioch: 'He submitted to baptism so that by
his Passion he might sanctify water' (Ephesians 18), and was known
to Cyril in Jerusalem: 'Christ washed in the River Jordan, and having
imparted the fragrance of his godhead to the waters, came up from
them ...' (*Catecheses* 21). The new Christian was then anointed, said
Tertullian, just as Moses had anointed Aaron: 'That is why the high
priest is called a Christ' (*On Baptism* 7). Wisdom motifs are linked to
baptism, 'that water of ours in which the sins of our original blindness
are washed away, and we are set at liberty to life eternal' (*On Baptism*
1). Restoring 'sight' was the gift of Wisdom: the oldest texts[45] say that
Jesus *anointed* the eyes of the blind man before he washed in Siloam

---

[45] P 66, Bezae, Sinaiticus.

and could see (John 9.6), and the risen LORD promised the gifts of Wisdom to the church at Laodicea — true riches, the white garment of eternal life and 'salve to anoint your eyes that you may see' (Rev. 3.18).

At the end of the fourth century, there was a change of emphasis, and the pattern of baptism became the dying and rising with Christ that Paul set out in Romans 6.4 and which was enacted dramatically by Easter baptism, especially in Jerusalem. This interpretation of baptism had been disputed for some time, as can be seen in the Gospel of Philip. 'By perfecting the water of baptism, Jesus emptied it of death. Thus we do go down into the water, but we do not go down into death' (CG II.3 77). This 'dying with Christ' interpretation, linked to the Exodus imagery that was natural for the Passover season and to Paul's imagery of the Red Sea as baptism (1 Cor. 10.1–2; Cyril of Jerusalem, *Catecheses* 19),[46] eventually superseded the older one, and the royal priesthood of all believers became less important. The Wisdom motifs remained. 'Beware of supposing that this ointment is mere ointment. Just as after the invocation of the Holy Spirit, the Eucharistic bread is no longer ordinary bread but the Body of Christ, so this holy oil, in conjunction with the invocation, is no longer simple or common oil, but becomes the gracious gift of Christ and the Holy Spirit, producing the advent of his deity. With this ointment, your forehead and sense organs are sacramentally anointed, in such wise that while your body is quickened with the visible oil, your soul is satisfied by the holy quickening Spirit' (Cyril of Jerusalem *Catecheses* 21.3). The mystery of the oil was given its fullest exposition by Dionysius: 'The ray of the most holy sacred things enlightens the men of God, purely and directly; it spreads its sweet fragrance into their mental reception'; 'In being initiated in that sacred sacrament of the divine birth, the perfecting anointing of the ointment gives us a visitation of the divine Spirit' (*Ecclesiastical Hierarchy* 484B, 476B).

The New Testament shows just how many of these aspects of baptism were present from the beginning: the forgiveness of sins and the gift of the Spirit (Acts 2.38), the spiritual birth giving access to the Kingdom of God (John 3.5), the washing of regeneration and renewal (Titus 3.5), enlightenment (Heb. 6.5; 10.32), sharing the

---

[46] Before they were baptized, the catechumens faced west to renounce Satan, before turning to the east to receive the light. A similar distinction between east and west is found in Sufism, where the west represents the world, fragmentation and dispersion, and the east, the light of God and unity.

death and resurrection of Christ (Rom. 6.4–5; Col. 3.1), putting on a new nature (Col. 3.10), and becoming a son of God (Rom. 8.14). The Christian passed from darkness to the Kingdom of the beloved Son (Col. 1.13), was called from darkness to light as the royal priesthood (1 Pet. 2.9), and was renewed in his mind (Eph. 4.23). These were not drawn from the conversion rites of contemporary Jews, but from the ancient ceremonies of priest making.

Chapter 6

TRANSFORMATION AND TRANSFIGURATION

They shall see his face.

Revelation 22.4

When the Servants of the LORD stand before the throne of God-and-the-Lamb, they worship him and they see his face. This is the climax of John's vision. 'Seeing the face of the LORD' must have been the most important part of Christian worship, but what did it mean? Since they proclaimed Jesus as the LORD, seeing the face of the LORD must have been associated in some way with the incarnation: 'The Word became flesh and dwelt among us ... we have beheld his glory' (John 1.14). John equated this with what Isaiah saw in his temple vision: 'He saw his glory and spoke of him' (Isa. 6.1–3; John 12.41). The setting of the Book of Revelation in the original temple, with its furnished holy of holies, suggests that 'seeing the face of the LORD' had been central to worship in the first temple. There is, as always, insufficient evidence for certainty, but many Old Testament texts do describe the LORD appearing, the glory of the LORD shining forth from the temple, the LORD dwelling in the temple. The changes as the texts were transmitted show that they were controversial, and so 'seeing the face of the LORD' may have been one of the differences between the first and second temples, one of the elements of the older cult that were restored in Christianity.

One strand in the Old Testament — and the strand that has had a disproportionate influence on reconstructions of Old Testament theology — was that of the Deuteronomists, so called because their ideals were drawn from, and expressed in, Deuteronomy. They were emphatic that the LORD could not be seen: for them, the meeting with the LORD at Sinai had been just a voice. 'The LORD spoke to you out of the midst of the fire; you heard the sound of words, but saw no form, *t*᷍*munah*; there was only a voice' (Deut. 4.12). The people saw only the Glory of God and they saw God speaking with a human being (Deut. 5.24). This is why any form, *ťmunah,* was forbidden (Deut. 4.15), along with graven images (Exod. 20.4; Deut 5.8, where AV and RSV translate the word as 'likeness'). On the other hand, Moses was distinguished from other leaders in Israel because he did see the form, *ťmunah,* of the LORD: 'With [Moses] I speak mouth to mouth, clearly, and not in dark speech; and he beholds *the form* of the LORD (Num. 12.8). The Psalmist gave thanks that he saw in a vision the face of the LORD, and was satisfied with his form (Ps. 17.15). The other (older, priestly?) account of the meeting at Sinai says that Moses, Aaron and his family, and the elders, 'saw the God of Israel; and there was under his feet as it were a pavement of sapphire stone, like the very heaven for clearness' (Exod. 24.10). God had feet, so at Sinai they saw a human form. Ezekiel saw a human figure: the likeness, *ďmut,* as the appearance, *mar'eh,* of a human (Ezek. 1.26). Moses asked to see the Glory of the LORD, and was told that he could see his goodness and know his Name, but he could not see the face/presence[1] of the LORD, 'for man shall not see me and live' (Exod. 33.20). The tradition is ambiguous here: the LORD used to speak to Moses face to face, as a man speaks to his friend (Exod. 33.11) and he spoke to him from between the two cherubim over the 'mercy seat', *kapporet* (Exod. 25.22); neither of these instances says that the LORD was actually seen. They could have been understood in the Deuteronomists' sense of recognizing the presence and hearing the voice. But Aaron was told that when he entered the holy of holies, the LORD would appear in the cloud over the *kapporet* (Lev. 16.2), so perhaps Moses did see the LORD when he stood in the same place.

In the Old Testament the issue is confused. There are two positions: the LORD could be seen — the temple tradition — or could not be seen, the later Deuteronomists' position. The New Testament is emphatic that the LORD was seen. An Aramaic prayer that has survived from the earliest worship is *Maranatha,* 'Come LORD'. They were praying for the LORD to appear, perhaps at the second coming (Rev. 22.20), perhaps in their place of worship. How else are we to understand: 'Where two or three are gathered together in my name, there am I in the midst of them' (Matt.18. 20). John opens his Gospel with the words: 'We have beheld his glory, glory as of the only Son from the Father' (John 1.14), thus rooting Christian tradition firmly in one particular strand of the Old Testament. 'Man shall not see me

---

[1] Face and presence are the same word in Hebrew, a plural form: *panim.*

and live' (Exod. 33.20) is exactly opposite to John's teaching that seeing the LORD brings eternal life: 'the life was made manifest, and we saw it and testify to it, and proclaim to you the eternal life which was with the Father and was made manifest to us' (1 John 1.2). How is this to be explained? In the Church, the LORD continued to appear to his people: Paul experienced a theophany on the road to Damascus (Acts 9.3–9); John saw the heavenly LORD and received letters from him, and then was given the little scroll (Rev. 2–3; Rev. 10.1–11[2]); and a mysterious young man with a lighted torch appeared when Thomas was baptizing Gundaphoros (Acts of Thomas 27).

There were two phases in the development of Israel's religion, and each created part of the text of the Old Testament. One of the changes concerned the vision of God: the older faith had spoken of seeing God, whereas some later writers denied that such a vision was possible. The two accounts of Sinai — one where the God of Israel was seen, and one where there was only a voice — are texts from different periods, from different 'schools'. The developments were not uniform, and so texts from the same period may exhibit two different views, or differing views may be apparent in the choice of words used for translations. When Moses was told to build the tabernacle, the LORD said to him: 'Let them make me a sanctuary, that I may *dwell* in their midst' (Exod. 25.8), but in Greek, this became: 'And you shall make for me a holy place, and I shall *be seen* among you' (Lxx Exod. 25.7). Why the difference? The Greek was later than the Hebrew, but when the Law of Moses was translated into Greek in Alexandria in the mid third century BCE,[3] the people there accepted that 'seen' was the meaning of 'dwell'. How could a Jew in Egypt at that time think that the LORD dwelling in the sanctuary meant that he was *seen* there?

THE LORD IN ZION

The Psalms were the hymn book of the temple, and in them we glimpse something of the ancient liturgy. In no way do they give a complete picture. Think in terms of reconstructing Christianity from the hymns of a modern hymn book that does not give the dates and

---

[2] See my book, *The Revelation of Jesus Christ*, Edinburgh: T&T Clark, 2000, pp. 180–199.

[3] During the reign of Ptolemy II (285–247 BCE), according to the story in The Letter of Aristeas, 172–181, 301–311.

authors of the hymns. There are compositions from various periods
and for various seasons of the Church's year. Some hymn books
group according to season or subject matter; others arrange the
hymns alphabetically. The Psalter presents similar problems, and we
do not know its system. There are texts from many periods, some
apparently associated with the great royal festivals, some commemorating the nation's history, and so on. There is, however, a recurring
pattern of imagery: the LORD was seen, his glory shone forth from
the temple. How the LORD was seen or how the glory shone forth we
do not know. The king or high priest in golden vestments perhaps?
What was literal? What was poetic? How did they organize and
choreograph temple ceremonial? What heavenly reality were they
expressing in their liturgy? Or what images of heaven were projections of the temple liturgy? Were the four living creatures around the
throne — the lion, the ox, the eagle and the man — in fact masked
priests, like those of Egypt and Assyria? We can only read what is there
or, given the sensitive nature of this subject, try to recover what was
once there.

The Psalms envisaged the LORD in Zion: the LORD dwelt, *yašab*,
there (Ps. 9.11). His dwellings, *miškanot*, were on his holy hill (Ps.
43.3); 'How lovely is thy dwelling place, O LORD of Hosts' (Ps. 84.1);
and 'The God of gods will be seen in Zion' (Ps. 84.7). This was the
place of his Glory: 'I love the habitation of thy house, and the place
where thy glory dwells' (Ps. 26.8). The LORD was enthroned in the
holy of holies that represented heaven: 'The LORD is in his holy
temple, the LORD's throne is in heaven' (Ps. 11.4). He was enthroned
on the cherubim in the holy of holies (Pss. 80.1; 99.1). Isaiah says that
in the year King Uzziah died he saw[4] the King, the LORD of Hosts in
the midst of the seraphim, 'sitting upon a throne, high and lifted up;
and his train filled the temple' (Isa. 6.1); 'Shout and sing for joy, O
inhabitant of Zion, for great in your midst is the Holy One of Israel'
(Isa. 12.6).

When Isaiah saw the LORD enthroned, he saw that his train filled
the temple (Isa. 6.1). The Greek text here says that his Glory filled
the temple. Isaiah heard the seraphim singing of his Glory filling the
whole earth (Isa. 6.3). Since the great hall of the temple represented
the creation, the Glory filling the earth and the Glory filling the

---

[4] He saw *ra'ah*, not *ḥazah*, which implies a visionary experience since related nouns
mean 'seer' and 'vision'. It must have been customary to use the word *ra'ah* for a
vision of the LORD.

temple was a distinction without a difference. How the LORD dwelt in the temple, how the Glory was envisaged, we do not know. Radiance caused by the reflected rays of the sun as it shone through the open door into the holy of holies is but one of several suggestions. The Targum, which is like the Greek text here, shows how later generations understood Isaiah's vision: 'the brilliance of his Glory' filled the temple, and Isaiah exclaimed that he had seen 'the Glory of the Shekinah of the Eternal King'[5] — the Glory of the Presence — but gave no detail of how this was made known. The Psalmist sang: 'Thou who art enthroned upon the cherubim, *shine forth*' (Ps. 80.1).[6] 'O LORD ... *shine forth*! Rise up, O judge of the earth ...' (Ps. 94.1–2). God *shines forth* from Zion (Ps. 50.2). The same verb *yapa'* appears also in the blessing of Moses: when the LORD came from Sinai and dawned from Seir, 'he shone forth' from Paran with his host of angels (Deut. 33.2). The Greek here uses the word for epiphany: 'The LORD *epephanen* from Seir ...' (Lxx Deut. 33.2). There is a clue in this ancient poem to the context of this 'shining forth': it happened when the LORD became King (Deut. 33.5). Shining was the sign that the LORD was in the temple, and his presence protected the city: 'Is not the LORD in Zion? Is her King not in her?' (Jer. 8.19). This 'shining forth' must be the context for John's triumphant assertion: 'We have beheld his glory' (John 1.14).

Seeing the LORD was described as seeing the face/presence of the LORD: 'I shall behold thy face', sang the Psalmist (Ps. 17.15), where the verb 'behold' is *ḥazah*, meaning 'see' in the visionary sense. He had prayed to the LORD in his distress, and knew that the LORD could visit him by night (Ps. 17.3): 'I shall be satisfied with your form, *t'munah*, on my waking' (Ps. 17.15, my translation).[7] He expected to see *the form* of the LORD. There are several examples of these 'night visions': the young Samuel at Shiloh saw and heard the LORD during the night, even though the word of the LORD was rare at the time, and there was no vision 'breaking through', *nipraṣ* (1 Sam. 3.1, 21, translating literally). Solomon went to the ancient holy place at Gibeon and saw the LORD in a dream by night (1 Kgs 3.5–15). He saw the LORD again, after he had built the temple, but we are not told where

---

[5] This phrase is used also in Tg. Isa. 33.17.

[6] The Targum here shows that losing sight of the face was being in exile. 'You whose Shekinah dwells among the cherubim ... restore us from our exile and make the brightness of your countenance shine upon us.'

[7] The Greek has 'I shall be satisfied by seeing your Glory'.

this vision occurred (1 Kgs 9.1). Daniel was granted a vision by night of 'one like a man' (Dan. 7.2, 13), and Zechariah in the temple saw in the night a man on a red horse (Zech. 1.8).

The verb *ḥazah*, to see as a visionary, is important evidence for the nature of temple 'seeing'. When Isaiah saw the LORD in the midst of the seraphim, the burning ones (Isa.6. 1–3), he must have seen through the temple veil to the Glory beyond. In other words, the LORD was shining forth for him: the veil between heaven and earth had been taken away. In the time of Samuel, vision rarely 'broke through'. Seeing beyond the veil, as at the transfiguration, and passing beyond the veil, were important themes for the early Christians too. They had confidence to enter the holy of holies, because Jesus had opened for them a way through the veil (Heb. 10.19–20). In the Liturgy of James, the earliest known liturgy, they prayed:

> We thank thee, O LORD our God, that Thou hast given us boldness for the entrance of thy holy place, which Thou hast renewed to us as a new and living way through the veil of the flesh of Thy Christ. We therefore, being counted worthy to enter into the place of the tabernacle of Thy Glory, and to be within the veil, and to behold the Holy of Holies, cast ourselves down before thy goodness.

Isaiah promised the upright that they too would see 'the King in his beauty', whilst sinners would fear the devouring fires of eternity (Isa. 33.14, 17) — the fires of the holy place. The Psalmist longed to see, *ḥazah*, the beauty, *no'am*, of the LORD and to contemplate his temple (Ps. 27.4). The *beauties* of the LORD are linked to the fullness of joy in his presence, and learning the path of life (Ps. 16.11). The Psalmist prays: 'Let your work be made clear to your servants, and your Glory to their children, and may the beauty, *no'am*, of the LORD God be upon us' (Ps. 90.17, my translation). The Greek text understood this beauty as brilliant splendour, *lamprotes*. This was the King shining forth — epiphany.

There are no details in these texts of who was seen — what the 'form' was like. The face/presence is described as beauty and Glory, but most frequently it is light that brings prosperity and deliverance, and seeing the face of the LORD is the response to prayer: 'Lift up the light of thy face upon us, O LORD' (Ps. 4.6, my translation); 'Let thy face shine on thy servant, save me in thy steadfast love!' (Ps. 31.16). When the LORD hid his face, there was disaster: 'Thou didst hide thy face, I was dismayed' (Ps. 30.7); 'Why dost thou hide thy face? Why dost thou forget our affliction and oppression?' (Ps. 44.24); 'Hide not thy face from thy servant; for I am in distress, make haste to answer me' (Ps. 69.17); 'Do not hide thy face from me in the day of my distress!' (Ps. 102.2). In despair, Israel felt that the LORD did not see: 'My way is hid from the LORD ' (Isa. 40.27). When the faithful worshipper saw the light of the LORD, he knew that he was secure: 'The LORD is my light and my salvation: whom shall I fear?'; ... 'Thou hast said, "Seek ye my face." My heart says to thee, "Thy face O LORD do I seek." Hide not thy face from me' (Ps. 27.1, 8–9); 'Blessed are the people ... O LORD, who walk in the light of your face/presence' (Ps. 89.15). This is the scene described in Revelation 21: 'The city has no need of sun or moon to shine upon it, for the Glory of God is its light and its lamp is the Lamb' (Rev. 21.23).

Several key texts are not easy to read. Sometimes this is due to the ambiguity of the Hebrew, where certain forms of two different verbs may be similar or even identical. The translator had to choose what seemed most reasonable to him, and would have made his choice according to what he already believed.

What, then, might the original of Psalm 68.35 have been? 'Terrible is God in his sanctuary, the God of Israel: he gives power and strength to his people.' The Hebrew has not 'in' but 'from' your sanctuaries, *mimmiqdašeyka,* but the Greek read the initial *m* as *b,* (easily done) thus giving 'in' or 'among', and then understood 'holy places' as 'holy ones,'[8] angels, a perfectly reasonable way to read the text. The Greek text therefore is: 'God is terrible among his angels.' Several versions[9] read 'sanctuary', singular, another complication that would exclude the Greek reading 'angels'. There are other possibilities: the Hebrew word 'terrible', *nr',* looks very similar to *n'r*— glorious, shining — and so the text could have been 'God shines from his sanctuary.'

There is a similar picture in Psalm 76.4, where God is 'shining' in Zion, more majestic than the 'mountains ***', the final Hebrew word being a problem. The Greek versions show the same confusion between *nr'* and *n'r*: The older Greek Lxx has 'you shine forth', *photizeis,* from *n'r*; the later Greek translation of Symmachus has 'shine forth', *epiphanes*; but the later Greek translation of Theodotion has 'fearful', *phoberos,* from *nr'.* The Targum has 'You are awesome O God, praised in the house of your sanctuary'. Psalm 76.4 could therefore be describing God as shining or fearful, 'more majestic than the *** mountains'. It is possible that *hrry,* 'mountains of' should be *hdry,* 'glories of', since 'd' and 'r' look similar in Hebrew

---

[8] Some Mss have *hagiois,* others *hosiois.* The meaning is the same.

[9] Thus Syriac, Targum and Jerome.

and were often confused. This happened in Psalm 110.3, a similar context, where the line could be 'upon the holy mountains' or 'in the glories of the holy place/the glories of holiness'. The second line of Psalm 76.4 is literally 'more excellent than the mountains of prey', which is how it appears in the AV. This makes little sense, and so the RSV used the Greek text and opted for 'more majestic than the everlasting mountains'. The problem is the last Hebrew word, *ṭareph*, which was represented above by ***. This word means 'prey', which makes no sense here, but a very similar one does: *śaraph*, a seraph. Psalm 76.4 could once have been: 'You shine forth, more majestic than the glories of the seraphim', which makes good sense.

These are two relatively simple examples to illustrate the problems facing any reconstruction of temple practice and belief. The problem in both Psalm 68.35 and Psalm 76.4 seems to be the shining of God among the angels in the holy of holies. The problem was epiphany — seeing the face or presence of the LORD.

When David brought the ark to Jerusalem, he appointed musicians, the Levites who were to serve before the ark of the LORD, to 'invoke, to thank and to praise the LORD the God of Israel' (1 Chron. 16.4). *Music invoked the presence.* The Holy One was 'enthroned on the praises of Israel' (Ps. 22.3), and the congregation praised and glorified the LORD and stood in awe of him (Ps. 22.23). Now 'hallelu-jah' is probably the most familiar word that has survived from temple worship, and is said to mean 'Praise the LORD.' Apart from Psalm 135.3, it always occurs at the beginning or end of the psalm, and is often kept in its original form even today. When hallelu-jah occurs at the beginning of a psalm, the old Greek simply transliterates: 'Allelouia' (Lxx Pss. 105, 106, 110, 111, 112, 134, 145, 146, 147, 148, 149, 150).[10] It must have been a significant temple term, whose meaning was known to those who needed the Scriptures in Greek. At the beginning of a psalm, hallelu-jah addresses the congregation: it is a plural form 'Praise the LORD'. The Hebrew root *hll*, however, means not only 'praise' but also 'shine'. Were the people commanded to make the LORD shine? Should we perhaps understand Psalm 22.23 as '*Make Him shine* ... make Him glorious ... stand in awe of Him.' rather than '*praise Him* ... glorify Him ... stand in awe of Him'? The hallelujah at the beginning of the Psalms would then be an instruction to the musicians to cause the LORD's face to shine, to invoke His presence:

---

[10] At the end of the psalms there is either translation, paraphrase or nothing: Lxx Pss. 104, 105, 112, 114, 115, 134, 145, 146, 147, 148.

'Make the LORD shine forth!' This was the first duty of the Levites: 'To invoke, to thank and to praise the LORD', and so they sang: 'Thou who art enthroned upon the cherubim, shine forth!' (Ps. 80.1). The Levites made music when the temple was consecrated, singing 'with one voice', and then the presence of the LORD came; the cloud of the Glory of the LORD filled the temple (2 Chron. 5.11–14). Once the LORD had been enthroned in his temple, the music invited the LORD to shine forth from the holy of holies, to show Himself as King: 'For dominion belongs to the LORD and he rules over the nations (Ps. 22.28).[11] He established his Kingdom.

A memory of this invocation, calling on the LORD to shine, has survived in an explanation of the liturgy written by Germanus, Patriarch of Constantinople 715–730 CE. He wrote: 'David exclaims allelouia, and says "Our God will come clearly/visibly, *emphanos*, and fire shall go before him."[12] For in Hebrew *al* means "he comes, he appears", *El* means "God" and *ouia* means "praise and sing hymns to the living God"' (*On the Divine Liturgy* 29). Of the three words, only *El* meaning God is correct, but Germanus must have known that allelouia was linked to the appearing of God, to theophany.

The radiant Glory of the Presence was later known as the Shekinah, 'the indwelling', and Kabbalah, which was the temple tradition as it survived and developed during the Christian era, used ritual and even magical practices to draw down the Shekinah which had again departed into heaven. A major study of the Kabbalah suggested, on the basis of the later texts and their temple imagery, that drawing the Shekinah down into the holy of holies had been at the heart of the original temple service. 'On the ground of these parallels, we can seriously consider the possibility that the Temple service was conceived as inducing the presence of the Shekinah in the Holy of Holies.'[13] In the original temple, *drawing down* would not have been necessary, since the presence of the LORD was there in the midst, but calling on the LORD to appear does seem to have been at the heart of the original temple cult. Perhaps this is why the first Christians called upon the LORD to appear: '*Maranatha*', Come LORD.

[11] This pattern appears at the climax of the Book of Revelation. The multitude in heaven sing 'Hallelujah' and then the LORD appears on earth, riding forth from heaven with his angels (Rev. 19.1, 3, 7, 11–16).

[12] The Greek version of Psalm 50.2b–3: 'God shines forth, our God comes ...'

[13] M. Idel, *Kabbalah. New Perspectives*. New Haven and London: Yale University Press, 1988, p. 168. See also below p. 168.

The writings of the Deuteronomists have a distinct hostility towards temple, monarchy and theophany, and many aspects of the temple were omitted or obscured in their writings. They denied that any form had been seen at Sinai (Deut. 4.12). In their history of the monarchy, Samuel warned that a king would be a disaster (1 Sam. 8.10–18), and most of the kings were shown to fall far short of the Deuteronomists' ideal. It is remarkable to have a national history presented as a catalogue of bad kings, and the destruction of the capital city blamed on their behaviour (2 Kgs 23.3–4). The Deuteronomists also disapproved of the temple. It was designed by foreigners, and Solomon had to impose forced labour on his own people to build it (1 Kgs 5.1–18); the cost was enormous, and Solomon had to sell part of his kingdom to the king of Tyre to pay the debts (1 Kgs 9.10–14). Given that these texts — 1 and 2 Samuel, 1 and 2 Kings — are the most frequently used source for reconstructing the history of the period, any attempt to describe the temple where the LORD appeared, and the royal high priest who probably represented the LORD, faces considerable difficulties.

Their description of the temple omitted certain details which are found elsewhere. These are not random details, but significant for any attempt to recover the older temple. It is as though the Deuteronomists wanted to rewrite the past and remove whatever theophany had implied. The Chronicler and the Deuteronomist both wrote accounts of Solomon's temple. The Chronicler said David had received a plan for the temple from the LORD, just as Moses had received detailed instructions on Sinai on how to build the tabernacle as the place where the LORD dwelt in the midst of his people (Exod. 25.8). Deuteronomy implies that Moses did not receive any plan for the tabernacle; on Sinai he received only the Ten Commandments: 'He added no more' (Deut. 5.22), and the Deuteronomists do not mention David receiving a temple plan from the hand of the LORD. The plan David received included the golden chariot throne (1 Chron. 28.18–19), but the Deuteronomist does not mention the throne. David had appointed temple musicians 'to invoke, to thank and to praise the LORD, the God of Israel' (1 Chron. 16.4), but the Deuteronomist does not mention them. Solomon set up a veil of blue, purple, crimson and white linen fabric to screen the cherubim of the holy of holies (2 Chron. 3.14), but the Deuteronomist does not mention this either. All of these — the throne, the veil and the music

— are important for understanding how the LORD appeared in the temple.

King Solomon's temple dedication prayer looks as though something was added that contradicted the original words of the prayer.[14] Solomon prayed: 'I have built thee an exalted house, a place for thee to dwell in for ever' (1 Kgs 8.13), but later in the prayer we find him saying: 'Will God indeed dwell on earth? Behold heaven and the highest heaven cannot contain thee; how much less this house that I have built!' (1 Kgs 8.27). Instead, the temple was to be the place of the Name: 'the place of which thou hast said, "My Name shall be there"' (1 Kgs 8.29). Nobody can be sure what this meant, but the same distinction is found in the Deuteronomist's account of Nathan's warning to King David. Here the contrast is first between a permanent temple and a tent: 'Would you build me a house to dwell in? I have not dwelt in a house since the day I brought up this people of Israel from Egypt to this very day, but have been moving about in a tent for my dwelling' (2 Sam. 7.6). Then there is the promise of a future house, but for the Name: '[Your son] shall build a house for my Name' (2 Sam. 7.13). We are invited to believe that the LORD was not 'in' the temple, and so the purpose of building the tabernacle (and the later temple) is immediately called into question.

Since the Deuteronomists and their successors were a major influence on the formation of the Old Testament — the collection and preservation of the texts that survived the destruction in 597 BCE, for example — there is a complex problem facing any attempt to reconstruct the original temple. There may be complete texts that never became canonical — 1 Enoch is a good example — and there may have been earlier versions of the Hebrew text underlying the present form, as the Qumran fragments suggest. The reason for the exclusion and alteration of those texts is very likely to be that they were evidence for the position the Deuteronomists sought to supersede. Any reconstruction that relies on their written evidence is therefore at a distinct disadvantage. Since conventional scholarship takes their canonical texts as the norm, a great deal has to be undone before any real progress can be made. Nevertheless, there are places in the Old Testament where the older temple theophanies can be detected. The texts that describe pilgrimages to the temple originally agreed with the Psalmist, that the pilgrim was hoping to see the face of the LORD, but in their present form, they are understood differently.

---

[14] This addition occurs also in the Chronicler's account, 2 Chron. 6.18.

Three times a year according to the ancient calendars — at the Feast of Unleavened Bread, at the Feast of Weeks and at the Feast of Booths — the men of Israel had to make a pilgrimage to the temple, 'to appear before the LORD' (Exod. 23.17; 34.23; Deut. 16.16). 'To appear before the LORD' is the usual translation, but the Hebrew actually says: three times a year shall all your men *see the face of the* LORD. Under the influence of the Deuteronomists and their spiritual heirs, it became the custom to read the letters differently, even though the Psalms show clearly what the original meaning must have been. None of these readings involves any change in the consonants of the text, just in the way they were understood and therefore pronounced:

- In Exodus 23.15 and 34.20, the text should be read 'none shall see my face with empty hands', or it could mean 'none shall see my face in an unworthy state'.[15]
- In Exodus 23.17 'each male *yr'h* to the face/presence of the LORD', the verb is read as a Niph'al, *yera'eh* and so the verse becomes 'each male shall appear before the face of the LORD'. The Samaritan text, however, has the accusative particle here instead of 'to' and so the letters *yr'h* must be read as the Qal form, *yir'eh*: 'each male shall see the face of the LORD'.
- In Exodus 34.23 the accusative particle occurs, and so there is no doubt that the verb *yr'h* is to be read as a Qal form: 'each male shall see the face of the LORD'.
- In Exodus 34.24 the infinitive construct form of the verb, *lr'wt* is Qal; the Niph'al would be *lhr'wt*. The text must mean: 'When you go up to see the face/presence of the LORD three times a year'.
- In Deuteronomy 16.16 the text is like Exodus 34.23, and so a Qal form is required: 'each male shall see the face of the LORD'.
- In Deuteronomy 31.11 there is the Qal infinitive construct and so it means: 'When all Israel comes to see the face of the LORD your God'.
- In 1 Samuel 1.22, Hannah planned to take her son 'to see the face of the LORD'.
- In Isaiah 1.12 there is the Qal infinitive construct and so it must mean 'When you come to see my face'.

---

[15] *reyqam* can mean either.

- In Psalm 42.2 the Psalmist longs to see God: 'My soul thirsts for God, for the living God. When shall I come and see the face of God?'

For each of these examples the Hebrew Lexicon says that the Qal form should be read. 'The verbs in all these passages were originally Qal, afterwards pointed Niph'al, *to avoid the expression 'see the face of Yahweh'.*[16]

Why should this have happened? The pilgrims with clean hands and a pure heart who are worthy to go to the holy place — 'Who shall ascend the hill of the LORD, and who shall stand in his holy place? (Ps. 24.3) — are described as *seeking the face* of the God of Jacob,[17] and promised blessing and vindication (Ps. 24.5–6). They prayed: 'May God be gracious to us and bless us, and make his face to shine upon us' (Ps. 67.1) — a sign of favour that would bring prosperity. The Greek here has 'May the LORD *epiphanai* his face upon us': (LXX Ps. 66.1): epiphany. The pilgrims prayed that the One enthroned on the cherubim would shine forth: 'Restore us O God; let thy face shine that we may be saved' (Ps. 80.1, 3, 7, 19). And the great high priestly blessing prayed that each person would see the face of the LORD: 'May the LORD bless you and keep you. May the LORD make his face/presence shine upon you and be gracious to you/give you life. May the LORD make his presence rise upon you and give you peace (Num. 6.24–6)[18]. The Greek translation here has the word for epiphany, and any interpetation of this verse was forbidden to Jews (Mishnah Megillah 4.10). Jesus said: 'Blessed are the pure in heart, for they shall see God' (Matt.5.8), and the climax of the Book of Revelation

---

[16] Brown, Driver, Briggs, *A Hebrew and English Lexicon of the Old Testament,* Oxford: Clarendon Press, 1962 edition, pp. 816, 908.

[17] The Hebrew is literally 'those who seek your face, Jacob'.

[18] The Syriac translator read *wyḥnk*, 'and be gracious to you', as *wyḥyk*, 'and give you life', but the Hebrew letters *y* and *n* are similar and so the confusion is understandable. The question is: which was the original? The covenant with the priests was a 'covenant of life and peace' (Mal. 2.5). One of Zechariah's symbolic staves was named 'beauty', *no'am*, and breaking that staff was the sign that the covenant had been broken (Zech. 11.7, 10). Perhaps Zechariah's sign of the broken staff related to losing the vision of the beauty of the LORD, or perhaps to losing the presence of the LORD in the temple. Both would have been consequences of the Deuteronomists' programme. Proverbs 29.18 warns that losing the vision results in social chaos. The text says, literally, that where there is no prophetic vision, the people unravel. The Apocalypse of Weeks, an enigmatic history incorporated into 1 Enoch, described the Deuteronomists' purge as the time when the people in the temple lost their sight and godlessly forsook Wisdom (1 En. 93.8).

shows the servants of God and the Lamb standing before the throne and seeing his face (Rev. 22.4)[19].

The Targums, which cannot be dated with certainty, but which preserve ancient tradition, treat the 'face' texts in two ways: either they adopt the Niph'al reading of the verb, and understand that the people appeared before the LORD rather than that the LORD appeared to the people, or they use other words to describe what was actually seen in the temple. All the Targums of Exodus and Deuteronomy reflect the Niph'al reading of the verb *yr'h*: that it was the people who appeared before the LORD, and not the LORD who appeared to the people. In the Targum of the Psalms, however, the LORD *does* appear, but the manner of the appearing is modified. The 'face' of the LORD is replaced by the Shekinah, the presence, for example Tg. Pss. 22.24; 27.8; 30.7; 42.2; 44.24 (which has 'the Shekinah of your Glory'); 69.17; 88.14; 102.2; 143.7; or it can be 'the brightness'[20] of the face, for example Tg.Pss. 4.6; 11.7; 24.6; 31.16; or by 'the splendour' of the face, as in Tg. Pss. 13.1; 67.1; 119.135; or by 'the Glory' of the face, as in Tg. Ps.17.15. Hiding the face becomes 'removing the Shekinah' as in Tg. Ps.22.24.[21] A key verse such as Psalm 17.15: 'I shall behold thy face in righteousness; when I awake I shall be satisfied with beholding thy form' becomes: 'In truth I shall see the brightness of your countenance; at the time when I awake, I shall be satisfied with the Glory of your face.' Psalm 42.2b, where the current Hebrew pointing gives, literally: 'When shall I come and be seen before God?' becomes: 'When shall I come and see the splendour of the Shekinah of the LORD?' *The pilgrim seeing the* LORD *in the temple must have been a part of*

---

[19] There is a curious episode in the Infancy Gospel of James, which may show one way in which the LORD revealed his face. Joachim and Anna, who were to become the parents of Mary, were childless, and Joachim was told that he could not offer gifts in the temple because he had not raised a child. As the great day of the LORD (the feast of Tabernacles?) drew near, Joachim learned that Anna was, at last, pregnant. He took his gifts to the temple, and said to himself, 'If the LORD has forgiven me, the plate that is upon the high priest's forehead will make this clear to me.' Joachim presented his offering and watched as the high priest went to the altar, 'and he saw no sin in himself'. 'Now I know that the LORD has become propitious unto me and hath forgiven all my sins.' What had Joachim seen? Did he perhaps see the golden plate shining? Since the golden plate was engraved with the Name, did it function as an oracle, and when it shone, did the worshipper know that the LORD had made his face/presence shine on him? (Infancy Gospel of James 4.5–5.1).

[20] *sbr*, which usually means 'hope'.

[21] See D. M. Stec, *The Targum of Psalms*, London and New York: T&T Clark/Continuum, 2004.

the older tradition. By reading crucial texts in another way, the ancient belief has been hidden.

THE WORD OF THE LORD

The Targums had several ways of describing the LORD, usually said to be reverent circumlocutions. The Glory of the LORD, the Name of the LORD and the Presence or Shekinah of the LORD often appear where the Hebrew text had simply 'God' or 'the LORD'. All have counterparts in the Hebrew text, for example the Glory of the LORD (Lev. 9.6; Isa. 60.1; Ezek. 1.28); the Name of the LORD (e.g. Isa. 30.27; Ps. 8.1); the Presence of the LORD, either as dwelling in the tabernacle, *miškan*[22] (e.g. Exod. 25.8; Ps. 46.4), or as the Presence/Face (e.g. Exod. 33.14; Isa. 63.9). The most frequent 'circumlocution', however, is 'Memra', usually translated 'Word', which has no obvious counterpart in the Hebrew text. It was not used to translate 'the word of the LORD' that came to the prophets; this was usually *pitgama* (e.g. Tg. Isa. 1.10; 2.1, 3). Philo, too, knew several titles for the LORD, the Second God, and all of these, except 'Logos', 'Word', can be found in or deduced from the Old Testament. This suggests that the Memra of the Targums and the Logos of Philo both represent a way of understanding the Old Testament that has been lost.

'Logos' can mean many things. Philo used it to mean God made visible, and so 'Word' is not an obvious equivalent. When the elders ascended Sinai with Moses, they *saw* the Logos (*Confusion of Tongues* 95–7). The LORD visible as his Angel was the Logos, and so when Hagar met the Angel of the LORD (Gen. 16.9), Philo says she met the Logos (*On the Cherubim* 3). The Hebrew text here is obscure, as so often with passages where the LORD was seen. Reconstructing from the Hebrew and the Greek, Hagar seems to say, 'You are a God who sees me. Have I seen the One who sees me and lived?' For Philo, this visible God was the Logos. The Logos was also 'God's Man' and 'the Man after his Image' (*Confusion of Tongues* 41, 146). 'The Image of God is the Logos' (*On the Special Laws* I.81). All these — and there are many examples[23] — show that the Logos was visible, suggesting that Philo used Logos in the sense of 'correspondence, relation'. This, in turn, suggests that the underlying Hebrew term was 'the appearance' of the LORD, *mar'eh*, or the vision of the LORD, *mar'ah*. In a consonantal text,

---

[22] Shekinah and *miškan* are both from the root *škn*, dwell.
[23] See my book, *The Great Angel*, London: SPCK, 1992, pp. 114–133.

these are identical, and suspiciously similar in sound and form to the elusive 'Memra'.

The 'appearance' of the LORD occurs so frequently in the Old Testament that it passes without comment, but there is never any description of what was seen. We do not know what Abraham saw (Gen. 12.7; 17.1). At Mamre, he saw the LORD as three men; that is to say, angels (Gen. 18.1–2). At least, that is how Josephus and later Jewish tradition understood the text (*Antiquities* 1.196; Genesis Rabbah L.2). Jacob saw the LORD standing by (or upon) a ladder (Gen. 28.12–13); the glory of the LORD appeared in a cloud (Exod. 16.10); the LORD appeared in a cloud over the mercy seat (Lev. 16.2); The LORD appeared to Samuel (1 Sam. 3.21); to David (2 Chron. 3.1); and to Solomon in dreams (1 Kings 3.5; 9.2). In Deuteronomy, there is no mention of the LORD appearing. Since Deuteronomy denied that the LORD was seen at Sinai — 'You heard the sounds of words but you saw no form' (Deut. 4.12) — this is not surprising.

These texts were later used by John of Damascus, writing in Palestine early in the eighth century CE, when he explained why Christians do have images. First he set out the Deuteronomists' case: 'It is impossible to make an image of the immeasureable, uncircum-scribed, invisible God' (*On the Divine Images* 1.7). But, he argued, the Incarnation has made images possible: 'It is obvious that when you contemplate God becoming man, then you may depict him clothed in human form. When the invisible one becomes visible to flesh, then you may draw his likeness' (1.8). John observed that written words and holy objects were also images. Both types — the tablets of the Law, Aaron's rod and the jar of manna — were kept in the ark, images to remind us of the past (1.13). He even implied that images were part of the unwritten tradition known to Basil: 'Since so much that is unwritten has been handed down in the Church, and is still observed now, why do you despise images?' (1.23). John drew examples from the Old Testament. The temple was full of pictures and images (1.20), but above all, God himself made the human in his image (3.26). Adam heard the sound of the LORD's feet in Eden; Jacob struggled with God — 'It is evident that God appeared to him as a man' — Isaiah saw the LORD as a man on a throne; Daniel saw one like a man ascending to the Ancient of Days. 'No one saw the divine nature, but the image and figure of what was yet to come' (3.26). This issue of seeing the LORD in human form was the key to his argument.

Unlike those passages in the Old Testament where the appearance of the LORD is not described, Ezekiel, the first temple priest, did say what he saw, and was careful to distinguish between the appearance, *mar'eh*, and the likeness, *d^emut*; that is, between what he saw and what it represented.[24] Only the Authorized Version is consistent in its translation of his chariot throne visions; other versions obscure this important distinction. The word *d^emut* implies the thought or concept preceding an action; that is, a plan.[25] (Ahaz brought back from Damascus *the plan* of an altar in 2 Kings 16.10.) The word *mar'eh* is the visible appearance. Ezekiel used the distinction more familiar in Plato, who lived some two centuries later. For Ezekiel, the *d^emut* was the invisible aspect of the Glory and the *mar'eh* was what he saw. Ezekiel saw the Glory manifested, shining forth from the invisible state, and he saw it as a human form: 'upon the likeness of the throne was the likeness as the appearance of a man … This was the appearance of the likeness of the glory of the LORD' (Ezek. 1.26, 28, AV). When the appearance of the glory of the LORD was seen on Sinai, however, it was a devouring fire (Exod. 24.17). The glory could be seen and represented in various ways. Ezekiel knew that the living creatures supported the throne, but he saw them as fire: 'As for the likeness of the living creatures, their appearance was like burning coals (Ezek. 1.13, AV)[26]. When a man of God appeared to Samson's mother, she said his appearance, *mar'eh*, was terrifying, like the appearance of an angel of God (Judg. 13.6). Daniel saw someone 'like the appearance of a man' (Dan. 8.15), and he was strengthened by 'one like the appearance of a man' (Dan. 10.18).

In his pairing of *d^emut* and *mar'eh*, Ezekiel shows how first temple priests related the invisible and the visible creation. Other texts show that elements of the invisible world did not always make themselves present in the same form. Enoch on his first heavenly journey saw 'those who were like flaming fire, and when they wished they appeared as men' (1 En. 17.1). The fallen angels could appear in many different ways to defile mankind (1 En. 19.1). Satan could appear as an angel of light (2 Cor. 11.14), the Spirit could appear as a dove (Luke 3.22). Those who were later described as Gnostic knew this too: Theodotus, a Gnostic quoted by Clement of Alexandria taught that the Son was 'drawn in outline in the beginning' (Excerpts

---

[24] For detail see my book, *The Great High Priest*, London: T&T Clark, 2003, pp. 178–84.

[25] This would correspond to John of Damascus's distinction between the invisible nature and the form in which it was seen.

[26] For detail see my book, *The Great High Priest*, London and New York: T&T Clark, 2003, pp. 179–84.

19). The 'beginning' was the holy of holies, and so he tried to describe the non-material state as flat, existing only in 'outline'. Sometimes this was described as the engraved state; each part of the creation had its own assigned place which was as much 'engraved' as were the divine laws.[27] Another 'gnostic' text says: 'The uncreated one brought forth the pattern of the uncreated, for it is from the uncreated that the Father brings forth into a shape. The created is a shadow of pre-existing things' (Valentian Exposition, CG XI.2.35). The belief that heavenly realities could be made present in different ways is important for understanding the Eucharist: 'This is my body.' Thus Dionysius could write of the Christian mysteries: 'The transcendent is clothed in the terms of being, with shape and form on things which have neither, and numerous symbols are employed to convey the varied attributes of what is an imageless and supra-natural simplicity' (The Divine Names, 592 B).

The Memra is closely linked to the phenomenon of anthropomorphism in Scripture. How was the human form of God to be explained? The two traditions of Targums — the Babylonian and the Palestinian — differ in their use of Memra. The Palestinian Targums (PT) use Memra far more often than the Babylonian (BT). Thus PT says that the human was created in the image of the Memra of the LORD (Neofiti Targum Gen. 1.27) whereas BT has the human created in the image of the LORD (Targum Onkelos). PT says the Memra of the LORD shut Noah into the ark (Targum Pseudo-Jonathan Gen. 7.16); PT says the Memra of the LORD killed the firstborn of Egypt (Targum Ps-J Exod. 12.29); the Memra of the LORD sits on his exalted throne to hear the prayers of his people (Targum Ps-J Deut. 4.7); 'Let the Memra of the LORD now be revealed ...' (Targum Ps-J Num. 10.35-36). These suggest that in PT the Memra was the LORD made visible.

Other characteristics of PT and BT may explain why BT stayed much closer to the Hebrew text, and PT so often used Memra. PT expands its translation with other material, especially temple material, where the LORD did appear. When Adam and Eve were driven from Eden, BT is close to the Hebrew text, but PT has the Glory of the Shekinah at the front of the east of the Garden of Eden, above the two cherubim (Fragment Targum and Neofiti Targum). In BT 'the sons of God'; that is, the fallen angels (Gen. 6.1–4), are the sons of the mighty, but in PT they are named as Semiḥazah and

---

[27] See *The Great High Priest*, esp. pp. 180–4.

Uzziel, or the sons of angels (Targum Ps-J and Neofiti margin). This is how they are described in 1 Enoch, a deposit of ancient temple lore, which suggests that PT was in touch with angel tradition that BT tried to sanitize. Rabbi Simeon ben Yohai, commenting on this story in the mid second century CE, said that the fallen ones were the sons of noblemen, and that anyone who called them sons of God was cursed (Genesis Rabbah XXVI.5). The date is significant: it was when the Christians were emphasizing the role of the sons of God. Rabbi Eliezer, teaching in Palestine in the mid third century, warned about the problems of translating texts in this way. 'He who translates a verse literally is a liar. He who adds to it commits blasphemy. For instance, if he translated "And they saw the God of Israel" (Exod. 24.10), he spoke an untruth; for the Holy One, blessed be He, sees but is not seen. But if he translated "And they saw the glory of the Shekinah of the God of Israel" he commits blasphemy, for he makes three: Glory, Shekinah and God.... (Midrash Hagadol Exodus 24).[28] The translation this Palestinian Rabbi condemned as blasphemy is that of the PT: 'And they saw the glory of the Shekinah of the LORD' (Targum Neofiti and Targum Ps-J Exod. 24.10). Note that it is *seeing the* LORD that is condemned, as is plurality. These suggest there was a reaction against Christianity which had retained/restored the temple traditions of theophany in human form, and the manifold but unified nature of the divine.

Anthropomorphism is a problem since it implies incarnation. In *The Incarnation of God*,[29] Jacob Neusner's study of the problem in the early centuries of Christianity, this Jewish scholar made some important observations. The 'incarnation of God' was, he said, a profoundly Jewish characteristic (p. 6). 'It is the representation of God as a human being who walks and talks, cares and acts' (p. 21). This way of 'framing a direct encounter with the living God' had no place in the early Christian centuries, but was developed in the era of the Babylonian Talmud, the sixth or seventh centuries CE, and then only in a community not threatened by Christianity. These teachers in Babylon 're-entered the realm of discourse about God that Scripture had originally laid out' (p. 28). When the earlier, Palestinian, Talmud was being formed, the community there faced the threat of the newly

---

[28] Quoted in R. Patai, *The Hebrew Goddess*, 3rd edn, Detroit: Wayne State University Press, 1990, p. 106.

[29] J. Neusner, *The Incarnation of God. The Character of Divinity in Formative Judaism*, Philadelphia: Fortress Press, 1988.

influential Christianity in the fourth century CE, and 'Judaic response took the form of counterpart exegesis' (p. 107), and they adapted their interpretation of Scripture to the new situation. They 'clearly treated with reticence and mainly through allusion, the perfectly available conception of God as incarnate' (p. 196). As a result, it was in the Babylonian Talmud in particular 'that God became Man' (p. 166). Thus in the earlier period, the Babylonian community represented the newer ways of the Deuteronomists and were, as a result, rejected by those who preserved the temple tradition of theophany in human form. Those who returned from Babylon to build the second temple were 'an apostate generation' (1 Enoch 93.9). The PT preserved the older temple ways, and the BT avoided them. If Neusner is correct, in the early Christian centuries, the situation was reversed. The Palestinian community had closest contact with the Church, and so had reason to distance itself from anthropomorphism and ideas of incarnation, whereas the Babylonian community did not have this problem and so 'God became man'.

THE MAN WHO SEES GOD

Philo, writing in Alexandria in the first century CE, knew that the very name Israel meant 'the one who sees God'. This 'occurs twenty three times in the Philonic corpus, and is expressed or implied in some twenty six additional texts'.[30] Philo does not explain it nor does he argue for it: he assumes that this meaning is well known,[31] presumably because his Greek version of the Scriptures said that the LORD *was seen* in the holy of holies (Lxx Exod. 25.8). Now, *'š r'h 'l* (ish ra'ah el, man sees God) is an unlikely origin for the name Israel, but there is another Hebrew word that could account for it: *šwr*, meaning 'behold'.[32] It occurs in Job 34.29: 'When he hides his face, who can behold him?' and in Job 35.14: 'Although you say you do not behold him' (my translation). Job is full of archaic forms, so perhaps this is the origin of 'Israel', the one who beholds God. Perhaps Philo had lost touch with the more ancient root of the name, but knew it had to mean 'he who sees God' and provided his own approximation. It simply appears in his text: 'for Israel means seeing God' (*Preliminary*

---

[30] J. Z. Smith, 'The Prayer of Joseph' in *Religions in Antiquity: Essays in Memory of E. R. Goodenough*, ed. J. Neusner, Leiden: Brill, 1970, pp. 253–94, p. 265.

[31] Like Germanus and the meaning of Alleilouia.

[32] Smith p. 266 n. 2.

Studies 51); 'Israel, he that sees God', (*Dreams* I.171), 'the nation that sees, even Israel' (*Dreams* II.44), 'Israel means seeing God' (*Dreams* II.173); 'Israel means seeing God' (*Questions on Genesis* III.49), 'Israel, a name meaning one who sees' (*Questions on Genesis* IV. 233)[33]. Sometimes we see Philo reading the Hebrew Scriptures in this way: 'The sons of Israel' (Lev. 15.31) becomes 'the sons of the seeing one' (*Allegorical Interpretation* III.15). Seeing God must have been fundamental to the Hebrew tradition as Philo knew it.

At times he gave additional explanation to set the term in a wider context. 'He calls Israel, though younger in age, his firstborn son in dignity, making it evident that he who sees God, the original cause of being, is the recipient of honour' (*Posterity and Exile of Cain* 63). 'He that sees God, drawn to Him by surpassing beauty (a reference to Isa. 33.17), has been allotted as His portion to Him whom he sees' (*Posterity* 92). 'Ishmael means "hearkening to God". Hearing takes the second place, yielding the first to sight, and sight is the portion of Israel, the son free born and first born; for "seeing God" is the translation of Israel' (*On Flight and Finding* 208). Explaining Exodus 19.6, the royal priesthood and holy nation, Philo wrote: 'Its high position is shown by the name; for the nation is called in the Hebrew tongue Israel, which, being interpreted is, "He who sees God ..." The sight of the mind, the dominant element in the soul, surpasses all the other faculties of the mind, and this is wisdom which is the sight of the understanding' (*Abraham* 57). 'Israel' could apply equally to the patriarch or to his descendants: 'The precious offspring of Israel who has the clear vision of God' (*The Sacrifices of Cain and Abel* 134). For Philo, those who lived in the knowledge of the One were rightly called 'sons of God', and he quoted Deuteronomy 14.1, 'You are the sons of the LORD your God', and Deuteronomy 32.18, 'the Rock who begot you' (Greek: 'The God who begot you'). They were exhorted to take their place under God's Firstborn, the Logos, the chief and ruler of the angels, 'the Man after his image, and he that sees, that is, Israel' (*Confusion of Tongues* 145–6).

Israel as 'the man who sees God' appears in rabbinic texts only in one late example[34] and this is almost certainly because Christian writers favoured the explanation 'the man who sees God'. Jerome, writing at the end of the fourth century, emphasized that 'a man seeing God' was a forced explanation of 'Israel'. He said it meant

---

[33] Also Leg.All. II.34; III.186; III.212; Conf. 56;72; 148, Migr. 113, 125, 201.
[34] Midrash on Hosea 9.10 in Seder Eliyyahu Rabbah XXVII, see Smith, p. 267.

'prince of God', as appears in the Targums and Midrash, and so he was presumably offering the interpretation current among Jews. 'He is aware of the hostility this observation will arouse among his co-religionists, some of whom were deeply suspicious of his association with Jews.'[35] Justin, who lived in Palestine some three centuries before Jerome, said the name meant 'man victorious over power' (*Trypho* 125), a possible understanding of Genesis 32.28, and presumably another Jewish interpretation. Josephus had had something similar: 'He commanded him to be called Israel, which in Hebrew means "the one that struggled with the divine angel"' (*Antiquities* 1.20).[36]

'The man who sees God' was adopted as the meaning of Israel by most Christian writers, all of whom could have drawn their inspiration from Philo. Seeing God always entailed understanding, an echo of the Enoch tradition that abandoning Wisdom meant losing the vision (1 En. 93.8). Israel as the one who sees God was applied in a variety of contexts: to the patriarch Israel, to Jesus, or to the Church. Thus Eusebius, listing heroes of the Old Testament, wrote: 'Israel ... the changed name indicates a man who sees God', and 'Israel means the one who sees God in the manner of the knowing and perceiving human mind' (*Preparation of the Gospel* 7.8 and 11.6). Clement of Alexandria explained that Israel had been punished by God because they had sinned wilfully. Their very name meant 'he that sees God, that is, understands God' (*Instructor* 1.9). Elsewhere he used 'Israel' in another context — explaining how philosophy related to theology: 'Philosophy is the study of Wisdom, and Wisdom is the knowledge of things divine and human, and their causes ... He who has received previous training is at liberty to approach Wisdom, which is supreme, from which grows up the race of Israel ... He who is really endowed with the power of seeing is called Israel' (*Miscellanies* 1.5). Hippolytus applied the name Israel to Jesus: 'Having received, then, all knowledge from the Father, the perfect Israel, the true Jacob did show himself upon earth and conversed with men. And who is meant by Israel but a man who sees God?' He then links this to John 1.14 (*Against Noetus* 5). Origen argued that there was an Israel according to the flesh but also a spiritual Israel, and it was to those lost sheep that Jesus had been sent (Matt. 15.24), to those who saw God and who were citizens of the heavenly Jerusalem: 'Israel is

---

[35] C. T. R. Hayward, *Interpretations of the Name Israel in Ancient Judaism and some Early Christian Writings*, Oxford: University Press, 2005, p. 311.
[36] For a fuller discussion see Hayward, pp. 330–51.

interpreted to mean "a mind", or "man seeing God"' (*First Principles* 4.1.21-2). Macarius expounded the theme of Israel leaving Egypt: 'For Israel is interpreted as being the mind contemplating God ... set free from the slavery of darkness, from the spiritual Egyptians' (*Homily* 47.5). Prayers in the Apostolic Constitutions apply Israel to the Church: 'For by [Christ] Thou hast brought home the Gentiles to Thyself for a peculiar people, the true Israel, beloved of God and seeing God'; 'O God Almighty ... who art by nature invisible and yet art known to all reasonable natures who seek Thee with a good mind and art comprehended by those that seek after Thee with a good mind; the God of Israel, Thy people which truly see, and which have believed in Christ' (Apostolic Constitutions 7.36 and 8.15).

Most famously, the name Israel appears in The Prayer of Joseph.[37] Jacob was recounting his struggle with the 'man' at Penuel, a place name meaning 'the face of God' (Gen. 32.22–32): 'I Jacob, whom men call Jacob but whose name is Israel, am he whom God called Israel, a man seeing God, because I am the Firstborn of every living thing to whom God gives life.' Jacob/Israel explained that he was the 'first minister before the face of God', an angel. Since Origen was writing about 230 CE, Israel as the man who sees God must have been known in Jewish circles well into the Christian era, since the Prayer of Joseph was 'in use', presumably in Palestine. Origen was born in Egypt, and he may well have known the early Gnostic text now known as 'On the Origin of the World' (CG II.5), an elaborate version of the Genesis creation story, peopled with heavenly beings. It describes a great chariot throne with cherubim and seraphim, surrounded by angels. On the right of the throne sat 'a first born called Israel', who was also named 'Jesus the Christ', and to the left of the throne sat the Virgin of the Holy Spirit.[38] Israel, the Firstborn, was an angel of the Trinity.

This is consistent with the Enoch tradition, that humans can become divine. In the Enochic histories there are examples of 'animals' who became 'men'; that is, humans who became divine. Noah was born a 'white bull', but after an archangel instructed him in a secret, he became a 'man' (1 En. 89.1). The transformation process

---

[37] See above, p. 82.

[38] This description of the Trinity — the One enthroned, the firstborn called Israel and the Holy Spirit, is very like that in the Ascension of Isaiah, an early Christian text reworked from a Jewish original. Isaiah ascended to heaven and saw the Great Glory, God Most High, enthroned, and on the right he saw Jesus the LORD, and on the left he saw the angel of the Holy Spirit (Asc. Isa. 10.7; 11.32–3).

was linked to knowledge imparted by an angel. Moses was a sheep who stood before the Lord of the sheep and became a man. He then built a house for the Lord of the sheep (1 En. 89.36). The enigmatic Apocalypse of Weeks, embedded in 1 Enoch, says that in the second week of history 'a man', clearly Noah, was saved, and in the third week 'a man', clearly Abraham, was chosen as the father of righteous descendants. In the sixth week 'a man', likely to be Isaiah, ascended and then the temple was burned (1 En. 93.4–8). The Old Testament does not mention the transformations: Noah was instructed by Yahweh (Gen. 7.1–4); Abraham saw the Lord (Gen.12.7; 17.1; 18.1), as did Jacob, who became the angel Israel (Gen. 28.12–17; 35.1). Moses was recognized as the servant of the Lord because he had spoken directly to the Lord and seen his form (Num. 12.8, referring to Exod. 3.2 and Exod. 24.10; also ben Sira 45.5). There is a hint of transformation into an angel in the tradition that his face shone when he came down from the mountain (Exod. 34.29).

There are many other examples in the Old Testament of people who saw the Lord, but there is no suggestion that they were transformed by the vision. Isaac saw the Lord, and built an altar to mark the site of the theophany (Gen. 26.2, 24). Gideon saw the angel of the Lord (Judg. 6.12), as did the parents of Samson (Judg. 13). The child Samuel saw the Lord at Shiloh (1 Sam. 3.21), and we learn that the more ancient name for a prophet had been a seer (1 Sam. 9.9), presumably one who saw the Lord. Philo implies as much, when he comments on this verse: 'He … is called not only the seer, but the seer of God, that is Israel' (*Who is the Heir* 78). The appearance of the Lord is not described in these passages. Even Isaiah's great temple vision of the King, the Lord of Hosts, does not describe the Lord (Isa. 6.1–5). Instead, we learn that His Glory fills the earth. It has been suggested that in second temple priestly texts and exegesis, the angels of the older temple, the hosts — whence the title Lord of Hosts — were described as the Glory.[39] The ancient poem about the Lord dawning and shining with his host of holy ones (Deut. 33.2) would have been understood as the Lord appearing in Glory. This is implied in Luke's account of the shepherds at Bethlehem: the *Glory* of the Lord shone around them, and they heard a *multitude* of the heavenly host (Luke 2.8–13). What was seen remains a mystery: a physical form, or a transforming moment of illumination, the imparting of 'knowledge'.

Philo, a contemporary of Luke, explained how 'seeing the Lord' was understood in his time, after centuries of Deuteronomists'

---

[39] See T. N. D. Mettinger, *The Dethronement of Sabaoth*, Lund: CWK Gleerup, 1982, p. 80.

influence. Beginning with the story of the Tower of Babel, when the LORD came to see what was happening, Philo emphasized that such anthropomorphism was a concession to the human mind. God, he said, fills all things. 'He has made his powers [i.e. his angels, his Glory] extend through earth and water, air and heaven, and left no part of the universe without his presence, and uniting all with all has bound them fast with invisible bonds that they should never be loosed.' He continued with a warning: 'This divine nature which presents itself to us as visible and comprehensible and everywhere, is in reality invisible, incomprehensible and nowhere' (*Confusion of Tongues*, 136–8). These ideas are perfectly compatible with the older temple tradition — that the Glory of the LORD was veiled by matter, but could shine though all the material world, and they survive in the Koran: 'Whithersoever ye turn, there is the Face of Allah' (2.115). *What is missing is the original belief that the 'fullness of God' could be present in one human being: 'For in him all the fullness of God was pleased to dwell'* (Col. 1.19); *'We have seen his Glory'* (John 1.14).

Trying to determine what was 'seen' or intended by the more ancient accounts of meeting the LORD is not easy. When the final form of the Pentateuch was compiled, memories of the temple had seeped into the ancient traditions of the tabernacle, and all these were heavily influenced by the Deuteronomists' assertion that the LORD could not be seen. The oldest Moses tradition knew the tent of meeting, located outside the desert camp, where the LORD descended in a pillar of cloud to meet with Moses at the door of the tent (Exod. 33.7–11), or to send his Spirit to the seventy elders (Num. 11.14–17, 24–30), or to speak with Moses, Aaron and Miriam and to confirm the supremacy of Moses over Aaron and Miriam (Num. 12.1–8). The LORD then left. The tent of meeting outside the camp was not part of the priestly tradition: it belonged ultimately to the Deuteronomists' desert tradition, which denied that the LORD was continually present in the temple, and so had the LORD descending to meet his people and then leaving.

The other tent, the 'tabernacle', was a pre-figuring of the temple, but the two names (tabernacle and tent of meeting) were sometimes combined, which makes tracing the two traditions more complicated. Moses erected a tabernacle, *mškn*, 'in the midst' of the camp and furnished it like the temple: veil, table, lamp stand and ark (Exod. 25.8–9). The people camped around it (Num. 2.2). The LORD spoke from above the *kapporet* (Exod. 25.22) or appeared there (Lev. 16.2). The Glory came forth or shone forth from the holy of holies: 'descend' is never used to describe the presence of the LORD in the priestly tradition.[40] The Glory 'abode', *škn*, on Sinai.[41] The Glory entered the tabernacle when it was completed (Exod. 40.34–8), but here the tabernacle is called 'the *mškn* of the tent of meeting', fusing the two tents. The post-exilic priestly writer in the Pentateuch 'reformulated the ancient tent tradition under the influence of Jerusalemite temple theology.'[42]

THE MAN OF LIGHT

The Glory of the LORD entered the tabernacle to take possession and consecrate it; the Glory entered the temple (1 Kgs 8.11); and Ezekiel had a vision of the Glory returning to take possession of the temple to be rebuilt in Jerusalem (Ezek. 43.1–5). This Glory, he said, was like the vision he had seen when Jerusalem was destroyed. Ezekiel, a priest of the original temple (Ezek. 1.3) has left us two descriptions of the Glory as he knew it, the only canonical descriptions of the Glory of the LORD. The Hebrew is, unfortunately, very difficult to read, possibly because the subject matter is so strange.[43] Several words occur only here, for example *bzq* (Ezek. 1.14), usually translated 'flash of lightning', and *qll*, 'burnished' (Ezek. 1.7), which only occurs elsewhere in Daniel 10.6, another vision of a heavenly being. Masculine and feminine forms are mixed, as are singular and plural. The vision seems to be a fiery, fourfold female figure, the Living One, above whom was the likeness of a throne where a human form was seated. The human — *'adam*, so no gender is indicated — was a fiery bronze figure, surrounded by the brightness of a rainbow. This was 'the appearance of the likeness of the Glory of the LORD' (Ezek. 1.28).

The Psalmist had seen the Glory of the LORD entering the temple in human form. He sang of the King of Glory entering the ancient doors (Ps. 24.7–9). He knew that the LORD was clothed with honour, majesty and light (Ps. 104.1–2). He also sang of a great procession — singers and minstrels entering the temple with 'my King, my God' (Ps. 68.24–5). What had he seen? Elsewhere in his world he might have seen a statue dressed in golden robes being taken into a temple,

---

[40] Mettinger, p. 86.

[41] Thus the Authorized Version.

[42] Mettinger, p. 85, summarizing the work of R. Schmitt.

[43] A comparison of modern translations, which differ quite widely, will show the difficulties of these passages.

but Jerusalem had no statues.[44] The King, the royal high priest, was God with his people, Immanuel, and so the King of Glory entering the temple was probably the human king in his role as the visible presence of the LORD. When there were no more kings in Jerusalem, the Aaronite high priest had that role, and the prescription for his vestments shows something of their original meaning. They were 'for Glory and for beauty' (Exod. 28.2), and the high priest wore the Name on his forehead (Exod. 28.36–7). When Enoch stood before the throne in heaven (i.e. in the holy of holies) to be consecrated as high priest, he was anointed and then vested with the Glory of the LORD: 'The LORD said to Michael, "Go, take Enoch from out his earthly garments, and anoint him with my sweet ointment, and put him into the garments of my Glory"' (2 En. 22.8).[45] The meaning of the vestments was long remembered: they had been the garments of God (Exodus Rabbah XXXVIII.8): 'It is because they are emanations of the supernal mysteries, and are made after the supernal pattern, that they are called residual garments, *bigde haš'rad*, inasmuch as they were made from what was left over of the supernal robes, of the residue of the ethereal celestial splendours' (Zohar Exodus 229b).[46]

Since the Glory came out into the temple as the high priest, there may be places in the Old Testament which describe the emergence of the high priest (royal or Aaronite) from the holy of holies. Isaiah spoke of the people in darkness who had seen a great light, and then described the 'birth' of a king among the angels: 'Unto us a child is born ...' (Isa. 9.6–7). This was the heavenly birth of the Davidic king, when he was begotten in the holy of holies, in the Glory of the holy ones (Ps. 110.3) and presumably then came forth into the temple court. The Glory of the LORD was the strength of the anointed king (Ps. 89.15–18). The Servant was appointed as a Light to the nations (Isa. 42.6; 49.6, cf. Luke 2.32); he saw the light (of the Glory) after his sufferings, and his soul was satisfied (Isa. 53.11 in the Greek and Qumran Hebrew, 1Q Is^a).[47]

---

[44] A. L. Oppenheim, 'The Golden Garments of the Gods', *Ancient Near Eastern Studies* 8 (1949) pp. 172–93. For a detailed study, see C. H. T. Fletcher-Louis, *All the Glory of Adam: Liturgical Anthropology in the Dead Sea Scrolls*, Leiden: Brill, 2002, pp. 68–84.

[45] Translation in R. H. Charles *Apocrypha and Pseudepigrapha of the Old Testament*, vol. II, Oxford: Clarendon Press (1913) 1968, p. 443.

[46] The passage continues: 'R Simeon said: "All the priestly robes were emblematic of the supernal mystery, having been made after the celestial pattern"' (Zohar Exodus 231a).

[47] Jesus expounded this version of this text to the disciples on the road to Emmaus (Luke 24.26). Nothing else in the Hebrew Scriptures fits.

Isaiah, the great temple prophet, frequently used this imagery of light: the Holy One of Israel was a light and a fire (Isa. 10.17). 'Let us walk in the light of the LORD' (Isa. 2.5; cf. Ps. 56.13); 'The LORD will be your everlasting light' (Isa. 60.20). The Psalmist, too, sang of the light of the face of the LORD: 'Lift up the light of thy face upon us, O LORD' (Ps. 4.6). Psalm 27 begins: 'The LORD is my light and my salvation' and then describes seeing the beauty of the LORD, and seeking his face. 'In thy light do we see light' (Ps. 36.9); 'He will bring forth your vindication as the light' (Ps. 37.6); 'Send out thy light and thy truth, let them lead me, let them bring me to thy holy hill and to thy dwelling!' (Ps. 43.3). The light of the face enabled the people to triumph over their enemies (Ps. 44.3). It became proverbial: 'In the light of a king's face there is life, and his favour is like the clouds that bring the spring rain' (Prov. 16.15). John wrote: 'In him was life, and the life was the light of men' (John 1.4).

Those who saw the light reflected the light. Moses' face shone when he came down from the mountain (Exod. 34.29). 'Look to him and be radiant' sang the Psalmist (Ps. 34.5). Seeing the light imparted knowledge to the seer,[48] who then reflected this radiance on to those who saw. The unknown hymn writer at Qumran wrote: 'I thank thee O LORD, for thou hast illumined my face by thy covenant ... I seek thee, and sure as the dawn, thou appearest as perfect light to me' (1QH XII); 'My light shall shine forth in thy Glory. For as a light from out of darkness, so wilt thou enlighten me' (1QH XVII). The priests at Qumran were blessed with the words: 'May you be as an angel of the presence ... May he make you holy among his people, and an [eternal] light [to illumine] the world with knowledge and to enlighten the face of the congregation' (1 Q Sb IV). Paul explained that this radiance was part of the Christian hope: 'And we all, with unveiled faces, beholding/reflecting[49] the Glory of the LORD are being changed into his likeness, from one degree of Glory to another' (2 Cor. 3.18). John's Jesus exhorted the crowd to believe in the light while they had it, and so become children of light (John 12.36).

The people of the restored temple looked for the light in their failing community, but Isaiah told them the light would return only when the temple and the community were fit to receive it: 'They seek me daily ... as if they were a nation that did righteousness and did not

---

[48] Another echo of 1 En. 93.8 — the link between Wisdom and the vision.

[49] *Katoptrizo* can mean looking into a mirror or reflecting like a mirror.

forsake the ordinance of their God' (Isa. 58.2); 'Your sins have hid his face from you' (Isa. 59.2); 'We look for light and behold darkness' (Isa. 59.9). Human sin had hidden the face/presence of the LORD (Isa. 59.2, cf. 'Blessed are the pure in heart for they shall see God' Matt 5.8). Later tradition described the presence as the Shekinah, the 'dwelling' of the LORD in the temple. In the Enoch tradition, it was the sins of Enosh's generation that caused the Shekinah to return to heaven.[50] The bright image of the Shekinah had originally been on a cherub beneath the tree of life, and anyone who looked upon it was protected from all ills such as sickness, pain, demons or insects (3 En. 5.1–5) — reminiscent of the Psalmist's plea: 'Let thy face shine, that we may be saved' (Ps. 80.3). The Shekinah was the Glory seen by Ezekiel, resting above the living creatures, whose faces reflected the Glory they bore (3 En. 24.13). Isaiah's oracle of hope declared that the light and the Glory of the LORD would rise again on the truly restored city (Isa. 60.1–2), and the images in this chapter were used by John to describe the holy city that came down from heaven, where all the servants of the LORD saw his face in the place of everlasting light (Isa. 60.19–20; cf. Rev. 21.23–6; 22.3–5, 14–15).[51] The holy city of John's vision came to earth after the earthly Jerusalem, the wicked city, had been destroyed. He described it as a huge holy of holies, a golden cube (Rev. 21.16), where all the servants of the LORD not only see the vision but are taken into it (Rev. 22.3–5). This is the Kingdom, where God and the Lamb, a Unity, are enthroned (Rev. 22.1). Jesus had spoken to Nicodemus about seeing the Kingdom and entering the Kingdom (John 3.3–5). Jesus had prayed that his disciples would be with Him, *to see His Glory* (John 17.24), and the final scene in John's vision is the faithful seeing the face of the LORD who is their light. In the Kingdom, they reign with Him for ever.

There is reason to believe that this vision of the King in glory and its realization was the original 'good news' of the Gospel. The Greek word *evangelion*, gospel, became the subject of bitter wordplay in the second century CE. Rabbi Meir said that it meant *aven gilyon*, the

[50] Another version of this tradition appears in Gen. Rab. XIX.7: the Shekinah left by seven stages of sin — Adam, Cain, Enosh, Noah's generation, the builders of Babel, the Sodomites and the Egyptians in the time of Abraham — and it returned through seven righteous men — Abraham, Isaac, Jacob, Levi, Kohath, Amram and Moses.

[51] The alternative way to read Psalm 37.29 was 'The righteous shall take possession of the land and cause the Shekinah upon it for ever', thus R. Isaac, Genesis Rabbah XIX. 7, reading *wayyaškinu*, they will cause the Shekinah to dwell, instead of MT *wayyiškenu*, and will they dwell.

worthless revelation, and Rabbi Johannan said it meant *avon gilyon*, the wicked revelation (Babylonian Talmud Shabbat 116a, a line censored from many texts). There was also an anonymous ruling that the *gilyonim* and the books of the heretics did not defile the hands, meaning they were not sacred (Tosefta Yadaim 2.13).[52] *Gilyonim* usually means empty spaces or margins, but here it is likely to derive from *galah*, reveal. Revelations and visions were clearly an important category of Christian writing, and the rabbinic taunts suggest that vision was a key element in the meaning of *evangelion*, gospel. The gospel of the Kingdom, then, was probably the vision that had been at the heart of the ancient temple cult. The Targums understood the coming of the Kingdom as a revelation, and revealing the Kingdom meant revealing the presence of God.[53] 'Your God reigns' (Isa. 52.7), became 'The Kingdom of your God has been revealed.' 'The LORD of Hosts will reign on Mount Zion' (Isa. 24.23) became 'The Kingdom of the LORD of Hosts shall be revealed in the mountain of Zion.' In Ezekiel, the Day of Judgement is understood as the Kingdom: 'Your doom has come to you, O inhabitant of the land' (Ezek. 7.7) became 'The Kingdom has been revealed to you, O inhabitant of the land.' 'Your doom has come' (Ezek. 7.10) became 'The Kingdom has been revealed.' At the Transfiguration, Jesus was the LORD shining forth. As in the ancient temple, this was the moment when the LORD became king, and so he had told Peter, James and John that some would see the Kingdom 'come with power' before they died. This was the Kingdom. When Jesus said that the Kingdom was in the midst (Luke 17.21), He was speaking of the original temple world view, with the LORD enthroned as King in the holy of holies: 'Build me a holy place, that I may dwell/ be seen in their midst.'

Maranatha was a prayer for the LORD to appear. 'Hallowed be thy Name' meant 'Show yourself to be the Holy One',[54] and 'Thy Kingdom come' was a prayer for the LORD to appear. The LORD's Prayer was thus rooted in the hopes and expectations of the temple

[52] The *gelyana* of Jesus Christ is how the Syriac version of the Book of Revelation begins.

[53] See B. D. Chilton, 'The Glory of Israel. The Theology and Provenance of the Isaiah Targum', Sheffield: Journal for the Study of the Old Testament Supplement 23, 1983, pp. 77–81.

[54] B. Lang, *Sacred Games. A History of Christian Worship*, New Haven and London: Yale University Press, 1997, p. 81 says that the authors of *Praying Together. Agreed Liturgical Texts* prepared by the English Language Liturgical Consultation, Norwich: Canterbury Press, 1988, were justified in giving this as the meaning.

that had been expressed in the ancient high priestly blessing: 'May the LORD bless you and keep you. May the LORD make his face to shine upon you and be gracious to you. May the LORD lift up his face upon you and give you peace' (Num. 6.24–6, my translation).

Chapter 7

CUP AND COVENANT

*Drink of it, all of you; for this is my blood of the covenant, which is poured out for
many for the forgiveness of sins.*

Matthew 26.27b–28

The Eucharist, the thanksgiving, is the central and defining act of
Christian worship, and yet its origins are far from clear. According
to the Synoptic Gospels, the Eucharist was instituted by Jesus at the
Last Supper which was a Passover meal. Jesus took bread and blessed
it, then took a cup of wine and gave thanks (Mark.14.22–3; Matt.
26.26–7). Luke says he gave thanks over both the cup and the bread
(Luke 22.17, 19). None of the Gospels records what Jesus said in
these thanksgivings, and it may be that the later forms of Eucharistic
prayers derive from Jesus' own words. 'The Eucharistic prayer is
the direct counterpart in Christian liturgy of Jesus' thanksgiving
at the last supper.'[1] Basil had spoken of 'unwritten traditions'[2] and
prominent among them was the Eucharistic prayer. Since his Jewish
contemporaries were forbidden to write prayers down (Babylonian
Talmud Shabbath 115b), this may have been why the Gospels do not
record the prayer of Jesus. Early descriptions of the Eucharist imply
that the prayers were not read from a text; Justin said that the one
presiding prayed and gave thanks in his own way (*Apology* 1.67). The
Didache, however, set out forms of prayer, but allowed that 'charis-
matics should give thanks in their own way' (Didache 10).

John's Gospel sets the Last Supper on the eve of Passover and does
not mention the Eucharist. The lambs were sacrificed during the
afternoon of the next day, that is, when Jesus died, and this was why
Paul described Christ as the paschal lamb who had been sacrificed

---

[1] A. Gelston, *The Eucharistic Prayer of Addai and Mari*, Oxford: Clarendon Press,
1992, p. 2.

[2] See above, p. 1.

(1 Cor. 5.7). Words recalling the Last Supper are part of most Eucharistic prayers — most, but not all. The earliest source outside the New Testament, the Didache, does not associate the Eucharist with the Last Supper and the death of Jesus. The ancient liturgy of the Church of the East,[3] in general and continuous use from time immemorial, does not link the Eucharist and the Last Supper.

Jesus' death was understood from the very beginning as atonement. Paul had been taught that 'Christ died for our sins in accordance with Scriptures' (1 Cor. 15.3), an allusion to Isaiah's fourth Servant Song (Isa. 52.13–53.12), which describes a high priest figure who bears the sins of others and sprinkles atonement blood. *This is not Passover.* The earliest interpretation of the death of Jesus also says it was the sacrifice of the Day of Atonement, offered by the great high priest (Heb. 9.11–14). Other early interpretations assume that the context was not just Passover but also the Day of Atonement. Justin compared Christ to the Passover lamb and then to the two goats of the Day of Atonement: 'The goats which were ordered to be offered during the fast, of which one was sent away as the scapegoat, and the other sacrificed, were similarly declarative of the two appearances of Christ: in the first, in which the elders of your people and the priests, having laid hands on him and put him to death, sent him away as the scapegoat, and his second appearance, because in the same place in Jerusalem you shall recognise him whom you have dishonoured and who was an offering for all sinners willing to repent' (*Trypho* 40). Justin does not describe the Day of Atonement accurately — the scapegoat was not sacrificed — which suggests he was using an existing interpretation he did not fully understand. The Letter of Barnabas reveals an early Christian understanding of Good Friday as the Day of Atonement: that was probably the original understanding. Tertullian said Christians observed the fast; that is, kept the Day of Atonement, 'on the day when the Bridegroom was taken away' (*On Fasting* 2), and Origen, expounding Leviticus, exhorted Christians: 'You who came to Christ the true high priest who made atonement for you, ... do not hold fast to the blood of the flesh.' (*On Leviticus*, Homily 9.10)

There was a clear pattern of associating the death, resurrection and second coming of Jesus with the Day of Atonement. Jerome, for example, writing about 400 CE, linked the resurrection, the second coming and the scapegoat — not an obvious association from a surface reading of the Bible. He understood Zephaniah 3.8: 'Wait for

---

[3] The Liturgy of Addai and Mari.

me, says the LORD, for the day when I arise as a witness, ... to gather nations, to assemble kingdoms, to pour out upon them my indignation, all the heat of my anger', as a reference to the resurrection, as do the Old Greek, Old Latin and Vulgate translations. 'The day when I arise' was 'the day of my resurrection', which, said Jerome, led to the reversal of the curse of Babel, the ingathering of the nations and the judgement. The scapegoat was Christ sent to the Church to take away sins, and he linked this to the Servant in Philippians 2, who was exalted after his sufferings. 'Unless we are prepared, the Sun of Righteousness will not rise for us' (*Commentary on Zephaniah* 3.8). Barnabas, Justin, Tertullian, Origen, Jerome all assumed the same pattern of connections.

Over the generations, the great liturgies of the Church developed, and one wonders what led to apparent innovations. Was it this same pattern of connections that linked the death and resurrection and the Eucharist, and then also the entire complex of imagery associated with the Day of Atonement? This pattern was not just the Day of Atonement as set out in the Old Testament, so it was not simply a creative handling of Scripture. It drew on a long-established web of myth and tradition. During the sixth century, for example, the Cherubic hymn was added to the liturgy, a hymn which compares the people to the host of angels who accompany the King. When the gifts of bread and wine are taken to the altar to be consecrated, the people sing: 'We who in a mystery represent the cherubim, and sing the thrice holy hymn to the life giving Trinity, let us now lay aside every care of this life ... That we may receive the King of all, invisibly escorted by the host of angels. Allelouia, Allelouia, Allelouia.' The usual explanation of this is that it represents the people acclaiming their king, just as the new Roman emperor was carried aloft on a shield by his soldiers, but this does not explain why they are called cherubim and angels.

Comparing the Cherubic hymn with its counterpart in the Liturgy of James,[4] the context becomes clear: 'Let all mortal flesh keep silent and with fear and trembling stand, for the King of kings and LORD of Lords advances to be slain and given as food to the faithful. Before him go the choirs of angels with every rule and authority, the many eyed cherubim and the six winged seraphim, veiling their sight and crying out the hymn: Allelouia, Allelouia. Allelouia.'[5] This is a temple

---

[4] Thought to be the ancient liturgy of the Church in Jerusalem.

[5] Fr Ephrem's translation.

theophany. Before the great psalm of Habakkuk, which describes the
Lord appearing in judgement, there was a profound silence: 'The
Lord is in his holy temple; let all the earth keep silence before him'
(Hab. 2.20). When the Lord shone forth, he came with his angels
and his holy ones (Deut 33.2–3). As the Lamb opened the seventh
seal, and prepared to come to earth, 'there was silence in heaven for
about half an hour' (Rev. 8.1). Then the mighty angel (the Lord)
appeared, wrapped in a cloud and wreathed with a rainbow (Rev.
10.1), and the Kingdom was established on earth (Rev. 11.15). The
twenty-four elders worshipped God and *gave thanks* (Rev. 11.16–17).
This theophany, according to the ancient song of Moses, was on the
Day of Atonement (Deut. 32.43). The Lord came forth to atone
the land of his people, the heavens praised him and the angels
worshipped. Thus the Old Greek text, but these lines are not in the
post-Christian Hebrew, only in the pre-Christian Hebrew found at
Qumran. They were an important proof text in the early Church:
'When he brings the first-born into the world, he says, "Let all God's
angels worship him"' (Heb. 1.6), yet they disappeared from the
Hebrew text in use today, from which the English version of the Old
Testament is translated.

By the eighth century, Germanus, Patriarch of Constantinople was
explaining that the angels were 'like the soldiers' who ran ahead to
proclaim the king. He quoted two psalms: 'Thou who art enthroned
upon the cherubim, shine forth/appear ... come to save us' (Ps.
80.1–2); and 'God sits upon his holy throne' (Ps. 47.8). Both these
psalms describe temple theophanies. Psalm 80 prays for the Lord to
appear in the temple, like the Maranatha prayer of the early church;[6]
and Psalm 47 is the psalm for new year, the first of the sequence of
festivals that included the Day of Atonement and then Tabernacles.
Germanus quoted Hebrews, that Christ is the great High Priest who
has passed through the heavens; that is, into the reality represented
by the holy of holies (Heb. 9.11, then 4.14). He then quoted John the
Baptist: 'Behold the Lamb of God who takes away the sin of the world'
(John 1.29); and then Psalm 50, 'Our God will come clearly, and fire
shall go before him' (Ps. 50.3, a slight paraphrase of the Greek text).
Finally, he explained that 'Allelouia' meant praise and sing hymns
because God is appearing. This is not the meaning usually given
to Allelouia, but may be the original meaning of the word: 'Shine

---

[6] See above p. 136.

LORD.'[7] The procession in the liturgy represented the theophany, the LORD shining forth: 'The fans[8] and the deacons are in the likeness of the six-winged seraphim and the many eyed cherubim, for in this way earthly things imitate the heavenly, transcendent, spiritual order of things.' (*On the Divine Liturgy*, 28, 29, 41).

Germanus' quotations are all drawn from texts linked to the complex of festivals around the Day of Atonement; *he was aware of their original meaning*. They are not wrenched from their context in order to illustrate a liturgical innovation. Considering, as we should, the whole passage and not just the verse cited to identify it, Psalm 47 proclaims the Kingdom of God at the new year festival; Psalm 50 tells of the LORD gathering his faithful ones, who made covenant with him by sacrifice, not a sacrifice of flesh and blood, but with the sacrifice of *thanksgiving*[9] (Ps. 50.14, 23); and Psalm 80 prays for restoration of the temple and the gift of life for those who call on the name of the LORD (Ps. 80.18). Germanus explains the procession as a theophany — the LORD appearing in his temple. The splendour of Byzantine liturgy seems far removed from a Jewish Passover celebration, and so the question must be: were these later elaborate theophanic forms a deviation from the original Eucharist, or were they expressing what was implicit from the beginning and had never been lost — that it was the theophanic procession of the Day of Atonement?

Narsai lived in the fifth century CE in Nisibis,[10] a city with a long-established Jewish community. He wrote about the mystery of the liturgy using temple imagery, and identified himself with Isaiah who had seen the LORD enthroned in the temple (Isa. 6.1–3). Like John he was invited into heaven (Rev. 4.1–2), where he saw the Lamb enthroned. He alluded to the 'mystery of the Righteous One'.[11] The bread and wine being taken to the altar, he said, signified Jesus' burial: 'the altar is a symbol of our LORD's tomb' but also 'a symbol of that throne of the Great and Glorious One'. He thought of the Christian priest celebrating the Eucharist as the high priest on the Day of Atonement, to whom the LORD appeared in the incense cloud over the ark (Lev. 16.2): 'the dread mysteries ... let everyone be in

---

[7] See above p. 142.

[8] The two *rhipidia*, ceremonial fans decorated with angel wings, that flank the consecrated elements, representing the seraphim of Isaiah's vision of the LORD enthroned, Isa. 6.1–3.

[9] Thus the Hebrew; the Greek text has 'sacrifice of praise.'

[10] Now Nusaybin, in south-eastern Turkey, near the border with Syria.

[11] See below p. 174.

fear and dread as they are performed ... the hour of trembling and great fear.' When the bread and wine were uncovered, there was the silence that precedes theophany: 'The mysteries are set in order, the censers are smoking, the lamps are shining, and the deacons are hovering and brandishing fans in the likeness of the watching angels. Deep silence and peaceful calm settles on that place: it is filled and overflows with brightness and splendour, beauty and power.' Narsai then described how the angels and the host of heaven worshipped, the cherubim, the seraphim and all the ranks of angels crying, 'Holy, Holy, Holy'. He was part of the vision of Isaiah.

The priest then summoned the Spirit to come down and dwell in the bread and wine, and make them 'the Body and Blood of Christ the King': 'The Spirit descends upon the oblation without change of place, and causes the power of His Godhead to dwell in the bread and wine and completes the mystery of our LORD's resurrection from the dead', just as the enthronement of the king in the temple had been his moment of resurrection.[12] After more prayers, 'the sacrament goes forth on the paten and in the cup with splendour and glory, with an escort of priests and a great procession of deacons. Thousands of watching angels and ministers of fire and spirit go forth before the body of our LORD and conduct it. All the sons of the Church rejoice, and all the people.' This is the firstborn coming into the world, and all the angels worshipping (Heb. 1.6). Narsai alludes again to Isaiah's exclamation about the mystery of the Righteous One in the holy of holies. The body of the risen LORD, wrote Narsai, 'pardons debts, purifies blemishes, heals diseases, cleanses and purges stains with the hyssop of his mercy.'[13]

The ancient Liturgy of Addai and Mari gives thanks for being raised from the fallen state of humanity, being resurrected, forgiven and enlightened in understanding. It is true that the form of the thanksgiving resembles the Passover thanksgiving in the Mishnah: 'We are bound to give thanks, to praise, to glorify, to honour, to exalt, to extol and to bless him who wrought all these wonders for our fathers and for us. He brought us out from bondage to freedom, from sorrow to gladness, from mourning to a festival day, from darkness to great light, and from servitude to redemption. So let us say before him Hallelujah' (Mishnah Pesaḥim 10.5). The content of the Christian

---

[12] See above p. 111.

[13] Homily 17, in R. H. Connolly, *The Liturgical Homilies of Narsai*, Cambridge: Cambridge University Press, 1909.

liturgy (that is, the reason for the thanksgiving) is very different: resurrection, forgiveness, enlightenment.[14] Bishop Serapion, in the mid fourth century in Egypt, described the sacrament as 'the medicine of life to heal every sickness ... and not for condemnation'. The Liturgy of St John Chrysostom prays for remission of sins, forgiveness of offences, communion in the Holy Spirit, inheritance in the Kingdom, healing of soul and body, and not judgement or condemnation. None of this is Passover; it is the Day of Atonement, when the whole earth is judged, cleansed and consecrated, the covenant is restored and the Kingdom established.

THE COVENANT

Matthew is the only Gospel writer to specify which covenant Jesus meant when he said: 'This is my blood of the covenant ...'[15] It was the covenant for the remission, *aphesis*, of sins. His Gospel was compiled for a community of Jewish Christians, for whom such matters as the temple tax were an important issue (Matt. 17.24–27). They knew of several covenants in their Scriptures, and so Matthew had to specify which was the covenant of the Last Supper. There had been covenants with Noah (Gen. 9.16); with Abraham (Gen. 15.18–21); with Moses and Israel at Sinai (Exod. 24.8); with King David (2 Sam. 7.12); and the new covenant prophesied by Jeremiah (Jer. 31.31–4). None of these was linked to Passover, and only Jeremiah mentions remission of sins[16]. Only one — at Sinai — involved blood which was used in the covenant-making ceremony and in which the phrase 'blood of the covenant' is found. The Exodus account has no hint that this was atonement, but the Targums expanded the text: 'Moses took half the blood and put it on the altar to make atonement for the people ... and said "This is the blood of the covenant"' (Exod. 24.8 and Targums Pseudo-Jonathan and Onkelos).[17] Only one covenant was broken —

[14] F. E. Brightman, *Liturgies Eastern and Western*, Oxford: Clarendon Press, 1896, p. 287.

[15] There is ongoing debate about what Jesus actually said: was this form of words grammatically possible in Aramaic? See M. Casey 'The original Aramaic Form of Jesus' Interpretation of the Cup', *Journal of Theological Studies* 41, 1990, pp. 1–12.

[16] The Sinai covenant was celebrated at Pentecost. Casey gives examples of 'covenant blood' in other contexts, e.g. circumcision, and notes; 'Jesus made creative use of this complex of tradition. Consequently, it does not matter that some of our sources for it are later than his lifetime' (!) p. 8. Since he deals only with the Markan form of the saying, he does not consider the 'remission of sins'.

[17] Was this the traditional understanding of Sinai, or a new interpretation in reaction to the Christian claim to the covenant of peace?

the one that had involved human obligation. The covenants with Noah, Abraham and David had been divine promises, but the Sinai covenant had been conditional: 'If you will obey my voice and keep my covenant, you shall be my own possession among all peoples' (Exod. 19.5; also Deut. 11.27–8; Deut. 26.62; Judg. 2.1–3).

How these aspects of the covenant related to each other is no longer clear. The fundamental covenant was the eternal covenant, also known as the covenant of peace, *šalom,* and it was the duty of the high priests to guard and preserve it. 'Peace' in this context meant integrity and wholeness, and so the high priests had to maintain the justice and righteousness, *mišpat* and *ṣedaqah* that were the signs of the covenant. The whole creation, the natural order and human society, flourished when kings and princes ruled with justice and righteousness: 'Then justice will dwell in the wilderness, and right-eousness abide in the fruitful field, and the effect of righteousness will be peace, *šalom* (Isa. 32.1, 16–17); 'Give the king thy justice, O God, and thy righteousness to the royal son. May he judge thy people with righteousness and thy poor with justice' (Ps. 72.1). The one who maintained the covenant was called the Righteous One, meaning the one who made things righteous. Everyone and everything was then safe within the bonds of the covenant. A breach of the covenant put everything and everyone in danger, and atonement was necessary to restore the bonds and protect those at risk.

There were two ways of explaining how the covenant bonds could be broken. The one set out most clearly in the Old Testament was breaking the Law of Moses, the Ten Commandments and all the other rules associated with the Sinai covenant. The other is implicit in much of the Old Testament, and clear in the New Testament: falling under the influence of evil angels who had conspired against God to set up a counter-covenant. There were, thus, two ways of accounting for human sin: deliberate action that required repentance, or evil supernatural influence from which the sinner had to be set free. Both views are represented in the New Testament: Jesus forgave the penitent and set people free from bondage to evil spirits. The Book of Revelation describes the defeat of Satan and his angels so that the Kingdom is established; the Old Testament shows how human sin was 'managed' so that the bonds of the covenant were maintained. The role of the priest was to teach what was right and exclude the sinner, but also to accept the penitent and offer a way back. The priest could then repair the damaged covenant bond, and protect the creation from the chaos — 'wrath' — that would otherwise have ensued.

There is a strange and gruesome story that illustrates what was meant by restoring the covenant of peace by atonement. Phineas, the grandson of Aaron, took violent action to protect his people from a breach of the covenant. One man had sinned by marrying a foreign wife, and plague had struck the whole people as a punishment. To avert further disaster, Phineas had killed the couple, and the plague was stopped. Phineas was rewarded by the Lord for his action: he was given 'my covenant of peace', to be, for him and his descendants, a covenant of perpetual priesthood (or rather, a covenant of priesthood of eternity), because he had made atonement for the people of Israel (Num. 25.6–13). Maintaining the covenant of peace was described as making atonement. In other words, atonement was protecting or repairing the bond of the covenant. This was the covenant specified by Matthew: the covenant for the remission of sins, maintained by the high priest or the king, and renewed by atonement. The link between the covenant of peace and atonement is clear.

Jeremiah's vision of a new covenant set the broken Sinai covenant in the context of the greater eternal covenant. Jeremiah — or rather, the disciple who compiled the prophecies — contrasted two visions of the future that were current in his time. Inherited liability for the sins of former generations was rejected in favour of personal responsibility: 'Every one shall die for his own sin' (Jer. 31.30). But this position too was rejected: sin would be forgiven and the basis of relationship with God would not be keeping commandments but knowing, that is loving, the Lord (Jer. 31.33–4). Jeremiah knew that teaching, the role of the priests, had failed. The Law had to be within the human heart, not imposed from without, just as Jesus was to teach in the Sermon on the Mount. This love was part of the order of creation: God's care for his people was unchanging like the movements of the stars, and beyond measure like the vastness of the heavens and the depths of the earth (Jer. 31.35–7). The new covenant would be the eternal covenant restored and renewed, but on a different basis. Hence the words of Jesus; 'A new commandment I give you, that you love one another' (John 13.34), and the allusion to the atonement sacrifice: 'We know love, that he laid down his life for us; and we ought to lay down our lives for the brethren' (1 John 3.16).

The greatest atonement ritual was the Day of Atonement, when the high priest took blood into the holy of holies and then brought it out to sprinkle in the temple.[18] It was part of the sequence of festivals for

---

[18] The temple rituals followed those prescribed for the tabernacle.

the old autumn new year. By the time the Pentateuch was compiled early in the second temple era, there was a new calendar with new year in the spring, but in the time of the monarchy the year began in the autumn. Because of the six-month shift in dates, the ancient calendar in Leviticus now had the 'new year' in the seventh month, and the tenth day of the seventh month set apart as a solemn penitential Sabbath, a day of fasting (Lev. 26.23–32). The Christians knew that this atonement was a covenant ritual, even though Leviticus does not use the word, since they compared Jesus' offering of his own blood to the blood offering of the Day of Atonement, by which he established a 'new covenant' (Hebrews 9.11–15). The Sinai covenant is here called the 'first covenant' and even this was not *restored* without blood (Heb. 9.19), which seems to imply that Jesus' action was also 'restoration'. The Greek verb here is the one used for the rededication of the temple, and so the sense of the Hebrews passage is likely to be covenant renewal.

The problem, as always, is what lay behind the Greek text of the New Testament. It is odd to have a book for the *Hebrews* written in Greek. In Hebrew, however, the verb from which the adjective 'new' derives always means 'renew', 'restore', as in 'You *renew* the face of the ground' (Ps. 104.30); 'Josiah *restored* the house of the LORD (2 Chron. 24.4) or 'they shall *repair* the ruined cities (Isa. 61.4). The sense of the passage in Hebrews could be that the covenant was renewed. The train of thought here continues with reference to purification, that nothing can be purified except with blood, to the sprinkling of the tabernacle and its vessels, and then to: 'without the shedding of blood there is no forgiveness, *aphesis*, of sins' (Heb. 9.22). This has nothing to do with the Sinai covenant as we know it: it is the covenant renewed on the Day of Atonement, when the tabernacle was sprinkled to reconsecrate it and make it fit for the LORD. Aaron was told to sprinkle blood to atone the tabernacle 'because of the uncleanness of the people of Israel, and because of their transgressions, all their sins'. He cleansed it and then reconsecrated it from all the uncleanness (Lev. 16.16.19). The process of reconsecration/purification was different from the initial consecration with holy oil (Exod. 30.20–33).

The words 'new' and 'covenant' are often found together in Christian discourse, with the resulting question: is the old covenant, meaning the Sinai covenant, no longer valid? A careful reading of the earliest sources, however, shows that 'new' was often a later addition to the text. In Matthew's account of the Last Supper, the 'new' covenant does not appear until the fifth-century Greek texts.[19] In Mark 14.24, 'new' does not occur until the fifth-century Greek text,[20] and in Luke, the cup of covenant is not mentioned at all in the Western Greek texts and most of the early Latin. The older liturgical books have no evidence either way. There were many people in the early centuries of the Church for whom the Last Supper was not about 'the new covenant', but about 'the covenant',[21] and it is possible that the 'newness' was a memory of the Hebraism: that the covenant was being renewed, restored, but on a new basis. The method of the Sinai covenant was superseded (Heb. 8.13), just as the evil powers had been defeated. Paul linked the two when he wrote: 'He cancelled the bond which stood against us with its legal demands ... nailing it to the cross. He disarmed the principalities and powers' (Col. 2.14–15). This was the gist of his complex argument in Romans: that Christian hope is rooted in an earlier system, the faith of Abraham rather than the demands of the Law of Moses.

The bonds of the great covenant of peace established and maintained both creation and human society, and breaking them brought disaster. The prophets had terrifying visions of total dissolution if the bonds were broken. Isaiah saw the earth and its people collapse because they did not know the LORD:

> The earth mourns and languishes/ is foolish,
> the fruitful land is weakened and languishes/ is foolish,
> the proud people of the earth are weakened,[22]
> the earth is polluted/godless under its inhabitants,
> because they have transgressed the laws,
> changed the divine decree,
> broken the everlasting covenant. (Isa. 24.4–5, my translation)

As so often happens with prophetic oracles, wordplay is part of the message. The Psalmist had sung of the earth established in/with Wisdom (Ps. 104.24), and the prophet responded with a word that means both 'languished' and 'foolish'. The earth was established with Wisdom and collapsed with foolishness. The word for 'mourns' is the same as the word for 'grow green',[23] and so those hearing the first line would have heard 'the earth grows green' and then realized,

---

[19] The Codex Alexandrinus, fifth century and the Codex Bezae, which may be earlier.

[20] Codex Alexandrinus.

[21] Or about something rather different, as we shall see in the discussion of the bread, see below pp. 202ff.

[22] The Hebrew text is not clear here. This is one possible meaning.

[23] *'abel* can mean both mourning and meadow.

as they heard the rest of the oracle, that the meaning was exactly the opposite. Hosea gave a similar picture: there was no knowledge of God in the land, and so the commandments were broken. 'Therefore the land mourns, and all who dwell in it languish' (Hos. 4.3). The disaster was caused by rejecting knowledge and Wisdom. Isaiah's vision of the peaceful kingdom, the wolf lying down with the lamb, has the earth full of *the knowledge of the LORD* (Isa. 11.9). In the earliest Eucharistic prayers, the Church gave thanks for the gift of knowledge, presumably because this was the sign of the restored covenant. The prayer over the bread, according to the Didache, was: 'We give thanks to thee our Father, for the life and knowledge thou hast made known to us through thy servant Jesus' (Didache 9).[24]

The bonds of the covenant were broken by the misuse of knowledge. This is symbolized in the Old Testament by the story of Adam and Eve who rejected the fruit of the tree of life — their intended food — and chose instead the forbidden tree, whose fruit gave knowledge of good and evil (Gen. 2.9, 16–17). The tree of life gave Wisdom (Prov. 3.18), denied to those who had chosen the other tree (Gen. 3.24), but restored as the food of the faithful Christian (Rev. 2.7; 22.14). Adam and Eve had been lured into this choice by the snake, the clue that links this story to the myth of fallen angels who appear briefly in Genesis 6. Genesis says nothing of the origin of the snake. The detail of the story is found in 1 Enoch, a book used as Scripture by the early Church who would have known that the 'sons of God' — the mighty angels — rebelled and bound themselves in a counter-covenant. They brought their knowledge to earth and taught how to use the resources of the earth without the law of the Great Holy One. They taught metalworking to make weapons; they taught the use of drugs to destroy life; they taught astrology and prediction. They filled the earth with violence and bloodshed, and the earth cried out for *justice* (1 Enoch 6–9). The earth cried out for the covenant to be restored.

THE DAY OF ATONEMENT

The temple in Jerusalem represented the whole creation — 'all things visible and invisible': the outer hall represented the visible creation and the holy of holies behind the veil represented the invisible world of God and the angels. When the high priest renewed the covenant of peace and thus restored the creation, the ritual performed was a

---

[24] See below pp. 206ff.

cleansing of the temple. The prescriptions in Leviticus 16 are ancient and not always easy to follow, but the account in the Mishnah shows how the complex ritual was performed in the time of Jesus. The high priest took blood[25] into the holy of holies and sprinkled it seven times with a whip-like motion.[26] Then he sprinkled the temple veil, then the golden altar of incense, and finally poured out the remaining blood under the great outdoor altar (Mishnah Yoma 5.4–6). This removed the pollution caused by sin.

Most people never entered the temple itself; only the priests went in. Since the temple represented the whole creation, sins committed far away from the holy place also polluted the temple and, conversely, cleansing the temple restored the whole of society and creation. Having cleansed the temple, the high priest then transferred the sins to the head of the scapegoat, who was driven out into the wilderness, bearing all the iniquities of Israel. By the time of Jesus, the goat was marked with red wool tied to its horns (Mishnah Yoma 4.2), to warn of its sin-laden state. The logic of this ritual is that the high priest himself must have been 'bearing' the sins of Israel if he was able to transfer them to the goat. Because he wore the Name, he was able to absorb any iniquity that was in the people's offerings and thus make them acceptable (Exod. 28.38), and it seems that he also absorbed and bore the sins that he removed from the temple. This was the original significance of the commandment not to wear the Name in vain, for 'the LORD would not hold him guiltless who takes[27] his Name in vain' (Exod. 20.7).

Blood represented life, and nobody, Israelite or stranger, was allowed to consume it (Lev. 17.11–12). The blood of the atonement ritual gave new life to the creation by cleansing and consecrating it, ridding it of all the pollution caused by sin, and the life came out from the holy of holies, from heaven, to restore the creation. The earliest Christian preaching interpreted the death of Jesus in this way: 'my blood of the covenant which is poured out ... for the forgiveness (*aphesis*, putting away) of sins.' He had taken his blood into heaven as the offering, and the Church was waiting for her great high priest to emerge and complete the renewal of the creation. 'Repent therefore and turn again, that your sins may be blotted out, that times of refreshing may come forth from the presence of the

---

[25] First blood from a young bull and then blood from a goat.

[26] Jesus used a similar motion, John 2.15.

[27] Literally 'bears' or 'takes up'.

LORD, and that he may send the Anointed One appointed for you, Jesus, whom heaven must keep until the time for fulfilling all that God spoke by the mouth of his holy prophets of old' (Acts 3.19–21, my translation).

The atonement ritual involved two identical goats (Mishnah Yoma 6.1). They were chosen by lot: one to be sacrificed and one to be the scapegoat. Leviticus 16.8 is usually translated 'one lot for the LORD and one for Azazel', but this creates huge problems. Why was an offering made to Azazel, the leader of the fallen angels? This form '*for* the LORD', '*for* Azazel', is reminiscent of personal seals, which also had the form 'for X',[28] and it may be that the lots were in fact engraved seals attached to the goats. The Hebrew preposition 'for' can also mean 'as', and with the latter meaning, the goats bearing the seals would have represented the LORD and Azazel. This is confirmed by a line in Origen, the great Christian biblical scholar writing in the mid third century CE. He knew that the scapegoat sent out into the desert represented Azazel (*Celsus* 6.43), and that Leviticus was not prescribing an offering *to* Azazel. The scapegoat was *as* Azazel, which means that the sacrificed goat must have represented the LORD. Since the high priest also represented the LORD, the Day of Atonement ritual was the LORD offering himself to renew the creation.[29] In the liturgy of St John Chrysostom, this appears as: 'For thou art he that offers and is offered, both he that receives and he that is given', part of the prayer of the Cherubic hymn. 'In him was life' said John (John 1.4). The climax of Hebrews is the declaration that the Anointed One did not take the blood of goats and calves, but his own blood, thus securing an eternal redemption (Heb. 9.12). The covenant was renewed and restored.

THE DAY OF JUDGEMENT

The Day of Atonement ritualized the myth of the day of the LORD which was the Day of Judgement. In the annual celebration in the autumn, when the Day of Atonement was followed by the Feast of Tabernacles, the cleansing was followed by restored fertility; but there was also the longer perspective, that there would be a great day in the future when the LORD would appear to judge and restore the

---

[28] See p. 122.

[29] The actual death of a high priest literally enabled sinners to return. Fugitives were allowed to return when the high priest died, (Num. 35.28; Philo, *Flight* 106).

earth. The day of the LORD is often mentioned in the Old Testament, and Amos implies it was a feast day: 'Woe to you who desire the day of the LORD ... It is darkness and not light ... I hate, I despise your feasts ...' (Amos 5.18, 21). Other prophets just warned of the coming judgement: 'For the LORD of Hosts has a day against all that is proud and lofty ...' (Isa. 2.12); 'Wail for the day of the LORD is near ...' (Isa. 13.6); 'The day of the LORD is coming ... a day of darkness and gloom' (Joel 2.1–2). 'On that day' also expressed the hope for a bright future on a restored earth: it was the day of the LORD's triumph: 'The LORD alone will be exalted in that day' (Isa. 2. 11); 'In that day the mountains shall drip sweet wine, and the hills shall flow with milk ...' (Joel 3.18). The largest collection of these predictions is in the last three chapters of Zechariah, and these were to have an important role in Christian expectation: the people of Jerusalem would look on the one they had pierced (Zech. 12.10 cf. Rev. 1.7); a fountain would flow in Jerusalem to cleanse the people from all sin (Zech. 13.1); nations would gather for battle against Jerusalem, but the LORD himself would appear with his angels on the Mount of Olives (Zech. 14.1–5); living waters would flow from Jerusalem, and the LORD would become King over all the earth (Zech. 14.8–9 cf. Rev. 22.1–5).

The day of the LORD was the time when the Kingdom was established on earth. Elijah would return to warn when it was imminent, to give people a chance to repent. The day was a time of judgement on sinners and the enemies of God's people, but it was also a time when the earth would be restored to miraculous fertility, and people would live in peace and harmony. The Book of Revelation is a vision of the day: 'I was in the Spirit on the LORD's day ...' (Rev. 1.10). John's vision describes the judgment, the coming of the LORD, and establishing the Kingdom on earth. Jesus told his disciples that some of them would see the Kingdom before they died, and then Peter, James and John saw him transfigured. In that they had seen Christ in glory, they had glimpsed the Kingdom. They asked Jesus about Elijah: surely he had to come first, to warn of the day, but Jesus said 'Elijah has come' (Mark 9.1–13). Jesus was teaching about the day and the coming of the LORD. This is why the Church prayed: 'Thy Kingdom come; thy will be done on earth as it is in heaven.' They also prayed: 'Maranatha.' In each case they knew that the Kingdom and the LORD were always present, in the midst. They prayed for the Kingdom and the LORD to appear. In the Gospel of Thomas, Jesus says: 'The Kingdom of the Father is spread out upon the earth, and men do not see it' (Thomas 113).

The myth of Judgement Day is not found in the Old Testament, even though knowledge of it is often assumed. The full story is found in 1 Enoch, which describes how the rebel angels brought their knowledge to earth and instructed the human race in how to use this knowledge without respecting the law of the Great Holy One. As a result, the earth was utterly corrupted and cried out to heaven for release. One version of the story has the four archangels coming to earth to destroy the children of the fallen angels and to bind Azazel, their leader. He would be imprisoned in a pit in the desert for seventy generations, and then brought out to face judgement and the abyss of fire (1 Enoch 10.1–14).[30] This is a scene in the Book of Revelation, when an angel seizes the ancient serpent and imprisons him in a pit for a thousand years. Then he is released and after a great battle, thrown into the lake of fire (Rev. 20.1–3, 7–10). Another version of the myth in 1 Enoch has the Great Holy One coming forth from his dwelling to bring the judgement and establish his Kingdom, bringing light and peace: 'He comes with ten thousands of his holy ones, to execute judgement upon all and to destroy the ungodly' (1 Enoch 1.9). This was the key text in the letter of Jude: 'Behold the LORD came with his holy myriads to execute judgement on all ...' (Jude 14–15).

After the judgement, the archangels were told to 'heal the earth which the [fallen] angels have corrupted, and proclaim the healing of the earth, that they may heal the plague, and that all the children of men may not perish through all the secret things that the [fallen angels] have disclosed and taught their sons' (1 Enoch 10.7). Now 'plague' was the sign that the covenant had been broken: when Korah usurped the right to burn incense, a priestly privilege, plague broke out as punishment for the sacrilege (Num. 16.46); when Phineas killed the erring couple, there was plague (Num. 25.9). The effect of the fallen angels was plague, because they had broken the covenant of peace and destroyed the earth. This was sacrilege. The high priest's duty to make atonement meant renewing the covenant, removing the plague and restoring the earth. This established the Kingdom. In the Book of Revelation, when the 'kingdom of the world has become the kingdom of our LORD and of his Anointed One', the twenty-four elders *give thanks* to God that it is time 'for the dead to be judged, for rewarding thy servants, the prophets and saints, and those who fear thy name, both small and great, and *for destroying the destroyers of the*

---

[30] This section of 1 Enoch is a composite ancient text, with many variations.

earth' (Rev. 11.15–18). This is the destruction of the evil angels — one way in which restoring the covenant was described.

The LORD coming to judge and atone the earth is the climax of an ancient poem known as the Song of Moses (Deut. 32.43). The Hebrew text is difficult: 'Rejoice, ye nations with his people, for he will avenge the blood of his servants, will take vengeance on his enemies and will atone his land his people.' The form of this verse found at Qumran is longer than the Masoretic Hebrew text:

> Heavens praise his people [or rejoice with him], all *'elohim* bow down to him
> For he avenges the blood of his sons and takes vengeance on his adversaries,
> And requites those who hate him and atones the soil of his people.'
> (4Q Deut^q)

The old Greek is very similar to the Qumran Hebrew, but longer, the text corresponding to the first line being:

> Heavens rejoice with him, and let the sons of God bow down to him
> Nations rejoice with his people, and acknowledge him all you angels of God.

The exact state of these lines in the time of Jesus is important, because they were a proof text for the early Church: 'When he brings the firstborn into the world, he says "Let all God's angels worship/ bow down to him"' (Heb. 1.6). *The poem describing the LORD coming on the Day of Atonement was a prophecy of the coming of Jesus. It was a procession of angels from heaven, like the Cherubic hymn.* Hebrews does not quote the Greek Old Testament, but seems to use a translation of the older Hebrew from Qumran. This vital line disappeared from the later Hebrew text, and thus an important link to Christian origins was lost. Jesus coming on the Day of Atonement had been part of the earliest expectation.

Another text known in the time of Jesus, The Assumption of Moses,[31] is generally thought to be an expansion of this part of Deuteronomy. It shows how people imagined the LORD coming on the Day to establish the Kingdom:

> Then his kingdom will appear throughout his whole creation
> Then the evil one will have an end.
> Sorrow will be led away with him
> Then will be filled the hands of the angel who is in the highest place appointed
> He will at once avenge them of their enemies

---

[31] Only one text is known, in Latin, which seems to have been translated from Greek. The original was probably Hebrew or Aramaic, so nuances could have been lost in the translations.

The heavenly one will go forth from his kingly throne
He will go forth from his holy habitation with indignation
and wrath on behalf of his sons. (Ass. Mos. 10).

The greatest angel becomes a priest — his hands are filled with incense[32] — and he rises from his throne to bring judgement. The evil one, Azazel, is led away, and the kingdom is established. The LORD emerges on the day as the High Priest to perform the atonement described in Deuteronomy 32: to atone the soil of his people.

A third text from the time of Jesus adds more to the picture of the day of the LORD. The Qumran Melchizedek text (11QMelch) describes the Day of Atonement at the end of the tenth jubilee that is also the day of the LORD. Melchizedek, the Great High Priest, was expected to deliver the sons of light from the hand of Satan and make atonement. Only parts of the text survive, but it was woven around a series of quotations from the Hebrew Scriptures and this helps in reconstruction. The (fallen) *'elohim* were to be judged (Ps. 82.1); the messenger would bring peace and proclaim the kingdom of God (Isa. 52.7); the anointed prince would come to Jerusalem (Dan. 9.25); and it would be the day — not the day of the LORD's favour, but the day of Melchizedek's favour. Isaiah 61.2 was applied to Melchizedek. This is the passage Jesus read in the synagogue at Nazareth: 'The spirit of the LORD is upon me, because he has anointed me ... To proclaim the year of the LORD's favour' (Luke 4.18–19, my translation). He added: 'Today this scripture has been fulfilled in your hearing.' Jesus was bringing the day.

From these three mutually consistent contemporary texts — the Song of Moses, the Assumption of Moses and the Melchizedek text — it is possible to reconstruct what the first Christians expected on the day. The Anointed One, Melchizedek the Great High Priest, would emerge from his holy place and come to earth with his host of worshipping angels: he would banish Azazel and his horde: establish the Kingdom: and atone the land, that is, purify and heal it. The Letter of Barnabas, at the latest a second-generation text, compared the Parousia to the 'second goat', a comparison that makes no sense apart from the original Day of Atonement context when the high priest brought out the blood of the goat from the holy of holies. This was the LORD emerging to renew the creation, and was the original expectation of the second coming: 'times of refreshing from the presence of the LORD' (Acts 3.19). 'The point of there being two

---

[32] This is the Hebrew idiom for ordaining a priest.

similar goats is that when they see him coming on the Day, they are going to be struck with terror at the manifest parallel between him and the goat' (Barn. 7). It is clear that the theophanic procession of the Cherubic hymn enacts the scene in the ancient Song of Moses that is quoted in Hebrews: 'When he brings the firstborn into the world, he says "Let all God's angels worship him"'. This suggests that it was implicit in Christian worship from the beginning. 'We who in a mystery represent the cherubim, and sing the thrice holy hymn to the life giving Trinity, let us now lay aside every care of this life ... That we may receive the King of all, invisibly escorted by the host of angels. Allelouia. Allelouia. Allelouia.'

This sequence is the framework of the Book of Revelation, which presents the myth in its original temple setting, being worked out in the history of the first forty years of the Church. As in the Assumption of Moses, the great angel received the incense (Rev. 8.3). The text is usually translated 'another angel', but in the Hebrew or Aramaic that underlies Revelation, 'another' and 'afterwards/next' are written in the same way, *'hr*, and so here, and at 7.2, 10.1, and 18.1, it means 'afterwards'. It is the mighty angel (Rev. 5.2), who was seen on the throne. *After this* he was given the incense, *after this* he came forth from his holy place to bring the destruction of Jerusalem (Rev. 18.1: 'Babylon' is Jerusalem). *After this* the angel imprisoned the ancient serpent (Rev. 20.1–3), and then the Kingdom was established and the earth renewed: 'Behold I make all things new' (Rev. 21.1–5). The final act of the rite of atonement in Christianity became the hope for the second coming: 'That times of refreshing may come from the presence of the LORD' (Acts 3.19); 'When the LORD Jesus is revealed from heaven with his mighty angels, inflicting vengeance' (2 Thess. 1.7). This was the earliest Christian hope, before the revelation to John that the return of the LORD would be in another way. The new teaching was inserted into Revelation, in the correct place in the historical sequence, before the fall of the city: 'Afterwards I saw the mighty angel coming down from heaven ... "You must prophesy again"' (Rev. 10. 1, 11).

THE OFFERING

Emerging to judge and renew the earth was the final act of the ritual. It began with the sacrifice of the goat to represent the LORD, and concluded with the expulsion of the scapegoat. Both goats were used to show how the death of Jesus fulfilled what the temple rite had prefigured. 'He entered once for all into the holy place, taking not the blood of goats and calves but his own blood, thus securing an eternal redemption' (Heb. 9.12). Cyril of Alexandria (died 444 CE) wrote: 'We must perceive the Immanuel in the slaughtered goat … the two goats illustrate the mystery' (Letter 41). The two goats, not just the one. Barnabas also saw the rejection of Jesus prefigured in the sufferings of the scapegoat. 'And what do they do with the other [goat]? The other, he declares, is accursed. Now see how plainly the type of Jesus appears. Spit on it, all of you, thrust your goads into it, wreathe its head with scarlet wool and so let it be driven out into the desert … the one that is accursed wears the wreath. That is because they shall see him on that day clad to the ankles in his red woollen robe and will say, "Is not this he whom we once crucified, and mocked and pierced and spat upon? Yes, this is the man who told us he was the Son of God"' (Barn. 7).

The act of atonement had inspired the poem in Isaiah 53 which the Church saw as a prophecy of Jesus. The ancient high priest (or sacral king, in the time of the monarchy) acted as an interceptor of divine wrath. Aaron had stood between the living and the plague-stricken after the rebellion of Korah, and had prevented further disaster (Num. 16.47–8). The mysterious Servant in Isaiah's poem had the same role: 'The LORD laid on him the iniquity of us all' (Isa. 53.6). The inspiration for the Servant poem had been Hezekiah, smitten with plague because he had destroyed the altars of the LORD and left his city vulnerable to enemy attack, but then he was redeemed.[33] The plague was transferred to his enemies, and there was a 'wasting sickness among the stout warriors of Assyria' (Isa. 10.16). The key to the role of the Servant is in the Hebrew verb, *pg'*, a word that cannot easily be translated. It occurs in Isaiah 53.6: 'The LORD *laid on him* the iniquity of us all', and in Isaiah 53.12: '*He made intercession* for the transgressors.' The Servant was the one who interposed himself. The rewriting of the Korah story in the Wisdom of Solomon captures this well: '[Aaron] withstood the anger and put an end to the disaster … he intervened and held back the wrath … showing that he was thy Servant' (Wisd. 18.21, 23). Holding back the wrath was the sign of the Servant even at the end of the second temple period when the Wisdom of Solomon was written. In the Book of Revelation, this was

---

[33] See my paper 'Hezekiah's Boil', *Journal for the Study of the Old Testament* 95 (2001), pp. 31–42.

the role of the angel of the dawn who held back the wrath until he had marked the chosen with the seal of the Living God (Rev. 7.1–8).

Jesus knew that this Servant poem described his role. Matthew, writing for Jewish Christians, linked Jesus' work as a healer to his role as the sin-bearer, and quoted the Servant poem (Matt. 8.17 quoting Isa. 53.4). When Jesus joined the disciples on the road to Emmaus, he explained to them that they were slow to believe the prophecies, that the Messiah had to suffer before he entered his glory (Luke 24.26). Now the present Hebrew text of the Old Testament has no prophecy of the Messiah suffering and entering his glory. Indeed, the whole question of a suffering Messiah is vexed: where did the Christians find this idea — or was it their own innovation? Until the Dead Sea Scrolls were found, that question could not be answered, but this Servant poem in the great Isaiah scroll (1Q Isa.ᵃ) has some different readings. The Servant is not 'marred beyond human semblance' (Isa. 52.14) but anointed beyond human semblance; that is, transfigured[34]. After his sufferings he sees the light, that is, the light of the Glory (Isa. 53.11), but the word 'light' is not found in the present Hebrew text. Jesus must have known Isaiah as it is in the Qumran scroll and known that this poem described the role of the Messiah. The Targum understood the poem as a description of the transfigured Servant Messiah who cleansed and restored the temple and established the Kingdom: 'Behold my servant the Messiah shall prosper ...' (Tg. Isa 52.13). His appearance was not marred, but he had 'a holy countenance' (Tg. Isa. 53.2). The Targum remembered that the Servant had restored the polluted temple: 'He shall build the sanctuary that was polluted because of our transgressions, and given up because of our iniquities' was the explanation of: 'He was wounded for our transgressions and bruised for our iniquities' (Tg. Isa. 53.5). The sins of the people would be transferred to their enemies (like transferring the sins to the scapegoat) (Tg. Isa. 53.8), and the purified remnant of his people would 'look upon the Kingdom of their Messiah' (Tg. Isa. 53.10).

The original temple scheme — and the detail is lost to us in time and poetic allusion and the activities of second temple editors, but was known to Jesus and his contemporaries — had the high priest himself as the sin-bearer and as the sacrifice, but in the ritual a goat was substituted for each role. How the stricken sin-bearer related to the triumphant emerging high priest cannot be reconstructed from the surviving Hebrew Scriptures. There are hints in Isaiah 53 where it

---

[34] The difference is one letter.

seems that the Servant died, and then his days were prolonged. This implies resurrection, which had been one of the mysteries of the holy of holies, as we have seen. The anointing and enthronement of the king was his resurrection, his 'raising up'. A 'Messiah', an anointed one, was by definition resurrected. The link between suffering and enthronement was known to the early Church, as can be seen in Philippians 2. Paul seems to be quoting from an established sequence of ideas when he describes the role of the Servant:

> Christ Jesus ... emptied himself, taking the form of a servant, being born in the likeness of men. And being found in human form, he humbled himself and became obedient unto death, even death on a cross. *Therefore* God has exalted him and bestowed on him the Name that is above every name, that at the Name of Jesus, every knee should bow, in heaven and on earth and under the earth, and every tongue confess that Jesus Christ is LORD, to the glory of God the Father (Phil. 2.7–11).

The key word is: 'therefore'. The early Church knew a pattern in which the Servant who suffered was exalted and enthroned as the LORD, and this is the pattern of the Eucharist: the sacrifice is offered and enthroned, and then emerges from heaven to feed the Church. The link between atonement, resurrection and Parousia is found in the Day of Atonement.

Atonement as enthronement is glimpsed in the vision of the Man in Daniel 7, another important text in the early Church. Daniel described a vision of fiery thrones in heaven surrounded by a vast throng. He had seen four great beasts rising up from a stormy sea, and each had been overthrown. Then he saw a human figure going up to heaven with clouds. It seems that he too emerged from the sea. He came to the 'Ancient of days' and was 'presented before him' (Dan. 7.13), and then he was given 'dominion and glory and kingdom, that all peoples, nations and languages should serve him; his dominion is an everlasting dominion, which shall not pass away, and his kingdom one that shall not be destroyed' (Dan. 7.14). 'Presented before him' could imply no more than being presented at court, but the temple context of the vision suggests a temple meaning for the verb: 'he was offered'. The word means 'bring near', but also 'offer', the meaning in Ezra 6.17 and 7.17.[35] This was the self-offering of the Man before he was enthroned in the Kingdom, the original of the Eucharistic offering that was also enthronement.

---

[35] Dan. 7.13, Ezra 6.17 and 7.17 are all Aramaic passages of the Old Testament.

The same vision is found in 1 Enoch 47, but with more detail. This is part of the 'parables'[36] of Enoch, described as 'the vision of Wisdom' (1 Enoch 37.1). The parables are three visions of the holy of holies that describe the role of the Messiah. He has three titles: Righteous One, the Son of man, the Chosen One[37] — all titles used for Jesus.[38] In the first parable, the Righteous One appears and brings light and judgement. Enoch then sees the righteous and chosen ones in the dwelling place of the LORD of Spirits (Enoch's name for the LORD of Hosts). This is like Revelation 4, with a throng blessing and praising around the heavenly throne, extolling the power of the Creator and joining with the powers of heaven to sing 'Holy Holy Holy is the LORD of Spirits. He fills the earth with Spirits' (1 Enoch 39.1–14). Enoch then learned the secrets of the creation. In the second parable, Enoch saw the heavenly vision that was realized on the Day of Atonement — the myth of the ritual. On that day, the Chosen One was enthroned in glory, and heaven and earth were transformed (1 Enoch 45.3–5). Then he saw two figures: the One before Time,[39] and a human figure with a face like an angel's — presumably he was radiant, transfigured. This was the Son of man who was to bring judgement. The words here are very like the Magnificat: 'He will hurl down the kings from their thrones and kingdoms, because they neither exalt nor praise him, nor humbly acknowledge where the gift of their kingdoms came from' (1 Enoch 46.5). Then the blood of the Righteous One and the prayers of the righteous ones were taken up to heaven, along with the blood of the righteous ones. The singular and plural forms — Righteous One, righteous ones — suggest that the Man figure in some way represented the others. His blood represented their blood. There was joy in heaven as the blood of the Righteous One was received, and the 'number of righteousness' was achieved (1 Enoch 47.1–4). Then the books of judgement were opened. The third parable is a collection of pieces about the judgement. The kings and the mighty were commanded to look at and recognize the

---

[36] In Hebrew, and so in the Enoch tradition, a parable can be either a wise saying or a vision.

[37] 1 Enoch is an Ethiopic text, probably translated from a Greek text that had been translated from Hebrew or Aramaic. In other words, there may be inaccuracies and a loss of nuance, for example, in these titles.

[38] Righteous One in Acts 3.14; Son of Man throughout the Gospels, Chosen One is the original Hebrew of Isaiah 42.1, the words Jesus heard at his baptism, Mark 1.11.

[39] Often translated the 'Ancient of Days', but the title means the one who is outside time and is its origin.

Chosen One on his throne (1 Enoch 62.1). There are fragments of a poem about the cosmic covenant, and how the fallen angels tried to learn its secrets (1 Enoch 69.13–25), and the section ends with a description of the Son of man on his throne in triumph, and Enoch being transformed into one of the angels (1 Enoch 69.26–71.17).

There are striking similarities to the Book of Revelation: the multitude around the heavenly throne singing 'Holy Holy Holy'; the Lamb on the throne 'standing as though it had been slain' (Rev. 5.6); the human figure with a radiant face (Rev.1.1 6); the number of the martyrs that had to be completed (Rev. 6.9–11); the prayers of the holy ones rising from the land (Rev. 8.4); the books of judgement opened (Rev. 20.12). The Parables, however, reveal more about what happened in the holy of holies, especially the offering of the blood of the Righteous One that inaugurated the judgement (1 Enoch 47.1–4). After the offering, the Son of man was 'named' 'before the sun or heavenly signs were created, before the stars of heaven were made' (1 Enoch 48.2–3). In the world of the temple, this means that he was given the Name in the holy of holies, which represented the state before the visible creation. All people on earth then worshipped and praised the one who had been 'chosen and hidden in his presence before the creation of the world' (1 Enoch 48.5–6). He had received the manifold Spirit, just as the Lamb in Revelation had the sevenfold Spirit (1 Enoch 49.3; cf. Rev. 5.6). This must have been the background to the 'hymn' in Philippians 2: the Servant who suffered death, and was then exalted and given the Name. Everyone then worshipped the Servant, and recognized that he was the LORD. Recognition was important: in Isaiah's Servant poem the kings are struck dumb when they see him (Isa. 52.15); John knew that every eye would see the one who had been pierced, and the tribes of the earth would wail (Rev. 1.7); and Barnabas knew there would be astonishment when the returning LORD was recognized as the second goat (Barnabas 7).

The Man figure in the Book of Revelation is called the Lamb. This is wordplay that is characteristic of temple texts: in Aramaic, the word 'young one' *talya'* was used for both a lamb and a servant, and so 'Servant' can be substituted for 'Lamb' throughout. The fact that the Servant was represented in the sacrifice by a goat is not a problem! There was a theological reason for keeping the animal figure, however, since in the visionary tradition which dealt with things on earth and in heaven, the characters had to be distinguished. All the heavenly beings were 'men', and all the mortals were animals, clean or unclean depending on whether or not they were enemies. Thus Jesus' parable of the sheep and the goats describes the judgement of mortals by the Son of man and his angels (Matt. 25.31). The Lamb enthroned shows that humanity has been restored to heaven.

Scholars have recognized the similarity between these scenes in 1 Enoch and the Song of Moses.[40] 1 Enoch describes the offering that preceded the LORD emerging from the holy of holies to avenge the blood of his sons and to atone the land of his people. Self-sacrifice and enthronement were a temple sequence. They have also recognized that the Enoch passage is similar to Isaiah's poem about the suffering Servant,[41] the one who sees the light of the glory after his suffering, 'the Righteous One, my Servant' (Isa. 53.11), who makes many righteous and bears their iniquities. This is a high priestly role, as can be seen from the otherwise inexplicable words at the beginning of the poem: 'he shall *sprinkle* many nations' — *yazzeh*, the word used in Leviticus 16.19 for the sprinkling on the Day of Atonement. Other translations are often offered, on the ground that the Hebrew is obscure, but read in context, it is perfectly clear.[42] The Servant was also made a sin offering, *'ašam*, a special term for the offering used to avert the plague that was a sign of wrath.[43] In other words, the Servant was the sacrifice to renew the covenant bonds and prevent the wrath. The Hebrew text of Isaiah 53.10 is: 'You make his soul an *'ašam ...*', where 'soul' is the word translated in Leviticus 17.11 as 'life', the life in the blood that makes atonement. The Servant then poured out his life/blood, bore the sin of many and put himself *to intercept* their transgressions. 'Intercept' is the same verb as 'laid on him' in Isaiah 53.6. This is the role of the high priest, ritualized as 'absorbing' the sins whilst sprinkling the blood in the temple, and then transferring them to the scapegoat. The final act of the Day of Atonement was to pour out the remaining blood under the altar — just as the Servant poured out his soul. In Philippians 2, this becomes: 'he poured himself out, taking the form of a servant, born in the likeness of men' (Phil. 2.7, translating literally). 'This is my blood of the covenant,

---

[40] E.g. D. Olson, *1 Enoch. A New Translation*, North Richland Hills, Tex.: Bibal Press, 2004, p. 90.

[41] E.g. M. Black, *The Book of Enoch or 1 Enoch*, Leiden: Brill, 1985, p. 209.

[42] The Greek of both Aquila and Theodotion is *rhantisei*, sprinkle; the Vulgate has *asperget*; the AV has sprinkle. The RSV has 'startle'; GNB has 'marvel'; NEB has 'were aghast at'.

[43] The Philistines sent an *'ašam* to take away the wrath when they returned the captured ark (1 Sam. 6.3).

which is poured out for many for the *putting away* of sins' (Matt. 26.28, my translation).

The Servant who poured out his blood was 'the Righteous One who makes many righteous'(Isa. 53.11) by bearing their iniquities. This was the role of the high priest before he transferred the iniquities to the scapegoat. The Righteous One restored the 'righteousness' that was a sign of the covenant. Peter described Jesus as the Holy and Righteous One, the Author of Life, before explaining that the final Day of Atonement had been inaugurated: 'Repent and turn again, that your sins may be blotted out, and times of refreshing may come from the presence of the LORD' (Acts 3.19). The Targum of Isaiah has preserved the older temple context of the Righteous One in its rendering of Isaiah 24.16, which in the Old Testament reads, enigmatically: 'From the ends of the earth we hear songs of praise, of glory to the Righteous One. But I say "I pine away, I pine away. Woe is me! For the treacherous deal treacherously and the treacherous deal very treacherously."' Isaiah 24 as a whole describes the destruction of the everlasting covenant vv. 4–13, the judgement vv. 17–22 and then the Kingdom, the reign of the LORD of Hosts in Jerusalem, v. 23. The meaning of the key passage about the Righteous One is obscured in the way the Hebrew text is usually read and translated.

The Targum's paraphrase, however, shows that the meaning was not lost: it was the Day of Atonement. 'From the sanctuary, whence joy is about to come forth unto all the inhabitants of the earth, we have heard a song of praise for the Righteous One. The prophet said: "The mystery of the reward of the Righteous One has been shown to me, the mystery of the punishment of the Wicked One has been revealed to me." Woe to the oppressors, for they shall be oppressed, and to the spoiling of the spoilers, for they shall be spoiled.'[44] The judgement is then described in graphic detail, as in the Hebrew text: the earth staggering under the heavy weight of sin, the LORD punishing the rulers of heaven and earth and then the Kingdom appears: 'For the Kingdom of the LORD of Hosts shall be revealed in the mountain of Zion and in Jerusalem, and before the elders of his people in glory' (Tg. Isaiah 24.16, 23b). This is what the Psalmist saw as he agonized over the problem of evil: 'When I thought how to understand this, it seemed to me a wearisome task, until I went into the sanctuary of God; then I perceived their end' (Ps. 73.16–17). This is the theme of

---

[44] The vision in Ps. 73.15–20 is similar.

the Book of Revelation, but there the emerging figure is called the Angel or the Lamb.

Establishing the Kingdom was restoring the covenant by atonement and by the 'bearing' of sin, but the link between 'bearing' sin and forgiveness is often lost in translation. There are places where the verb *naśa'*, literally 'bear' or 'carry', is more appropriately rendered 'forgive'. The role of the Righteous One is implicit in the Law of Moses, in the way that the consequence of sin is described. A person who had deliberately broken a law had to 'bear' his own guilt; that is, could not be forgiven. Anyone who failed to bear witness when he had evidence had to bear his own iniquity (Lev. 5.1). A couple who contracted an illicit marriage had to bear their own iniquity (Lev. 20.17), and an adulterous couple had to 'bear their own sin' (Lev. 20.20). Anyone who ate forbidden meat would defile himself and bear his own sin and die (Lev. 7.18; 22.9). Anyone who cursed God would bear his own sin, and die (Lev. 24.15–16). Anyone who failed to observe Passover without good reason would be cut off from his people and bear his own sin (Num. 9.13). The LORD's forgiveness of the penitent was the priests 'bearing' the iniquity of the sinner. They did this by atonement sacrifice and by eating the sin offering (Lev. 10.17). Eating the sacrifice transferred the 'iniquity' to the one who had eaten, and he then bore it.

The same verb, when the LORD is the subject, is usually translated 'forgive': 'Who is a God like you, bearing [i.e. forgiving] sin?' (Mic. 7.18). Job asked, 'Why do you not bear my transgression and cause my guilt to pass away?' (Job 7.21).[45] 'Carrying' iniquity was the role of the LORD, of the high priest and of the scapegoat, suggesting that in the ritual the high priest and the scapegoat represented the LORD. The literal translation of Psalm 32 is: 'Blessed are those who are borne [the verb is *nś'*] in respect of transgressions and covered in respect of sin … Blessed is the man to whom the LORD imputes no iniquity … I acknowledged my sin to thee, and I did not cover my own iniquity; I said, "I will confess my transgressions to the LORD"; then thou didst carry the iniquity of my sins.' (Ps. 32.1–2, 5, my translation). The verb atone, *kpr*, does not occur, but this passage describes the process perfectly. The role of the LORD and his manifestation, the Righteous One, was to maintain the covenant by bearing away anything that would have destroyed it and left the people without protection from sickness, enemies, droughts and disasters.

---

[45] In each case, translating literally.

The role of the Righteous One, the sin-bearer, is implicit in that the great punishment for sin was to be 'cut off' from the people: the sinner who had to bear his own iniquity was cut off. He was outside the covenant bond and therefore beyond its protection. The priest could make atonement for the penitent or unwitting sinner, but whoever sinned 'with a high hand' 'that person shall be utterly cut off, his iniquity shall be upon him' (Num. 15.30–31). The LORD declared through Ezekiel: 'As I live ... I will be King over you ... I will make you pass under the rod, and I will bring you into the bond of the covenant. I will purge out the rebels from among you, and those who transgress against me' (Ezek. 20.33, 37–8). 'I will remember my covenant with you in the days of your youth, and I will establish with you an everlasting covenant ... and you shall know that I am the LORD, that you may remember and be confounded and never open your mouth again because of the shame, when I atone for you everything that you have done, says the LORD Yahweh' (Ezek. 16.60, 62–3). This was also the role of the Servant: 'Surely he has carried [*nś'*] our sicknesses ... He was pierced for our transgressions, smitten for our iniquities, upon him was the chastisement that made us whole', is one possible translation of Isa. 53.4a, 5. But double meanings were characteristic of temple tradition: 'pierced' and 'polluted/ profaned' are both *ḥll*, and this is the opposite of *qdš*, holy; 'chastisement', *mwsr*, is the same word as 'the bond of' the covenant (Ezek. 20.37); and 'stripes' is not the commonest meaning of *ḥbrt*: the word usually means to unite, for example 'joining together' the tabernacle curtains (Exod. 26.4, 10). Isaiah also said of the Servant: 'Surely he forgave our sicknesses ... He was polluted by our transgressions, crushed by our iniquities; the covenant bond of our peace was his responsibility, and by his joining us together we are healed.' This implies that the role of the sin-bearer was to bring people back and keep them within the bonds of the restored covenant.[46] Paul was using this image when he wrote that God justifies (that is, 'makes righteous' in the covenant sense) and so nothing could separate that person from 'the love of God in Christ Jesus' (Rom. 8.33, 39).

Mary Douglas, in her study of biblical purity laws, observed that they did not set members of the community apart from one another.

---

[46] The Righteous One appears in Isa. 3.10, where the Hebrew is obscure and seems to mean: 'Tell the Righteous One that he is good'. The Old Greek reads the Hebrew differently — or reads different Hebrew: '... saying "Let us bind the Righteous One, for he is vexatious to us."' The Righteous One is associated with bonds, but here used as an attack upon him.

On the contrary, they were rules for keeping the community together: 'The more closely we look at the biblical rules of sacred contagion, the more marked appears the difference between the Bible system and other systems of contagious impurity. We cannot avoid asking why the priests defined laws of purity that did not make parts of the congregation separate from or defined as higher or lower than the rest.' She concluded that ideas of washing and cleansing have imported into Leviticus a range of meanings that are not there in the original. To atone originally meant to 'repair' or to 'cure a sickness', 'to make good a torn covering'.[47] The covenant was restored by the self-offering of the Righteous One, the Man whom Daniel saw ascending and offering himself before he was enthroned. Although the present book of Daniel was compiled in the second century BCE, during the Maccabean war, it was the reworking and interpretation of older prophecies. The Man vision did not originate with Daniel. After Nathan had promised David that his son would build the temple, the king prayed, and it seems that he spoke of a man ascending. The Hebrew text is opaque, but reconstructing from the Greek also, it could have been: 'You have caused me to see the crowning of the man whom you caused to ascend, O LORD God', or 'You have caused me to see in the midst the man on high ...' (1 Chron. 17.17). The Greek text understood that this was a vision of a man, and that the king had been 'raised up'. The original text is probably beyond recovery, but the state of this text (and of many similar texts) raises an important question: why is it unreadable? Why has the vision of the Man been obscured?

Three psalms depict the ascent of the Man. 'Of old thou didst speak in a vision to thy faithful one, and say: "I have set the crown upon one who is mighty, I have lifted up/exalted one chosen from the people. I have found David, my servant; with my holy oil I have anointed him; ... He shall cry to me, "Thou art my Father ..."" And I will make him the firstborn ...' (Ps. 89.19–20, 26–7). David was not a name: it was a royal title, the beloved, as can be seen from Isaiah's parable of the vineyard: 'Let me sing for my beloved, a song for my loved one [my David] concerning his vineyard ...' (Isa. 5.1). We have here, then, the beloved Servant, exalted and anointed, a son in that he addresses God as Father, and the firstborn. The two other psalms, 89 and 110, describe the 'birth' of the divine son. The king, when

---

[47] Mary Douglas, 'Atonement in Leviticus', *Jewish Studies Quarterly* 1 (1993–4), pp. 114, 117.

he was set on Zion, heard the words: 'You are my son, today I have begotten you. Ask of me and I will make the nations your heritage, and the ends of the earth your possession.' (Ps. 2.7–8). Scholars have recognized that this psalm describes the same temple ritual as Daniel's vision of the Man ascending.[48] The king was set at the right hand of the LORD, and established as a priest for ever (or as a priest of eternity) 'after the order of Melchizedek'. The crucial part of this psalm, which described how the human became the divine son, is now unreadable in the Hebrew, but reconstructed from the Greek text, it may once have read: 'In the glory of the holy ones, [or in holy array] I have begotten you.' Part of the process was 'dew' (Ps. 110.3–4). The Christians understood that Melchizedek's priesthood came by resurrection. His priesthood was contrasted with that of Aaron, whose family became priests by descent and having the family name (Heb. 7.11, 16). Melchizedek had 'arisen' — the word means 'resurrected' — and had become a priest 'through the power of indestructible life' (Heb. 7.11, 15–6). Since he did not die, he was a priest for ever.

From these three psalms we have some idea of the ancient temple ritual for the birth of the son of God: the Man went up to the throne with clouds; that is, he entered the holy of holies with incense to offer himself. There, among the angels of the holy of holies, he was 'born' as the divine son, the firstborn. He was anointed — this is probably the 'dew', since the anointing oil is compared elsewhere to dew (Ps. 133.3) — and installed as the Melchizedek priest. The description of Enoch's consecration as the angel high priest may have derived from these texts, or may be an independent witness to the ritual. Either way, it shows how the consecration was imagined in the time of Jesus. Enoch rose up through the heavens until he stood before the throne, where the archangel Michael removed his earthly clothing, anointed him with perfumed myrrh oil that was like dew, and then vested him in garments of divine glory.[49] Enoch knew that he had been trans-formed into an angel (2 Enoch 22.8–10), which means that he was

---

[48] For example, A. Bentzen *Messias-Moses Redivivus-Menschensohn*, Eng. trans. *King and Messiah*, London: Lutterworth Press, 1955.

[49] Aaron's vestments were specifically 'garments of holiness for glory and for glory' (Exod. 28.2). Both Hebrew words mean the divine glory: the first, *kbd*, occurs in e.g. Exod. 24.16, the glory on Sinai; Exod. 40.34, the glory in the tabernacle; Ezek. 1.28, the glory in human form that left the temple; Ps. 26.8, the glory that dwells in the temple. The second word, *tp'rt*, is the glory as in Ps. 89.17, the glory of their strength; Ps. 96.6, the glory and strength of the LORD; Isa. 60.7, the house of the LORD's glory; Isa. 63.15, the habitation of your glory; Isa. 64.11, the house of our holiness and glory.

resurrected (cf. Luke 20.36, where Jesus deems angels, sons of God and the resurrected as equivalent terms). Isaiah knew that the angels sang when the divine son was born: 'To us a child is born, to us a son is given, and the government will be upon his shoulder, and his name will be called Wonderful Counsellor, Mighty God, Everlasting Father, Prince of Peace' (Isa. 9.6). Some Greek texts gave not four names but one: he shall be called 'the Angel of Great Counsel'. Then the firstborn emerged from heaven, and all the angels were told to worship him as he came to bring judgement to his enemies and atonement for the land of his people. This was the theophany of the Cherubic hymn.

EUCHARIST AND ATONEMENT.

Memories of the original Day of Atonement in the temple shaped the Eucharistic liturgies. How and where these traditions had been preserved is not known, but there are too many correspondences for this to be coincidence. Limiting the setting to Passover and a domestic scene offers no obvious basis for the ideas of atonement and resurrection, nor for the theophanic procession as the LORD emerges from heaven. Imagining the early Eucharist as re-presenting the covenant sacrifice that put away sins and led to the judgement and renewal of the creation fits better with the available evidence. It explains how a human sacrifice — albeit represented by goats — was part of the temple cult. It also addresses the assumption made by Dillistone in his influential book *The Christian Understanding of Atonement*: 'From the New Testament there come hints, suggestions, even daring affirmations of a comprehensive cosmic reconciliation.' Since he doubted this could have come from Hebrew thought, he concluded: 'It was not until early Christian witnesses found themselves confronted by pagan systems in which a full theory of cosmic redemption played a prominent part that the effect of the work of Christ upon the cosmos began to receive serious consideration.'[50] The eternal covenant renewed on the Day of Atonement accounts for all this. It explains the sequence in the Book of Revelation, which must, surely, be a description of Christian worship. The creatures around the throne — in temple tradition these were called the cherubim (Ezek. 10.20) — sing 'Holy, Holy, Holy,' and give thanks for the glory of the Creator (Rev. 4.8–11). After the Lamb

---

[50] F. W. Dillistone, *The Christian Understanding of Atonement*, Philadelphia: Westminster Press, 1968, p. 47.

has been enthroned, they sing a new, that is a renewing, song, and the whole creation joins in the hymn of praise (Rev. 5.6–14). This is why the Sanctus — 'Holy, Holy, Holy, Lord God of Hosts, Heaven and earth are full of your glory' — is part of the eucharistic prayer.

As early as the Letter of Barnabas, the Day of Atonement was being used to explain why Jesus drank the sour wine as he died (Matt. 27.48; Mark 15.36; John 19.30). He was preparing himself to be the Day of Atonement sin offering. Now the Letter of Barnabas is attributed to the Levite from Cyprus (Acts 4.36), and it certainly shows considerable knowledge of the Old Testament and of temple customs, some of which differ from those known in other sources. It explains how it was possible for Christians to 'drink blood', even if theirs was only a symbolic drinking. There is a passage in the Mishnah which suggests that if the Day of Atonement fell on a Friday, some priests consumed raw the goat offered as the sin offering (Mishnah Menaḥoth 11.5), which seems to contradict the ruling that no blood could be consumed. Barnabas mentions a similar custom, but with more detail, and quotes a text that is not found in our present Old Testament: 'And what does it say in the prophet? "Let them eat of the goat which is offered for their sins at the fast, and, note this carefully, let all the priests but nobody else, eat of its inward parts unwashed and with vinegar"' (Barn. 7). When Jesus drank the sour wine, Barnabas explained, he was preparing himself to be that Day of Atonement sacrifice, to be eaten by the priests. 'When I am about to offer my body for the sins of this new people of mine, you will be giving me gall and vinegar to drink. That is why you shall be the only ones to eat, while the people of Israel are fasting and lamenting in sackcloth and ashes' (Barn. 7).

This remarkable quotation[51] not only links the crucifixion to the Day of Atonement, but says that Christians are the new priesthood, since they consume the sin offering and thus bear the sins, just as the priests consume the inward parts. According to the Old Testament, the rule for the Day of Atonement had been that 'the LORD's portion' was burned on the altar whilst the rest of the carcase was burned outside the desert camp or temple (Lev. 4.8–12; Lev. 16.23–7; Mishnah Yoma 7.6). The rule for other atonement sacrifices had been that the priests ate the offering in order to bear the sin and make atonement, if the blood of that offering had *not* been taken into the holy of holies (Lev. 10.16–20). The context

---

[51] It is part of the New Testament in the fourth century Sinai Codex, so must have been of considerable importance in the early Church.

here suggests a debate within the high priesthood about atonement procedure. Clearly, there was more than one set of rules for the sacrifices. There is confusion over the two goats for the Day of Atonement sacrifice: both being described as the sin offering (Lev. 16.5), but elsewhere distinguished as one for a sin offering and one as the sin offering of atonement (Num. 29.11). Eating the central part of the sin offering (that is, the LORD's portion, 'bloody and unwashed') was how the Church remembered the Day of Atonement, and linked the vinegar offered to Jesus and the vinegar mixed with the LORD's portion before it was eaten by the priests. This explains the otherwise difficult commandment of Jesus — to consume, albeit symbolically, his blood. There may be a memory of this practice surviving in the Orthodox Church, where the central portion of the loaf is removed during the celebration of the Eucharist, and mixed with wine in the chalice. Whatever the age of this custom, in the fourth century CE, the central portion of the sacrifice, mixed with wine, was described and prescribed as the words of Jesus in the New Testament.

Strangest of all must be the special ritual performed by the mediaeval popes in the Lateran basilica on Maundy Thursday. Anyone visiting Rome in the Middle Ages would have been told of the temple relics in the Lateran. The high altar was no more than a case for the ark of the covenant, and it also housed the seven temple candlesticks, the rod of Moses and the rod of Aaron, and the tablets of the ten commandments. During the Mass of Maundy Thursday, the cardinals removed the table, the *mensa*, of the altar, leaving the Pope to celebrate alone on the hollow altar which was said to be the ark. He used a relic of the blood of Christ. There is some evidence for this unusual celebration as early as the seventh century. This means that the Pope marked Maundy Thursday with the ritual of the Day of Atonement, blood upon the ark in the holy of holies. The difference was the Christian dispensation, when there was no longer a temple veil, and so the Pope performed his ritual in full view of all the congregation. A sermon of Pope Innocent III, about 1200 CE, made it quite clear what was happening: 'In this manner he is commemorating that the high priest once a year went into the holy of holies with blood.'[52] The origin of the Eucharist in mediaeval Rome was remembered as the Day of Atonement.

---

[52] See S. de Blaauw, 'The solitary celebration of the supreme pontiff. The Lateran basilica as the new temple in the mediaeval liturgy of Maundy Thursday', in *Omnes Circumadstantes*, ed. C. Caspers and M. Schneiders, Kampen: Kok Pharos, 1994, pp. 120–143.

Chapter 8

BREAD AND WISDOM

He took bread and when he had given thanks he broke it and gave it to them saying,
'This is my body.'

Luke 22.19

Bread is the common element in the various forms of the Eucharist: with bread then wine, or with wine and then bread, the Emmaus supper when the disciples recognized the risen LORD as he broke bread, and Thomas's Eucharist in India, where there was only bread. 'Breaking bread' was probably the earliest description of the Eucharist (e.g. Acts 2.46; 20.7). According to the New Testament, the bread was 'my body' and 'in remembrance'. At the Last Supper, Jesus took bread, blessed it, broke it, gave it to his disciples to eat and said: 'This is my body' (Matt. 26.26; Mark.14.22; Luke 22.19; 1 Cor. 11.24). Then, according to Matthew, Mark and Paul (1 Cor. 11.25), he gave the covenant cup. Justin also described the cup after the bread, although he made no mention of covenant (*Apology* 1.66). This sequence — bread then cup — has passed into Christian liturgy as the essential form of the Eucharist. Other ancient sources are different, for example the earlier texts of Luke have a cup *before* the bread without mentioning the covenant, and no covenant cup afterwards. The words 'This is my body' are found in all the sources, but 'broken/given for you' and 'do this in remembrance of me' are only in Paul (1 Cor. 11.24) and the longer Luke (Luke 22.19). John implies 'the body' when the miracle of the loaves was followed by the discourse on the flesh and blood of the Son of man (John 6.53), which was the new manna, the bread from heaven. The Didache, however, did not mention 'the body'. 'My body' and 'my remembrance' may have been unique to Jesus with no association other than the Last Supper, or they may have been building on and transforming an existing custom. There is little hard evidence, only glimpses and allusions. We can only speculate.

The early witnesses that do not mention the covenant cup include the Codex Bezae and several Old Latin texts. This raises important questions about the Eucharist, since the Codex Bezae is now thought to represent a very early text tradition, 'written at a time when there were still people who had known Jesus and the first generations of his disciples, and who knew the difficulties they faced within Judaism ...'[1] Since Luke's addressee, Theophilus, is now thought to be the high priest who served between 37 and 41 CE,[2] the question is: why was the cup that represented atonement not mentioned? Luke has no teaching about atonement, as is well known, but did he avoid atonement teaching because he was writing for a high priest? Or was it the sensitive matter of consuming 'blood'? Matthew specified which covenant was intended at the Last Supper precisely because he was writing for Christians of Jewish origin.[3] Since he did not specify 'which' bread was intended, it must have been clear to his Jewish Christians what was meant by 'my body'. For Luke's community, the bread was the only symbolic element in the meal: he knew a Eucharist without covenant blood. The words over the cup *before* supper (Luke 22.18) are part of the words over the covenant cup *after* supper in other accounts (Matt. 22.29; Mark 14.25): '... from now on I shall not drink of the fruit of the vine until the Kingdom of God comes.' A special cup *before* the bread is the order implied in one of Paul's references (1 Cor. 10.16), and is prescribed in the Didache: 'Begin with the chalice ... then over the broken bread say ...' (Didache 9). The order of the elements may have been variable, but an account of the Last Supper, such as the early Lucan text, that omits all reference to any covenant cup is a great problem, and serves to emphasize the importance of the bread. In the Acts of Thomas there are several accounts of a Eucharist after baptism using only bread, and described in various ways: 'breaking bread', with no cup mentioned (A.T. 27); or 'the Eucharist of the holy body and blood', with only bread used even though it represented the body and blood (A.T. 49); or just bread and water (A.T. 121); or bread alone as 'the bread of life' (A.T. 133). What, then, did the bread signify, that it could stand alone as a Eucharist?

---

[1] J. Ruis-Camps and J. Read-Heimerdinger, *The Message of Acts in Codex Bezae*, London: T&T Clark, 2006, p. 1.

[2] R. Anderson, 'À la recherche de Théophile', in *Saint Luc, évangéliste et historien* (Dossiers d' Archéologie 279 [2002–3] pp. 64–71.

[3] See above, p. 173.

Which Bread?

The Last Supper has usually been understood as a Passover meal, where Jesus took the bread and wine on the table and gave them a new meaning for his disciples. This could explain 'the remembrance', since Passover was a memorial, *zkrwn*, (Exod 12.14; 13.9), a word used elsewhere, for example for the bronze covering of the altar to 'remind' Israel that only Aaron's family could be priests (Num. 16.40), or for the standing stones to remind Israel how they crossed the Jordan (Josh. 4.7). Each man was obliged to consume the Passover lamb, the unleavened bread and the bitter herbs, and to consider that he himself had come out of Egypt (Mishnah Pesaḥim 10.5). If the Last Supper was a Passover, the words of institution could have developed from the special blessings for that meal. The sacrifice of Isaac, remembered at Passover,[4] was another 'memorial', when the Lord was asked to remember the binding of Isaac. The broken ' body' could have been an allusion to Isaac.

Another possibility is that the bread after the meal was the *afikomen*. The Passover was the night when the Messiah was expected to appear,[5] and the custom after the meal was to eat the *afikomen*, a word that first appears in the Mishnah (Mishnah Pesaḥim 10.8), but whose meaning is much disputed. Clearly Greek in form, it is thought to represent *aphikomenos*, 'the one who comes', and so to represent the expected Messiah. This suggestion was set out by Daube, an Orthodox Jewish scholar, but he assumed that such a custom must have existed in Jesus' time, in order to make sense of the Eucharist that was developed from the Passover meal: 'The institution of the Eucharist as recorded in the New Testament pre-supposes a ritual essentially ... like that of "The Coming One" ... Had not ritual of the kind preserved in the Jewish Passover Eve service existed, and had Jesus suddenly produced a cake of unleavened bread and said of it, "This is my body", his disciples — to put it mildly — would have been perplexed.'[6] Such an interpretation of the bread would explain Paul's words: 'For as often as you eat this bread and drink this cup, you proclaim the Lord's death until he comes' (1 Cor. 11.26), and it could explain 'my body'.

Since, however, John's account of holy week makes it unlikely that the Last Supper was a Passover, or even that the Eucharist was

[4] See above, p. 27.
[5] See above, p. 26.
[6] D. Daube, 'He That Cometh', lecture given in St Paul's Cathedral, London, October 1966, published by the Council for Christian-Jewish Understanding.

instituted at the Last Supper, other bread imagery may be relevant to the origin of the Eucharist. The bread eaten at the Last Supper was described in the Synoptic Gospels as 'bread', *artos*, not unleavened bread, *azumos*, but this does not necessarily indicate that the Last Supper was not a Passover. Most cereal offerings in the temple were unleavened, except certain types of peace offering and the wheat loaves offered at Pentecost (Lev. 7.13; 23.17), and so *artos* could imply unleavened Passover bread even if 'unleavened' is not mentioned in the immediate context. The bread at an ordination, for example, was unleavened, but was described simply as 'bread', *artos* (Lev. 8.31). More significant is John's calendar for holy week: if the crucifixion was on the eve of Passover (John 19.14), the Last Supper could not have been a Passover. Furthermore, there are no references to eating the Passover lamb, nor to the bitter herbs which were obligatory. It has been suggested that Luke 22.15–16 expresses an unfulfilled wish: 'I have earnestly desired to eat this Passover [but this is not to be] …, for I tell you I shall not eat it until it is fulfilled in the Kingdom of God.' In other words, the next Passover Jesus would eat with his friends would be the feast in the Kingdom.[7]

There were other communal meals which may explain the symbolism of the bread. The Therapeuts[8] assembled to hear their president expound the Scriptures, and then they sang hymns before sharing a frugal meal of leavened bread and herb-seasoned salt. This was to distinguish their food from the shewbread, which was unleavened bread set out with pure salt, and was reserved for the highest rank of priests. Philo's account implies that the Therapeuts were a priestly group, but not high-priestly (*Contemplative Life* 81–2). This community of men and women wore white robes, ate no meat and drank only water; the Therapeuts lived in the state required of priests when they offered sacrifices (73–4). Most of the women were unmarried, having chosen rather to be impregnated by spiritual rays in order to behold the truths of Wisdom (68). The Essenes were a similar group, whose new members were not allowed to share the common meal until they had served three years' probation and sworn 'tremendous oaths' (Josephus, *War* 2.139). The Messianic Rule from Qumran describes a ritual meal with the Messiah, when bread and wine are blessed, but the words of the blessing have not survived

---

[7] First suggested by F. C. Burkitt, *Journal of Theological Studies* ix (1908) pp. 569–72.

[8] See above p. 8.

(1QSa II). Another suggestion is that the Last Supper was friends meeting in a private house for religious discussion and a meal on the eve of Sabbath or a festival, as had become the custom in Jesus' time. John describes a meeting of friends (John 15.14: 'I have called you friends'), and so Jesus' farewell discourse could have been his teaching at a such a gathering immediately before Passover. In these *kiddush* ceremonies, the cup was offered first, then the bread, the order in the original Luke and the Didache. The words of institution would then have developed from the blessings of the *kiddush*.[9]

Perhaps the 'bread as body' represented the flesh of the sin offering, the body of the goat that was consumed by the priests on the Day of Atonement. The distinction between body and blood in the Eucharist implies the two elements of a temple sacrifice, where the blood and the carcase were treated separately. Having bread to represent the sacrifice would accord with the vegetarian lifestyle of the Therapeuts, who, in the fourth century CE were remembered as the forerunners of Christian monks (Eusebius, *Church History* 2.17). The Letter of Barnabas was emphatic that this custom of eating the flesh of the sin offering was the reason for Jesus drinking sour wine before he died (Matt. 27.48; Mark 15.36; John 19.29–30) — to prepare himself as the holiest portion of the sacrifice which had to be eaten raw with sour wine (Barn. 7).

Had the Last Supper been a 'temple' rite, albeit in a private house, this could also explain the foot washing. Any priest serving in the temple area had to immerse himself as purification each day, before beginning his duties (Mishnah Tamid 1.1-2), but a further sanctification was needed before he entered the temple itself: he had to wash his hands and feet. The temple complex became increasingly holy as one approached the centre, and so the great hall was second only to the holy of holies: 'the holy place [i.e. the great hall] is still more holy, for none may enter therein with hands and feet unwashed' (Mishnah Kelim 1.9). Holiest of all was the holy of holies, which only the high priest could enter. Jesus' words to Peter resemble the temple regulation: 'He who has bathed does not need to wash except for his feet' (John 13.10). This suggests a temple context for the bread of the Last Supper, a food received by priests in the temple. The obvious allusion is to the Bread of the Presence: 'every Sabbath day ... Aaron and his sons shall eat it in a holy place, since it is for him a most holy

---

[9] Oesterley, pp. 167–92 summarizes the work of various scholars who propose this.

portion ...' The Bread of the Presence was also a 'memorial' (Lev. 24.5–9).

The Fourth Gospel encoded Jesus' teaching about the bread in the feeding miracle, which was one of the signs that Jesus was the Messiah, the Son of God. The crowds declared Jesus to be the promised prophet and tried to make him king (John 6.14–15; 20.30–31). Jesus then taught about the food that 'endures to eternal life' (John 6.27) and about the Bread of God 'which comes down from heaven and gives life to the world' (John 6.33), finally declaring himself to be the bread of life [or the living bread] (John 6.35). Jesus contrasted himself with the manna, which came from heaven but did not give eternal life (John 6.48–50). The Jews did not understand, and asked how Jesus could give his flesh to be eaten, and the eucharistic teaching that followed used the terms 'flesh' and 'blood' not 'body' and 'blood'. John may have been reflecting accurately the Hebrew usage, where 'flesh', *baśar*, was the usual word for the human body. Thus the holy oil was not to be put on the *bodies* of [ordinary] men (Exod. 30.32); the high priest had linen garments on his *body* (Lev. 6.10; 16.4); the leper washed his *body* as part of the ritual to recognize that he was cured (Lev. 14.9). Discussing the precise equivalent in Hebrew for the Greek *soma*, body, Barr observed: 'It is notorious that classical Hebrew has no such word, except marginally. Only later Hebrew, the usage of the Hellenistic period, develops one.'[10] It seems that the Synoptic Gospels and Paul transposed into Greek ideas the original eucharistic words of Jesus, which were preserved by John as *flesh* and blood. Centuries earlier, and so the usage could have changed, Job used 'flesh' in the sense of his physical body: 'without my flesh I shall see God' (Job 19.26), meaning 'after I have left my human body'. The bread of the Eucharist, then, represented the LORD in the flesh — the familiar term 'in*car*nate'. This is another possible explanation of 'my body'.

The Didache was very different, prescribing: 'Over the particles of bread say: "We give thanks to thee our Father for the life and knowledge thou hast made known to us through thy servant Jesus ... As this broken bread, once dispersed over the hills, was brought together and became one loaf, so may thy Church be brought together from the ends of the earth into thy Kingdom"' (Didache 9). This seems to be an entirely different tradition: life and knowledge

---

[10] J. Barr, *The Garden of Eden and the Hope of Immortality*, Minneapolis: Fortress Press, 1993, p. 112.

made known through Jesus and associated with the bread, and the joining together of what had been scattered. The bread scattered on the hills alludes to the feeding miracle, and the prayer to become one loaf is reminiscent of Paul's words: 'We who are many are one body, for we all partake of the one bread' (1 Cor. 10.17). Ignatius wrote of 'the one common breaking of bread, the medicine of immortality and the sovereign remedy by which we escape death and live in Christ Jesus for evermore' (Ephesians 20). The motifs here are not sacrifice and atonement, as they were with the cup of wine, nor Passover, nor body and memorial, but life, knowledge and unity, which are Wisdom motifs.

In the wordplay characteristic of temple tradition, the life and knowledge of the Didache prayer could have implied a living body, since the antitype would have been a corpse associated with death and foolishness. This pairing does work as Hebrew wordplay. The root, *nbl*, has several distinct meanings: foolishness, lewdness, withering, drooping, or being a corpse. What seem to us distinct meanings may not have been so to the ancient speakers of Hebrew: folly, *nᵉbalah*, and dead body, *nᵉbelah*, both describe the state without Wisdom. Isaiah had used similar imagery when he described the whole creation collapsed and *withered* — the same root — because the eternal covenant had been broken (Isa. 24.4-6). When the Didache linked life, knowledge and becoming one loaf, this looks like covenant renewal expressed in terms of Wisdom and bread: Jesus the living bread who gave life, knowledge and unity. The feeding miracle was the breaking and giving of the bread, but the Eucharist — 'We who are many are one body for we all partake of the one bread' (1 Cor. 10.17) — showed that the pieces remained One. This is another Wisdom motif: 'Although being One she is able to do all things, and remaining in herself she renews all things, and in every generation, passing into holy souls, she makes them friends of God and prophets' (Wisdom of Solomon 7.27).

The Gospel of Philip has preserved some important allusions to the sacraments. 'The LORD did everything in a mystery: a baptism and a chrism and a Eucharist and a redemption and a bridal chamber' (CG II.3.67). The washing and the anointing were two parts of the initiation; perhaps the Eucharist and redemption were also two parts of the one celebration: the redemption being the wine/blood, and the bread the Eucharist. Philip linked the mysteries to three stages of entering the temple: the holy place (the temple courtyard), the holy of the holy one (the great hall), and the holy of holies 'the place where the high priest entered alone' (CG II.3.69). The text is broken, but the correspondence seems to be: 'Baptism is the holy place' and 'baptism has the resurrection',[11] suggesting that baptism was the priestly washing in the temple court; then, logically, the mystery of the great hall would have been the Eucharist; and then 'the holy of the holy ones is the bridal chamber'. The Gospel of Philip, despite the broken text, seems to preserve a coherent temple scheme for the Christian sacraments, consistent with what we have deduced from other sources: the Christians were the new high priesthood, with a temple context for baptism, Eucharist and the final state of union implied by entering the holy of holies, the scene in Revelation 22.[12]

In the LORD's Prayer the Christian prayed for bread: 'Give us this day our daily bread' is the usual translation of Matthew 6.11.[13] The prayer was said three times a day, according to the Didache, and also by all the people immediately before receiving the bread and wine. Having prayed 'thy Kingdom come', they are unlikely to have been asking, at this point, for ordinary food. The 'daily' bread was the eucharistic bread. Now 'daily', *epiousios*, has always been a problem because the word is rare. Jerome (died 420 CE), knew the Hebrew Gospel in which the word was *mahar*, 'tomorrow':[14] 'Give us today the bread of tomorrow', and this is offered as an alternative translation by some English versions. Jerome rendered *epiousios* as *supersubstantialis*, a word he seems to have invented, which implies that it was supernatural bread. 'Tomorrow' had a special significance for the early Christians: it meant the great Sabbath rest, when the Son would return to establish the Kingdom and the true Sabbath begin. Barnabas explained that the six days of creation symbolized the eras of history, with the sixth day as the human era, and the seventh, the Sabbath, yet to come (Barnabas 15). The 'bread of tomorrow' was the Sabbath bread, the Bread of the Presence, or its Christian counterpart, the bread of the Kingdom.[15]

There were two temple practices exclusive to the high priests: entering the holy of holies to offer the blood on the Day of Atonement, and eating the Bread of the Presence each Sabbath. Now the community in the Damascus Document listed among 'the hidden things in which all Israel had gone astray' (that is, the malpractices

---

[11] See above p. 111.
[12] See below p. 232.
[13] Luke 11.3 has 'Give us each day ...'
[14] Jerome on Psalm 135, and Matt. 6.11.
[15] For detail see my book, *The Great High Priest*, pp. 101–2.

of second temple Jerusalem) the Sabbath and the Day of Fasting, i.e. the Day of Atonement (CD III, VI). Jesus took the high priestly rituals of these days — the Bread of the Presence and covenant blood — and it is entirely possible that he made them his own, since he was remembered as the Great High Priest. The 'Damascus' community also described themselves as 'men of the new covenant' (CD VIII) who, nevertheless, were restoring the ancient covenant with their ancestors (CD IV). Since the Eucharist was celebrated weekly, or even more frequently, one root of eucharistic practice is likely to lie in a weekly observance, and this indicates the Bread of the Presence. The high priest (by the time of Jesus it was all the priests) ate the Bread of the Presence each Sabbath, when fresh loaves were set out in the temple, and the loaves that had been there for a week were brought out and eaten (Lev. 24.8; Mishnah Menaḥoth 11.7).[16] It was described by the Targum of Onkelos as the most sacred of all the offerings (T.O. Lev. 24.5–9).

THE BREAD OF THE PRESENCE

The Bread of the Presence was the only cereal offering taken into the temple; the table for the bread was as holy as the ark, these being the only items in the tabernacle that were wrapped in three coverings for transport in the desert (Num. 4.5–8). The loaves were spread out[17] on the golden table, together with incense and wine (Exod. 25.29–30).[18] As with so many temple practices, nothing is said of the meaning, but there are enigmatic references to feasts in the temple, associated with theophany. The elders who saw the God of Israel on Sinai and then ate and drank is an encoded reference to temple practice (Exod. 24.11), as are the familiar words of Psalm 23: 'Thou preparest a table before me.' The Bread of the Presence was not 'consumed' by the LORD: no part of it was burned as an offering. The LORD had no need of food: 'If I were hungry, I would not tell you; for the world and all that is in

---

[16] There were twelve huge unleavened loaves, each measuring some 0.8m × 0.4m with projections 'horns' at the ends about 14 cm high, made from fine flour. They were baked within the temple area, and a special mould was used (Mishnah Menaḥoth 11.1–2).

[17] The AV and the RSV translate the word as 'row', Lev. 24.7, but 'spread out' was significant.

[18] The Greek says there was salt too, Lxx Lev. 24.7. There were golden 'cups' in Solomon's temple, 1 Kgs 7.50.

it is mine ... Offer to God a sacrifice of thanksgiving' (Ps. 50.12, 14). The Bread of the Presence was the LORD feeding his priests.

Paul, the longer texts of Luke, and Justin (*Apology* 1.66) say the bread was the remembrance, *anamnesis*, of Jesus, and retelling the story of the Last Supper became a central part of the eucharistic liturgy, just as retelling the story of the Exodus was central to Passover. This was not always so. The Didache does not mention the Last Supper, nor does the oldest form of the liturgy of Addai and Mari. What was this 'remembrance'? If, as seems likely, Jesus' words were not in Greek but in Hebrew or Aramaic, there is an interesting ambiguity. Underlying *anamnesis*, remembrance, must be a form derived from the root *zkr*, remember. There was a type of cereal offering known as the *'azkarah*, a word only found in priestly texts, and usually translated 'memorial offering' (e.g. Lev. 2.2, 9, 16; 24.7;[19] Num. 5.26). It always comprised frankincense, oil and cereals in the form of fine flour, roasted grain, or unleavened bread (Lev. 2.2, 4, 14). Some of the cereal and oil was burnt with the frankincense as a pleasing fragrance for the LORD; the rest became a most holy food for the high priests (Lev. 2. 3, 10).

But *zkr* has another meaning: 'invoke'. When David appointed Levites to serve before the ark, they had to *invoke*, to thank and to praise the LORD (1 Chron. 16.4). Moses was told the Name by which to *invoke* the LORD (Exod. 3.15). Thus too Psalm 6.5: 'In death there is no *invoking* thee, and in Sheol who can praise thee?' Psalms 38 and 70 both have the title 'for the *memorial* offering',[20] but they include such lines as: 'Make haste to help me' (Ps. 38.22) and 'Hasten to me O God' (Ps. 70.5), which suggest they were sung as invocations. It seems that the cereal offering was an invocation, and the most holy of all these offerings was the Bread of the Presence. Jesus' words over the bread 'in remembrance of me' may also have meant 'to invoke me'.

The biblical prescription for the Bread of the Presence is ambiguous and seems to say that the incense, rather than the bread, was the 'memorial' offering (Lev. 24.7), but the Targums (Onkelos and Neofiti), show that the bread itself was the 'memorial' offering. The special status of this bread was known in the time of Jesus, as can be seen in the way it was taken in and out of the temple. 'On the table of marble they laid the Bread of the Presence when it was brought in, and on the table of gold they laid it when it was brought out, since what

---

[19] The Lxx only uses *anamnesis* of the shewbread.
[20] In Ps. 38, the Greek has 'the memorial offering on the Sabbath'.

is holy must be raised and not brought down' (Mishnah Menaḥoth 11.7). The bread had acquired holiness whilst in the temple and could no longer be placed on a marble table: gold was the material of temple furnishings. Was the Bread the vehicle of the Presence? Malachi implied that the bread was the means of theophany: the LORD would not 'lift up his face/presence' on polluted bread (Mal. 1.9, translating literally).

The bread became a 'most holy food' for the high priests (Lev. 24.9). Now 'most holy' does not mean 'more holy than holy' — it means actively holy, able to impart holiness. Moses had to anoint the tabernacle furnishings 'that they may be most holy; whatever touches them will become holy' (Exod. 30.29). The most holy bread that the high priests ate imparted holiness to them. The bread was also an eternal covenant, and the command to eat was an eternal statute (Lev. 24.8–9). No other offering was designated 'an eternal covenant'. Since the Sabbath was itself an eternal covenant, marking the completion of the creation (Exod. 31.16–17), one possibility is that the Bread of the Presence set out and eaten each Sabbath was a memorial of the eternal covenant, the covenant which Jesus renewed with his blood.[21] Were the high priests being fed with the means to maintain the eternal covenant? As with so many temple practices, the surviving texts describe only the outward act, and do not give its meaning. There may, however, be a clue in the Hebrew text of Leviticus 24.9, which says, literally: 'And *she* shall be for Aaron and his sons, and they shall eat it [i.e. the bread].' Bread is usually a masculine noun in Hebrew, as here, 'it' being in the masculine form. 'She' does not refer to the loaf. The Samaritan text has another feminine form in this verse: 'for *she* is for him the most holy ...' rather than 'it is for him a most holy portion ...' What was feminine about the holy food that empowered the priests to maintain the covenant?

There were many differences between the teaching and practices of the first temple and the second, and one of these concerned the Bread of the Presence. Enoch described the second temple as a place where impure bread had been placed on the table before the holy of holies, the offering of sheep and shepherds who had lost their vision (1 Enoch 89.73–4). This bread must have been the Bread of the Presence as this was the only cereal offering taken into the temple. Malachi warned the priests of the second temple that they

---

[21] See above pp. 173–8.

had offered polluted bread,[22] such that the LORD would not 'lift up his face upon them and be gracious to them ...', quoting the high priestly blessing (Mal. 1.8–9; Num. 6.25–6). The bread was associated with the LORD appearing, just as the elders had feasted when the God of Israel appeared on Sinai. The disciples, to whom Jesus appeared 'in another form' (Mark 16. 12), recognized him at Emmaus when he broke the bread (Luke 24.30–31).[23] The words of Malachi (Mal. 1.11) were seen as a prophecy of the Eucharist: 'From the rising of the sun to its setting, my name is great among the nations, and in every place incense is offered to my name and a pure offering,'[24] was cited in Didache 14 and by Justin (*Trypho* 41). The early Church saw the eucharistic bread as the Bread of the Presence, and Cyril of Jerusalem, in the mid fourth century, still taught that the Bread of heaven had replaced the Bread of the Presence (*Catecheses* 22.5), replacing the impure bread of the second temple.

Bread 'of the Presence' is usually said to mean 'bread set out in the presence of the LORD', but this way of reading leads to some redundancies in the text, for example 'You shall set the Bread set out in the Presence in my presence always' (Exod. 25.30, translating literally). If, however, the Bread was the sign of the Presence, the means by which the LORD was present, much as Ezekiel distinguished between the heavenly reality and the visible form it took,[25] this would account for the special status of the bread. 'Presence' in Hebrew is the same word as 'face', a plural form *panim*, and there are several places where 'Presence' is used to mean the LORD himself. 'My Presence will go with you' (Exod. 33.14) was translated into Greek as 'I *myself* will go with you'; and 'He brought you out of Egypt with his own Presence' (Deut. 4.37) became 'He *himself* led you out.' Most emphatic was the clarification introduced into the Greek of Isaiah 63.9. The Hebrew has: 'The Angel of his Presence saved them', but the Greek has: 'Not an ambassador nor an angel, but *he himself* saved them.' Perhaps Bread of the Presence should be understood in the same way — the means whereby the divine was present.

'Invocation' over the bread, the bread acquiring holiness whilst it was in the temple, the bread imparting holiness to the priests,

---

[22] Hebrew and Greek both have 'bread' not 'food' as in some English versions.

[23] The Codex Bezae of Luke seems to preserve many original Jewish elements, see Reid Heimerdinger, op. cit. n. 1, p. 202. When the disciples recognized the LORD, it was at Oulammaous, the Lxx name for Luz, the original name for Bethel (Gen. 28.19). Luz means 'almond tree' and was associated with Wisdom.

[24] In the priestly texts, *minḥah* always means a cereal offering.

[25] See above pp. 150–1.

all these suggest that the origin of the eucharistic epiclesis is to be found in the invocation over the Bread of the Presence. Basil said the words of epiclesis were part of the unwritten tradition, i.e. the first temple tradition handed down from the apostles,[26] and the writings of the Jewish mystics who also preserved temple tradition suggest that invoking the Presence in the temple was central to the original cult. 'We can seriously consider the possibility that the temple service was conceived as inducing the presence of the Shekinah in the holy of holies.'[27] Such an idea is familiar in the Old Testament, but usually described differently. The glory of the LORD filled the tabernacle when it was completed (Exod. 40.34), and the glory, appearing as a cloud, also filled the temple when it was consecrated (1 Kings 8.10–11). Ezekiel, a priest, described the glory, and this presumably is what the other writers had in mind when they said that the glory filled the holy place. The glory appeared as a huge bright cloud, with a fiery heart in which Ezekiel saw the fourfold living Creature and the throne with the human likeness (Ezek. 1.1–28). When he received the vision of the future temple, he saw the glory of the LORD return (Ezek. 43.2–5).

The Psalmist prayed for the LORD to come (Pss. 38.21–2; 70.1, 5, the 'memorial offering' psalms), and the greatest blessing was to see the face of the LORD.[28] The tabernacle was built so that the LORD could dwell, *škn*, (whence shekinah) in the midst (Exod. 25.8) — but in what form? The Davidic king 'was' the LORD, sat on the throne of the LORD and was worshipped (1 Chron. 29.20, 23).[29] The high priest wore the Name of the LORD (Exod. 28.36), and the bread in the temple was known as the Bread of the Presence/Face. Perhaps Bishop Serapion in fourth century Egypt still knew this when he prayed with unmistakable echoes of the high priests and the shewbread: 'Let thy holy Logos come and dwell (*epidemesato*) upon this bread, that the bread may become the body of the Logos ... a medicine of life for the healing of every sickness, and for the strengthening of all advancement and virtue. Not for condemnation ... and not for censure or reproach.' Two generations earlier, the Christians in Syria had prayed with similar allusions: 'We offer ...

---

[26] See above p. 1.

[27] M. Idel, *Kabbalah. New Perspectives*, New Haven and London: Yale University Press, 1988, p. 168.

[28] See above, p. 1.

[29] The AV here gives an accurate rendering of the Hebrew, rather than a paraphrase.

this bread and this cup, giving thanks ... because you have made us worthy to stand before you as priests ... and we beseech you ... to send your holy Spirit on this sacrifice ... to show/declare/make plain (*apophene*) that this bread is the body of your Christ ... that they who partake may be strengthened in godliness.'[30]

The Bread of the Presence was 'spread out', which in Greek became *prothesis*: '[Moses] set out on the table the *set out* bread' (Exod. 40.23, Lxx 40.21). The bread could be simply the *prothesis* (Lxx Exod. 40.4). In the New Testament, the Bread of the Presence was 'the spreading out, *prothesis*, of the loaves (Heb. 9.2), and according to the Gospel of Philip, Jesus was called the Eucharist because he was the one spread out (CG II.3.63). Here 'spread out' is said to mean 'crucified', suggesting that an earlier usage was known but not fully understood. It was probably a reference to Jesus as the 'spread out' bread, in other words, the bread of the Eucharist was the Bread of the Presence. The same terminology, *prothesis*, passed into Christian liturgy for setting out the offerings, or for the place where the offering was set out, to the north of the altar. The table for the Bread of the Presence had been on the north side of the tabernacle/temple (Exod. 40.22).

WISDOM'S FOOD

One of the most important differences between the first temple and the second was the place of Wisdom. 'Josiah's reform' was not so favourably viewed by all who lived through it. The account in 2 Kings 23 tells how the temple vessels 'for Baal, for Asherah and for all the host of heaven' were removed and destroyed, how the Asherah was taken from the temple, burned, beaten to dust and cast over common graves; that is to say, it was utterly desecrated. Then the places where women had woven hangings for Asherah were broken down, places described in our present text as the houses of male prostitutes. The same consonants can be read as 'holy ones, angels', and so Josiah may have destroyed the shrines of the angels, part of the cult of Asherah.[31] Jeremiah has an account of the same events, but told rather differently. Refugees who had fled to Egypt after the destruction of Jerusalem in 586 BCE refused to accept what Jeremiah said: that the disaster had been caused by their sins (Jer. 44.16–20). It has been caused, they

---

[30] The Apostolic Constitutions Book 8.12 in F. E. Brightman, *Liturgies Eastern and Western*, Oxford: Clarendon Press, 1896, pp. 20–21.

[31] Cf 'Wisdom is the mother of the angels' (Gospel of Philip), CG II.3.63.

said, by abandoning the worship of the Queen of Heaven, for whom they had burned incense, poured out libations, and made loaves 'to represent her' (translating literally). She had protected her city, and since abandoning her, they said, 'we have lacked everything and have been consumed by the sword and by famine' (Jer. 44.18). There is a third account in 1 Enoch 93.8: just before the temple was burned, the priests lost their vision and abandoned Wisdom. The banished Queen of Heaven was Wisdom, represented by a tree-like object, the asherah, in all probability the original menorah, and by loaves. She gave vision to her priests.

Isaiah knew the Queen of heaven as the woman about to give birth to Immanuel (Isa. 7.14), the Virgin daughter of Zion who scorned the Assyrians when they came against her city (Isa. 37.22–3). Isaiah's contemporary Micah knew her as the mother of the great shepherd of Israel (Mic. 5.3–4), and as the daughter of Zion and the daughter of Jerusalem to whom the Kingdom would return (Mic. 4.8). She was the mother of the King, the Anointed One. Isaiah knew that her great tree had been felled, but that the royal seed was preserved in its stump. The mysterious words at the end of Isaiah's call vision condemn his people to living with what they had chosen — life without Wisdom. They would hear and not understand, see and not perceive (Isa. 6. 9–10) until she was restored to her land. 'Until great is the Deserted One in the midst of the land' is the other way to read 'Until the forsaken places are many in the midst of the land' (Isa. 6.12b). After Josiah's purge, the anointing oil was hidden (Babylonian Talmud Horayoth 12a), another way of saying that Wisdom had left the temple. Nobody was anointed, and so Wisdom had no children. Philo, giving 'the hidden meaning of the literal words', said that Wisdom, 'through whom the universe came into existence' was the 'mother of the high priest.' His head had been anointed with oil and so his mind had been illuminated with a brilliant light (*Flight* 108). According to the Gospel of the Hebrews, Jesus said that his mother was the Holy Spirit.[32] Origen also knew that the temple furnishings represented 'the secrets of mysterious Wisdom' (Homily 4, *On Numbers*).

Wisdom was remembered by the descendants of Jeremiah's refugees. Papyri from the fifth century BCE were found in the south of Egypt at Elephantine, records of a community that had been estab-

---

[32] See above p. 110.

lished there for over a century[33]. They came from Judea, offered only
cereals, incense and libations in their temple — there was no animal
sacrifice — and they had women's names among their divinities.
Marx has shown that the cereal offerings were originally a separate
system parallel to the blood offerings, but integrated with them when
the Pentateuch was compiled. The cereal offering took precedence
(or perhaps retained its precedence) over the blood offerings,[34]
which may explain why the Bread of the Presence was remembered
as the most sacred of all the offerings. If it had represented the bread
of the Queen of Heaven, this would explain why 'she' was given to the
priests as they ate the bread.

Centuries later, a Jew in Egypt wrote The Wisdom of Solomon.
Wisdom had instructed Solomon (Wisdom 7.22), and given him
immortality (8.13). She was the Holy Spirit (9.17), a spotless mirror
of the working of God (7.26). Another Wisdom book, The Wisdom
of ben Sira, depicts Wisdom as she was known in Judea, early in the
second century BCE. Much has been overwritten to ascribe to the Law
what had formerly been Wisdom imagery, but she is unmistakable:
she meets her devotee like a mother and a wife, she gives him the
bread of understanding and the water of wisdom (ben Sira 15.2-3).
'Those who eat me will hunger for more, and those who drink me
will thirst for more' (ben Sira 24.21). This is very like the Eucharist
of bread and water in The Acts of Thomas 121, when he invoked 'the
compassionate mother, the one that reveals the hidden mysteries ...'
before breaking bread at dawn and seeing a human figure appear
(A.T. 27).

Although it is not customary to look for her, and therefore not
to recognize her, Wisdom and her bread are mentioned in the Old
Testament. Wisdom built her house of seven pillars and summoned
the simple (the word can also mean deceived) and those lacking
sense. Her food gave wisdom. She offered bread and wine, so that
her disciples could leave those who had been deceived, live, and
walk straight/be happy in the way of discernment (Prov. 9.1, 4–6).
The final verb with the two meanings is *'šr*, wordplay on Asherah,
one of the names of Wisdom. The Greek has an extra line: 'Leave
foolishness so that you may reign for ever....' Wisdom's bread, then,

---

[33] A. E. Cowley, *Aramaic Papyri of the Fifth Century BC*, Oxford: Clarendon Press,
1923.

[34] This is the thesis of A. Marx, *Les Offrandes Végétales dans l'Ancien Testament*, Leiden:
Brill, 1994.

gave wisdom, understanding, life and kingship. Later tradition linked the tabernacle and the Bread of the Presence to Wisdom: 'The House of Wisdom is the tabernacle, and Wisdom's table is the Bread of the Presence and wine (Leviticus Rabbah XI.9). This was also the bread and wine that Melchizedek — representing the older priesthood in Jerusalem — offered to Abraham (Gen. 14.18). When he instructed Abraham in the priesthood, he gave him the Bread of the Presence, and the wine for libations, and there follows a reference to Wisdom's table in Proverbs 9 (Genesis Rabbah XLIII.6). Presumably this was the bread and wine that the angels gave to Levi when he was made a high priest (T. Levi 8.5).

What might have been said to those who received the bread that represented the Wisdom, the Queen of Heaven? 'Take, eat, this is myself that I am giving to you?' And what might have been said to the high priests as they received the Bread of the Presence? We can only speculate, but Clement of Rome, at the end of the first century CE, wrote in words reminiscent of Wisdom's bread: 'Through [Jesus Christ the High Priest] we can look up to the highest heaven and see, as in a mirror, the peerless perfection of his face, through Him the eyes of our hearts are opened, through him our dim and clouded understanding unfolds like a flower to the light; for through Him the LORD permits us to taste the Wisdom of eternity' (1 Clem. 36). Bishop Serapion prayed at the Eucharist: 'Make us living men ... Give us Holy Spirit that we may be able to tell forth and enunciate thy unspeakable mysteries'; 'Make us wise ... by the participation of the body and the blood.' The prayer over the bread in the Didache was: 'We give thanks to thee our Father, for the life and knowledge thou hast made known to us through thy servant Jesus' (Didache 9). In the New Testament, the 'Hebrews' were warned about apostasy: 'For it is impossible to restore again to repentance those who have once been enlightened, who have tasted the heavenly gift, and have become partakers of the Holy Spirit, and have tasted the goodness of the Word of God and the powers of the age to come' (Heb. 6.4–5). The bread of Wisdom was part of the earliest teaching, and the Orthodox Church still reads Proverbs 9 on Maundy Thursday, linking the Last Supper and Wisdom's table. The ikon of the communion of the apostles shows Wisdom as the host.

Proverbs reveals more about Wisdom. She had been rejected by her people and warned them what would happen if they did not return to her, another reference to Josiah's temple purge. Her name was a plural form — 'Wisdoms' — a sure sign of divinity (Prov. 1.20), and she longed to pour out her Spirit on her people (Prov. 1.23). But the simple/deceived loved being that way; fools hated knowledge, and would eat the fruit of their own choosing. 'The simple are killed by their turning away, and the complacence of fools destroys them' (Prov. 1.32). In contrast, 'O the *happiness* of the man who finds Wisdom' (Prov. 3.13). She is more precious than silver, gold or jewels, she gives a long life of peace, pleasantness, prosperity and honour. She is the tree of life to those who grasp her; 'those who hold her fast are called *happy/on the straight path*.' (Prov. 3.13–18). 'Happiness' is from *'šr*, wordplay on Asherah, and so this poem begins and ends with allusions to the banished Queen. She was the tree of life — presumably this was her symbol — and the *asherah* desecrated by Josiah must have been the tree of life. The 'fools' had been deceived into eating other fruit.

Another account of Josiah's purge is the story of the Garden of Eden. In Jewish tradition, the temple represented the Garden of Eden, and Adam was the first high priest.[35] The human pair lost their temple when they rejected the tree of life and chose instead the fruit of the other tree. The story implies that the fruit of the tree of life was intended as their food, since only one tree was forbidden (Gen. 2.16–17). The risen LORD promised to faithful Christians that they would eat again from the tree of life (Rev. 2.7; 22.14), in other words, they would eat the food of Wisdom and return to the true temple. A damaged piece of the Gospel of Philip contrasts the two trees and their fruit. 'The one bears animals, the other bears men' is fairly clear, and the following passage seems to say that because Adam ate from the wrong tree, his descendants were also animals (CG II.3.71). Now 'animals' and 'men' in temple tradition indicate respectively humans and angels. In other words, had Adam eaten from the tree of life he would have been an angel, but, having eaten from the other tree, as the Genesis story relates, he became mortal. The Gospel of Philip later explains that the tree of the knowledge of good and evil is the Law (CG II.3.74), implying that the tree of life was contrasted with the Law, and represented the better way. Exactly the opposite appears in Deuteronomy, which was extolling the Law and represented the position of those who purged the temple: the Law of Moses was to become Israel's Wisdom; that is, to replace it (Deut. 4.6).

Wisdom's tree and its fruit appear also in 1 Enoch. On his second heavenly journey, Enoch saw a fragrant tree, the source of long life,

---

[35] See my book, *The Revelation of Jesus Christ*, Edinburgh: T&T Clark, 2000, pp. 19–20.

standing by the throne of the Great Holy One on a mountain in the south (1 Enoch 24.1–25.7). The archangel Michael, who was his guide, explained that after the great judgement, the tree would be transplanted northwards in a holy place beside the house of the LORD and its fruit would be given to the chosen ones. This was the tree of life, surviving in a community to the south of Jerusalem. On another journey to the east, Enoch passed over the Persian Gulf and saw a second tree, which his angel guide, Raphael, said was the forbidden tree from which Adam and Eve had eaten (1 Enoch 32.1–5). These heavenly journeys distinguished between two communities: the Jews in Babylon who had the tree of the knowledge of good and evil, and the Jews of Egypt who had the tree of life that would be restored to the temple to feed the chosen ones. In other words, Wisdom would return to the temple to feed her children. This is the final scene in Revelation: the tree of life by the throne in the holy of holies (Rev. 22.1–5), and its fruit promised to the faithful (Rev. 2.7). Narsai knew this: 'With food the evil one in the beginning slew us and made us slaves; and by food the Creator has now willed to quicken us.' (Narsai, Homily 21)[36].

The bread of the Eucharist gave Wisdom, life and knowledge. Barnabas prayed: 'May God, the Lord of all the world, give you wisdom, understanding, discernment and knowledge of his ordinances ...' (Barn 21). Jesus joined Bread of the Presence to the blood of the Day of Atonement, thus combining the two roles of the high priest. The blood restored the covenant and the bread of Wisdom maintained it. The Gospel of Philip knew the distinction between the two elements of the Eucharist and named them separately: they were redemption and Eucharist, the blood and the bread (CG II.3.67), and it was the invocation of the Presence in the temple that was the origin of the eucharistic epiclesis.

---

[36] *The Liturgical Homilies of Narsai*, tr. R. H. Connolly, Cambridge: Cambridge University Press, 1909, p. 58.

Chapter 9

MUSIC AND UNITY

*Be filled with the Spirit, addressing one another in psalms and hymns and spiritual
songs, singing and making melody to the LORD with all your heart.*

Ephesians 5.19.

Music had an important place in worship, according to one memory
of the ancient temple. The Chronicler said that David appointed
Asaph and his brethren as musicians to serve continuously before the
ark, even before the temple was built (1 Chron. 16.4–6; 37–42). When
the temple was consecrated, all the temple musicians robed in white
linen stood to the east of the altar, accompanied by 120 priests with
trumpets. They praised and thanked the LORD 'with one voice', and
then the Glory of the LORD filled the temple. 'Praise' here is the word
that also means 'shine', and it seems that the music made the Glory
visible in the temple.[1] When Hezekiah restored the temple, a huge
sacrifice was offered to mark the re-consecration, and the temple
musicians played until the burnt offering was consumed (2 Chron.
29.25–30). These same events were recorded by the Deuteronomist,
but he had a very different view. He did not mention the appointment
of musicians (2 Sam. 6.16–9), nor the music at the dedication of the
temple (1 Kings 8.1–11), nor the music at Hezekiah's re-consecration
of the temple (2 Kings 18.1–4). The Deuteronomist also denied the
vision of God (Deut. 4.12).

These two — the music and the vision — are connected, and
they seem to represent what the Deuteronomists sought to deny.
Christianity was clearly rooted in the non-Deuteronomic strand of
Israel's religion, and so the music and the vision were important in
the Church. The only throne vision that does not mention music is
the one like a son of man on the clouds in Daniel 7: Ezekiel saw the
throne and heard the voice of wings, like the voice of many waters,

---

[1] See above p. 142.

the voice of Shaddai (Ezek. 1.24; cf. 10.5); and John saw the throne and heard the Sanctus and the praise of the Creator (Rev. 4.8–11). Isaiah saw the LORD enthroned and heard the seraphim praising him: 'Holy, Holy, Holy is the LORD of Hosts, the whole earth is full of his Glory' (Isa. 6.3). Once he had heard the song, Isaiah could see the Glory of the LORD throughout the creation. The Glory and the music were one, and the voices that invoked the Glory were as one: Gregory of Nazianzus would write: 'The angelic choirs sing praise to God with psalms ... celebrating with a common voice from many mouths',[2] and singing 'with one voice' became an important element in Christian worship, representing the unity of the Christian community, but also their union with the angels and the harmony of the creation. Basil of Caesarea described the music of the monasteries of Pontus: 'What is more blessed than to imitate here on earth the chorus of angels?'[3] Perhaps the priests in the Jerusalem temple joined in the Sanctus — we cannot know — but this may be what the Psalmist meant when he declared that the LORD was enthroned on the praises of Israel (Ps. 22.3). The Church was to teach that singing with the angels was a sign of *theosis*, transformation into an angel. 'In this light, the soul, now equal in dignity with the holy angels ... and having learned to praise in concert with them ... is brought to the adoption of similar likeness by grace ...',[4] and there is no doubt that the Jerusalem priests were described as angels.

The Ascension of Isaiah, a Jewish text expanded by Christians, described Isaiah's ascent to stand before the throne. In the first heaven Isaiah saw two groups of angels, either side of the throne, singing alternately, but 'they all sang praises with one voice' (Asc. Isa.7.15). In the seventh heaven he saw the righteous people of the past, all praising with one voice, and he joined in their song. Then the angels approached and joined their worship (Asc. Isa. 9.28). The praise sent up from the six lower heavens was 'not only heard but seen' (Asc. Isa. 10.5).[5] Ignatius of Antioch knew this angel world, and could even have known this text, as he is said to have introduced this style of singing into the churches. 'Ignatius, who had conversed familiarly with the apostles themselves, saw a vision of angels hymning

---

[2] Gregory Nazianzus, *Carmina* 2.1.1.180, PG 37.991.

[3] Letter 2, PG 32.225.

[4] Maximus the Confessor, *Mystagogy* 23.

[5] The two mighty angels that took Enoch up to heaven were 'clothed in singing', 2 Enoch 1.5.

alternate chants to the Holy Trinity; after which he introduced this mode of singing ... into the Antiochian church, whence it was transmitted by tradition to all the other churches.'[6] It was this style of singing that Egeria heard when she visited Jerusalem in holy week in 386 CE. 'The pre dawn hymns and psalms are sung in alternate chant as too are the antiphons.'[7]

The Psalms show the importance of music in temple worship, but we could never have guessed this from the Deuteronomic histories. Musicians were appointed to invoke, to thank and to praise the LORD (1 Chron. 16.4). The Levites had to choose certain families to specialize in temple music, and they and their instruments were named in the list of temple servants (1 Chron. 15.16–24). There were golden instruments kept in the temple; the words translated 'snuffers' was understood by mediaeval rabbis to mean 'musical instruments' (1 Kgs 7.50).[8] The Psalter ends with a vivid picture of temple music: trumpets, lutes, harps, timbrels, strings, pipes and various types of cymbal (Ps. 150.3–5), but Amos warned that this was no substitute for right living (Amos 5.23). The courts of the temple were filled with music and dancing at Tabernacles (Mishnah Sukkah 5.4), and Levites in the temple court sang the Hallel[9] as the Passover lambs were sacrificed (Mishnah Pesaḥim 5.7). The Book of Revelation describes harps and singing (Rev. 5.8–9; also 14.2–3, 15.2), presumably the ideal for Christian worship.

Despite these visions of heaven, there were strong reservations about musical instruments, because of their association with pagan worship. Philo said that Moses had learned 'the lore of metre, rhythm and harmony and the whole subject of music' from the Egyptians (*Life of Moses* 1.23), and this was associated with the worship of the golden calf (Exod. 32.18–19; *Special Laws* 3.125). The early Christian commentaries on Psalm 150 reflect this unease: God permitted musical instruments in the temple because the Jews had meant well, or because God was making a concession to human weakness, just

[6] Socrates of Constantinople, died 450 CE, quoted in Eusebius, *Church History* 6.8.

[7] *Egeria's Travels* 24, in J. Wilkinson, *Egeria's Travels*, Warminster: Aris and Philips, 1999.

[8] See V. A. Hurowitz, 'Solomon's Golden Vessels and the Cult of the First Temple' in *Pomegranates and Golden Bells*, ed. D. P. Wright and others, Winona Lake, Ind.: Eisenbrauns, 1995, pp. 151–64.

[9] Psalms 113–18.

as blood sacrifice had been permitted.[10] Amos' warning was often quoted.

The Sabbath Songs found at Qumran described the praise in the temple, but whether the singers were angels or priests — or both — is not clear (e.g. 4Q 403.1). The singers were 'priests, God's righteous people, his host, servants, the angels of his Glory who would praise him'. This was not a new idea nor a sectarian viewpoint, because Malachi had described the priests as angels (Mal. 2.7). The risen LORD sent letters to his angels, that is, the bishops of the churches in Asia Minor (e.g. Rev. 2.1). Ignatius described the bishop and his clergy as God and his council of *'elohim* (Magnesians 6; Trallians 3 alluding to Ps. 82.1). In the fourth century CE, Cyril of Jerusalem explained the Lord's Prayer in terms of the angel priesthood. 'Thy will be done on earth as it is in heaven' meant 'As in the angels thy will is done, so on earth be it done in me O LORD' (*Catecheses* 23.14.)[11] A generation later, John Chrysostom wrote: 'Though the office of priesthood is exercised on earth, it ranks, nevertheless in the celestial order of things ... The Paraclete himself established this ministry, and ordained that men abiding in the flesh should imitate the ministry of angels' (*On the Priesthood* 3.4).[12]

The Apocalypse of Abraham, a Jewish text preserved by Christians, described the music around the heavenly throne as the first Christians would have known it. Abraham ascended to heaven with the smoke of his sacrifice, guided by an angel dressed as a high priest, named Yahweh-El, the 'Singer of the Eternal One'. Abraham saw what Ezekiel had seen: a great fire and the 'sound of many waters', which the angel said was the many voices of the Sanctus. The angel taught Abraham how to join in the song,[13] reciting the many names of God and describing the Eternal One as the dawning light. Abraham saw the living creatures by the throne, and his angel guide taught them 'the song of peace which the Eternal One has in himself... And I heard the sound of their sanctification, like the voice of a single man' (Ap. Abr. 18.11). From his place in the fire and the music, Abraham looked down on the creation and was able to see the (formerly) invisible angels in their ranks: 'the host of stars and the orders they were commanded to carry out, and the elements of the earth obeying

---

[10] Respectively Theodoret *On Ps. 150*, PG 80.1996, and John Chrysostom *Homily on Ps 150*, PG 55.497.

[11] Also known as *Mystagogical Lecture* 5.14.

[12] For detail see my book, *The Great High Priest*, pp. 103–45.

[13] Only the redeemed could learn the 'new song', Rev. 14.3.

them' (Ap. Abr. 19.9).[14] As he sang the song, Abraham saw the harmony of creation. Other versions of this story say that Abraham saw the heavenly city when he offered the sacrifice. Adam had seen it before he sinned (2 Baruch 4. 4–5), and had heard the song of the seraphim before he sinned (Testament of Adam 1.4).

Seeing the kingdom and hearing the song were one experience, and sin prevented both. Gregory of Nyssa (died 395 CE), the brother of Basil with whom our investigation began,[15] opened a Christmas Sermon with Psalm 118.27, the Tabernacles psalm. The LORD, he said, had appeared to restore the original unity of all creation, which was 'the temple of the LORD of creation'. The mouths of those who had once offered praise there had been closed by sin, and the symphony of celebration had ceased because the human creation did not join with the praises of heaven.[16] As a result of the work of Christ, people excluded by sin could rejoin the liturgy of heaven and earth, and so the Christians entered the holy of holies to worship with the angels. The earliest picture of Christian worship is exactly this: the servants of God-and-the-Lamb wear his name and they see his face (Rev. 22.3–5). Jesus taught that the pure in heart would see God (Matt. 5.8), not necessarily those who conformed to the physical purity requirements of the Jerusalem high priests. Out of the heart (that is, the mind) came true impurity (Mark 7.21–3), and these impurities appear again as impediments to entering the heavenly city (Rev. 22.15). Those with impure minds could not sing the song of the angels: their mouths, as Gregory said, had been closed by sin. Philo, Jesus' contemporary, had reached the same conclusion. 'It is not possible genuinely to express our gratitude to God by means of buildings and oblations and sacrifices... It must be expressed by hymns of praise, not such as the audible voice shall sing, but strains raised and re-echoed by the mind, too pure for eye to discern.'[17]

THE SOURCE OF CREATION

The temple was constructed to represent the whole creation, with the great hall as the visible world, and the holy of holies as the invisible

---

[14] The Apocalypse of Abraham survives only in six slightly different manuscripts in Old Slavonic. It is thought to be a Jewish text from the early second century CE, since it describes the fall of the temple in 70 CE and seems to be mentioned in *Clementine Recognitions* 1.32–3.

[15] See above p. 1.

[16] PG XLVI 1127–8. I do not know of an English version.

[17] Philo, *On Planting* 126.

world of God and the heavenly host. In the scheme of creation, the veil of the temple marked the boundary between the two states, corresponding to the firmament created on the second day (Gen. 1.6–8). The great hall and its furnishings represented the creation of the third, fourth, fifth and sixth days, and the holy of holies represented Day One. This was not 'the first day' since 'first' implied a temporal sequence with the visible creation; this was Day One, the Beginning and Source that was eternally beyond and yet within the material world. Everything that was 'within the veil' was given only to the high priests (Num. 18.7), and so they alone knew the secrets of Day One: 'The secret things belong to the LORD our God; but the things that are revealed belong to us and our children ...' (Deut. 29.29). As a result, the lore of the holy of holies did not appear in the public Scriptures.

The Christians, nevertheless, knew this lore and claimed that they had learned it from Jesus, their Great High Priest.[18] In the ancient Liturgy of James, the Christians gave thanks that they *could* enter the holy of holies: '... being counted worthy to enter into the place of the tabernacle of thy Glory, and to be within the veil, and to behold the holy of holies, we cast ourselves down before thy goodness'. The high priestly lore is important for understanding the roots of Christian worship, but what survives is found mainly in non-canonical texts such as Jubilees, and is implicit in the Greek Old Testament but not in the Hebrew.[19] Jubilees records what was revealed to Moses on Sinai — the history of his people until his own time. He saw the process of creation, including Day One when all the ranks of angels were created (Jub. 2.2). This list appears also in the Song of the Three Children (the Benedicite) that is found in the Greek, but not the Hebrew text, of Daniel. All the works of the LORD are summoned to sing his praises: first the angels, the powers and the weathers, and then the works of the visible creation.

The praise of the angels in Day One was at the heart of the creation, and their song was part of the process of creation. Simeon the high priest[20] taught that the world was sustained by three things: the Law, the temple service and deeds of loving kindness (Mishnah

---

[18] See above p. 51.

[19] This is why restricting 'biblical studies' to the Protestant canon based on the post-Christian Hebrew text of the Old Testament is so counterproductive. See my book, *The Great High Priest*, London: T&T Clark, 2003, pp. 294–315.

[20] Described simply as Simeon the Just, he could have been the Simeon who was high priest about 280 BCE, or the Simeon who was high priest about 200 BCE.

Aboth 1. 2), and the temple service, as we have seen,[21] sustained the creation that the temple represented. The final section of the Community Rule at Qumran set out the times — each day, each week and throughout the year — when praise was to be offered. The hymn itself lists the names of God Most High: My Righteousness, Author of my goodness, Fountain of knowledge, Source of holiness, Summit of Glory, Almighty Eternal Majesty. By their singing, the worshippers committed themselves to stay within the covenant and keep the 'engraved precept' on their tongues. 'He will wipe out my transgression through his righteousness ... my eyes have beheld his marvellous deeds and the light of my heart, the *raz nihyeh*.' This latter is difficult to translate, but perhaps 'the mystery of existence' — how things come to be. The sense is clear enough: by singing, the faithful committed themselves to the eternal covenant and both glimpsed and sustained the holy of holies, the source of life. This is what John saw and heard when he stood before the throne (Rev. 4.6–11).

John heard a longer form of the Sanctus: 'Holy, Holy, Holy is the LORD God Almighty, who was and is and is to come!' (Rev. 4.8). This is best understood as the expanded form of the Name, the Greek equivalent of the form in the Palestinian Targums, and therefore how it was understood in the first century CE. 'Yahweh' did not mean 'He who is' but rather 'He who causes to be', and Yahweh of Hosts should perhaps be understood as 'He who causes the Hosts to be'. He is the One who enables the many to exist, not as the result of a single act in the past, but as a continual process in and from the eternal state, prompted, it would seem, by the praises of the angels. When 'Holy, Holy, Holy' is sung in heaven, according to 3 Enoch, the throne of Glory sends forth its river of fire, and the great angels are crowned (3 Enoch 36, 39, 40). The Targums gave the Name as 'He who said to the world from the beginning "Be there" and it was; and is to say to it "Be there" and it will be.'[22] The process of creation was the great mystery of the holy of holies — how the One became the many, the invisible hosts and then the visible creation — and so John heard the heavenly song continue: 'for thou didst create all things and by thy will they existed and were created' (Rev. 4.11). The older creation story, known to Job, told how the morning stars sang as the world was created (Job 38.7), and the song of the angels was believed to be part of the process of creation and re-creation. One of the Qumran hymns

[21] See above pp. 178ff.

[22] The Fragment Targum to Exod. 3.14; Neofiti and Pseudo-Jonathan are similar.

describes the work of Day One: 'Loving kindness and truth are about his face; truth and judgement and righteousness are the pedestal of his throne. He divides light from obscurity, he establishes the dawn by the knowledge of his heart. When all his angels saw it, they sang' (11 Q5 XXVI).

Enoch heard the Sanctus as 'Holy, Holy, Holy is the LORD of Spirits; he fills the earth with spirits' (1 Enoch 39.12), and as he heard the song his face 'changed'. In another description, Enoch said his body melted and his spirit was transformed/transfigured (1 Enoch 71.11). He could then see the angels around the throne, and he learned the secrets of the creation — how the Kingdom was divided; in other words, how the Unity became the plurality of the heavenly hosts (the spirits) and then the plurality of the visible creation (1 Enoch 41.1). The LORD of the spirits filled the earth with his spirits. The Greek Old Testament and the Targum understood the Sanctus this way too: the temple, which represented the visible creation, was filled with his Glory (Lxx Isa. 6.1), rather than with 'his train', and so Isaiah saw the Glory in the creation as he heard the Sanctus: 'The whole earth is full of his Glory.' The Targum expanded the Sanctus: 'Holy in the highest heavens, the house of his Shekinah; holy upon earth, the work of his might; holy for endless ages is the LORD of hosts ...', and a similar expansion appears in the eastern liturgies: 'Holy God, holy and strong, holy and immortal have mercy on us.' This was the joining of heaven and earth, as John Chrysostom said of Isaiah's vision: 'Above the hosts of angels sing praise. Below, men form choirs in the church and imitate them by singing the same doxology.' In other words, all sing the Sanctus together.[23] Thus too Maximus the Confessor (died 662 CE): 'By the thrice holy hymn there comes about the union with the holy angels and elevation to the same honour, as well as the ceaseless and harmonious persistency in the glorification of God.'[24]

Filling the earth with Glory was the coming of the Kingdom, and worship anticipated the Kingdom. John saw this as the heavenly city coming to earth, but what he saw was a huge golden cube; that is, the holy of holies (Rev. 21.15–18). The state of glory, Unity and the angels was the setting of John's vision of Christian worship, and so 'On earth as it is in heaven' was understood in The Apostolic Constitutions as a

---

[23] Homily on Isaiah 6 (PG 56.97)

[24] *Mystagogy* 24, in *Maximus the Confessor*, tr. G. C. Berthold, The Classics of Western Spirituality, Mahwah, NJ: Paulist Press, 1985.

description of the heavenly praise on earth: 'As the heavenly natures of the incorporeal powers do all glorify God with one consent, so also on earth all men with one mouth and with one purpose may glorify the only, the one and true God by Christ his only begotten.'[25] Maximus too: 'The unceasing and sanctifying doxology by the holy angels in the Thrice Holy Hymn signifies, in general, the equality of the way of life and conduct, and the harmony in the divine praising which will take place in the age to come by both heavenly and earthly powers.'[26]

The Testament of Adam is another Jewish text, preserved and expanded by Christians, that reached its present form by the third century CE. Adam told his son Seth the hours of the night and day when each part of creation had to offer praise: the doves at the second hour of the night, for example, and the Sanctus of the seraphim two hours later. The Christian addition describes the ranks of angels and their praises, from the lowest rank who are the guardian angels of human beings up to the highest ranks — the cherubim and seraphim — who sing the Sanctus. The fragment of an early third century Christian hymn found at Oxyrhynchos is similar: 'all noble [creatures] of God together ... shall not be silent, nor shall the light bearing stars lag behind ... all the rushing rivers shall praise our Father and Son and Holy Spirit, all the powers shall join in saying Amen and Amen, power and praise ...'[27] The Hekhalot Rabbati[28] and 3 Enoch are Jewish texts from the same period which show how the heavenly praise was prompted by the praises of people on earth; in other words, it was human commitment that was vital to maintaining the harmony: 'And all the ministering angels ... when they hear the sound of the hymns and praises which Israel speaks from below, begin from above with "Holy, Holy, Holy"' (H.R. #179); 'When I opened my mouth and sang praises before the throne of Glory, the holy creatures below the throne of Glory and above the throne responded after me

---

[25] Apostolic Constitutions 2.56.

[26] *Mystagogy* 24.

[27] Papyrus XV 1786, quoted in J. Quasten, *Music and Worship in Pagan and Christian Antiquity*, Washington DC: National Association of Pastoral Musicians, 1983, p. 71.

[28] Thought to be the earliest collection of the 'throne mystic' texts, incorporating Palestinian tradition from the second and third centuries CE. The best introduction to this material is P. Schaefer, *The Hidden and Manifest God*, Albany; State University of New York Press: 1992, which shows its great relevance to understanding early Christian worship. There is a useful short summary in B. D. Spinks, *The Sanctus in the Eucharistic Prayer*, Cambridge: Cambridge University Press, 1991, pp. 36–9.

saying "Holy Holy Holy", and "Blessed be the Glory of the LORD in his dwelling place"' (3 Enoch 1). The same pattern of response occurs in the Liturgy of St John Chrysostom, composed a century or so later, where the Sanctus begins with the choir and is then taken up by the clergy/angels in the sanctuary.[29]

Isaiah heard the Sanctus (Isa. 6.3), Enoch heard it (1 Enoch 39.12), and John heard it (Rev. 4.8). Each heard the song in the context of the Day of Atonement, the only time the high priest entered the holy of holies, and so the only time he would have 'heard' the song. Isaiah heard the song and then experienced atonement: 'Your guilt is taken away, and your sin is forgiven' (Isa. 6.7). Enoch heard the song as he stood in the holy of holies, learned the hidden things (1 Enoch 40.2), and then saw the blood of the Righteous One brought to the throne (1 Enoch 47.1). John heard the song and then saw the slain and resurrected Lamb enthroned (Rev. 5.6); that is, the Glory in human form, the Servant, the Great High Priest. A memory of the temple known in the fourth century CE and attributed to R. Benaiah,[30] said that the Levites made atonement for Israel by their song.[31] Since atonement renewed the creation, this is the context for the psalms of renewal, 'new' and 'renew' being hard to distinguish in Hebrew.[32] Psalm 33 describes the 'new' song, and then how the LORD made the creation; Psalms 96 and 98 exhort the people to sing the 'new' song because the LORD reigns and the earth is established (thus too Pss. 144, 149). Isaiah told of the 'new song' and the singing of heaven and earth as the LORD restored his people (Isa. 42.10; 44.23; 49,13); John heard the 'new song' in heaven (Rev. 5.9; 14.3) and the angels marked the beginning of the new creation by proclaiming at Bethlehem: 'Glory to God, and peace on earth' (Luke 2. 14).

This link between the Sanctus and atonement — in the temple sense of the renewal and restoration of creation — may explain why the Sanctus was, from the earliest period, incorporated in the eucharistic prayers. Spinks has an interesting example of an 'interpolated Sanctus', comparing the anaphora of the Apostolic Tradition and that of the Ethiopic Apostles. The Sanctus appears at the point where the incarnation is described, implying that incarnation has filled the whole earth with the Glory.[33] 'The Word became flesh and dwelt

---

[29] I am grateful to Bishop Basil of Amphipolis for this reference.
[30] Early third century CE.
[31] JerusalemTalmud Ta'anit 4.2.
[32] See above p. 176.
[33] Spinks, op. cit. n. 28 above, p. 58.

among us ... and we have beheld his Glory' (John 1.14). It would not be hard to imagine — and this is speculation — the Sanctus as part of the ancient rite of atonement, when the life of the LORD, represented by the blood, was brought from the holy of holies to heal the earth. The angel hosts (i.e. the priests) were commanded to worship the LORD as he emerged to atone,[34] and this was a text so important in the early Church and so controversial that it did not survive in the post-Christian Hebrew of Deuteronomy 32.43, but only in the Greek and in Christian usage: 'When he brings the Firstborn into the world, he says, "Let all God's angels worship him"' (Heb. 1.6) could well have been the original context of the Sanctus, and account for its association with the incarnation. Cyril of Jerusalem, writing in the mid fourth century CE, implied this when he explained the pattern of the liturgy. The worshippers, he said, joined themselves with the whole creation, visible and invisible, to sing the song of the seraphim, 'to mingle our voices in the hymns of the heavenly hosts.' Then they prayed for the Holy Spirit to come to the bread and wine, and then they prayed for peace and healing. This is recognizable as the pattern of the temple atonement: the LORD emerged, originally in the person of the high priest, but in the Eucharist in the bread and wine, to heal and restore the creation (*Catecheses* 23.6-10)[35].

In addition to the differences that developed in Hebrew texts of the Old Testament, the Jewish commentaries show that angels and Day One were much debated in the early centuries of Christianity. Jewish scholars argued about when the angels were created: 'R. Luliani b. Tabri said in the name of R. Isaac: "Whether we accept (that they were created on the second day or on the fifth); all agree that no angels were created on the first day"' (Genesis Rabbah III.8[36]). Such a controversy in Palestine strongly suggests that the angels of Day One were important for the Christians — as indeed they were. Their role in the holy of holies, Day One, was at the heart of Christian belief about the nature of the Church, the Kingdom, Unity and worship, and the song of the angels was set at the heart of the liturgy.[37]

[34] See above p. 185.

[35] Also known as *Mystagogical Lecture* 5.6–10.

[36] A compilation of explanatory material about Genesis, made in Palestine in the fifth century CE.

[37] The choir in a traditional church is by the altar, and often decorated with angels, to replicate the temple vision.

UNITY

According to the Genesis Rabbah, Day One was/is the state when
the Holy One was/is One with his universe (Gen. Rab. III.8). It is
the state described enigmatically by Paul, after the struggle to bring
the Kingdom: 'Then shall the Son also be subject to him that put
all things under him, that *God may be all in all*' (1 Cor. 15.28, AV).
Christian worship anticipated and realized this state of Unity, because
the Christians were angels on earth, and like the angels of Day One,
they were part of the Unity. When Jesus knew he was returning to the
holy of holies, the state beyond time and matter that was the Glory
of Day One, he prayed: 'Father, glorify thou me in thy own presence
with the glory which I had with thee before the world was made'
(John 17.5). He prayed that his followers would be One, included in
the unity that was the unity of Father and Son, 'perfectly One' so that
the world would know Jesus' divine origin (John 17. 20–3). Sharing
the unity of the angels/the Glory was proof that they were already
in/of Day One. Finally, Jesus prayed that his followers would be with
him to see his Glory (John 17.24) — the scene at the end of the Book
of Revelation: 'The throne of God and of the Lamb [shall be there]
and his servants shall worship him, and they shall see his face, and his
name shall be on their foreheads (Rev. 22.3–4). Paul pointed out the
practical implications of living in this state: those baptized into Christ
could no longer have any of the divisions characteristic of the material
state outside the holy of holies: 'There is neither Jew nor Greek, there
is neither slave nor free, there is neither male nor female; for you are
all one in Christ Jesus' (Gal. 3.28). John gave visionary expression
to it: he saw the great high priest emerging from the holy of holies
bringing the wrath of judgement, but he saw a sevenfold high priest:
there were seven angels wearing white linen and golden girdles, the
dress worn only by a high priest (Rev. 15.5–8).

Gnostic texts preserved memories of this unity: 'The Saviour was
a bodily image of the Unitary One. He is the Totality in bodily form'
(Tripartite Tractate CG I.5.116). The angels were all One, just as
the units of time were all one: 'The year came to be as a type of the
Saviour ... the 360 days came to be a type of the 360 powers that were
revealed by the Saviour ... In relation to the angels who came out of
these, who are without number, the hours and the moments of the
days came to be as a type' (Letter of Eugnostos CG III.3); 'They say
that our angels were put forth as a unity and are One in that they
came out from One. Now since we existed in separation, Jesus was

baptised that the undivided should be divided until he should unite us with them in the Fullness, that we, the many, having become one, might all be mingled with One which was divided for our sakes' (Excerpts from Theodotus 36).[38] Paul said: 'He is before all things and in him all things hold together ... For in him all the fullness of God was pleased to dwell.' (Col. 1.17, 19), and this had been the Jewish declaration of faith: the LORD our God (*'elohim*, a plural form) is One, as well as the hope of the early prayer: 'As this broken bread, once dispersed over the hills, was brought together, and became one loaf, so may thy Church be brought together from the ends of the earth' (Didache 9). John Chrysostom said: 'In the mysteries we are joined to each other, so that the many become one,'[39] and Dionysius explained what it meant to belong to the unity: 'Keep these holy truths a secret in your hidden mind. Guard their unity safe from the multiplicity of what is profane ...' The goal of the hierarchy, he said, was to enable beings to be as like as possible to God and to be at One with him: 'clear and spotless mirrors reflecting the glow of primordial light and indeed of God himself.'[40]

The angels are the Glory, the powers of God, and what was said of them sounds very like the ideal of the Church. Philo shows how 'the powers' in creation were understood in the first century CE: 'God is everywhere because he has made his powers extend through earth and water, air and heaven, and has left no part of the universe without his presence, and uniting all with all, he has bound them fast with invisible bonds that they should never be loosed' (*On the Confusion of Tongues* 136). These invisible bonds were the bonds of the eternal covenant, restored and maintained by the high priest, just as Isaiah's enigmatic servant had himself 'been' the covenant (Isa. 42.6). Binding on the Name of the LORD — as in baptism — had symbolized joining oneself to the LORD, and meant far more than just obeying the commandments.[41] The LORD was present in his angels, as can be seen from Josephus' version of the story of Mamre in Genesis 18: Abraham did not meet the LORD and two angels, as Genesis leads us to suppose, but he met three angels (*Antiquities* 1.196).

The fourfold name of the Messiah — Wonderful Counsellor, Mighty God, Everlasting Father, Prince of Peace — was the four aspects of

---

[38] In R. P. Casey, *Clement of Alexandria, Excerpts from Theodotus*, Studies and Documents 1, London 1934.

[39] Homily 79, On John, PG 59.426.

[40] Celestial Hierarchy 45 C and 165 A.

[41] See above p. 124.

the LORD before they were given their separate names as archangels: Uriel, the light of God who illumined the mind; Gabriel, the strength of God; Michael, the warrior;[42] Raphael the healer. In Enoch they are still the four presences/faces of God (1 Enoch 40.2), and the early Jewish mystical texts described the LORD as 'Tootrousia', derived from the Greek meaning four essences: *tetra* and *ousia*.[43] Plurality and Unity was far more ancient than the Christian formulation of the Trinity. Knowing the names, that is, the nature of the angels and how they are One, was the great secret of the holy of holies. The Jewish temple mystic exclaimed: 'When my ears heard this great mystery, the world was transformed over me in purity, and my heart was as if I had arrived in a new world. Every day it appeared to me, as if I was standing in front of the throne of Glory.'[44] Discussing these Jewish mystical texts, Schaefer observed: 'The texts show ... that it is almost impossible to differentiate between God and his angel.'[45] A Christian described this as standing in the Kingdom. His eyes had been opened and he saw everything differently, because he saw the Glory. This mystery of the unity of mystic, angel and the LORD is crucial for understanding, for example, Jesus' prayer after the Last Supper: 'The glory which thou hast given me I have given to them, that they may be one even as we are one, I in them and thou in me, that they may become perfectly one ... Father I desire that they also, whom thou hast given me, may be with me where I am, to behold my glory' (John 17.22–4).

The Glory, Day One, was the holy of holies, a name that means 'actively holy', 'imparting holiness.' When Moses consecrated the tabernacle vessels, they became most holy or holy of holies — the same Hebrew words underlie both — and whatever touched them became holy (Exod. 30.29). Similarly, all those who entered the holy of holies became holy ones, often translated 'saints': 'the saints' in Corinth (1 Cor. 1,2); 'the saints in Achaia' (2 Cor. 1.1); 'the saints at Philippi' (Phil. 1.1), etc. Being a saint meant being part of the Unity. Tertullian, about 200 CE, expounded 'hallowed be thy name' in this way — acquiring the holiness and becoming an angel: 'Yet when is the name of God not holy ... seeing that he hallows others from within himself, and those angels who stand around cease not to say to him Holy Holy Holy. We also, angels designate ... already here are

---

[42] 'Everlasting Father' is better rendered 'Father of booty'.

[43] In the Hekhalot Rabbati, ## 206, 219 in P. Schaefer, *The Hidden and Manifest God*, Albany: State University of New York Press, 1992, p. 21.

[44] Merkavah Rabbah #680, ibid., p. 114.

[45] Ibid., p. 116.

learning that heavenly address to God and that service of Glory that is to be.'[46] The unity was also expressed in terms of music. Clement of Alexandria, also about 200 CE, wrote: 'We want to strive so that we, the many, may be brought together into one love, according to the union of the essential unity ... The union of many, which the divine harmony has called forth out of a medley of sounds and division, becomes one symphony.'[47] John Chrysostom, teaching about the divided community that Paul knew in Corinth, wrote: 'There must always be one voice in the Church as though coming from one mouth',[48] and Ambrose, recognizing what Paul had said about women being silent in church, said they could sing as a sign of unity: 'For it is clearly a great bond of unity when the whole of the people come together in one choir.[49]

From the very beginning, Christian writers compared the music of their worship to the harmony of the angels. At the end of the first century, Clement of Rome wrote to the divided community in Corinth: 'Think of the vast company of angels who all wait on him to serve his wishes ... In the same way ought we ourselves, gathered together in a conscious unity, to cry to him as it were with one voice, if we are to obtain a share of his glorious great promises' (1 Clem. 34). Ignatius, at about the same time, wrote: 'Your clergy ... are tuned to their bishop like the strings of a harp, and the result is a hymn of praise to Jesus Christ from minds that are in unison and affections that are in harmony ... Join this choir, every one of you, let there be a whole symphony of minds' (Ephesians 4). In a century of bitter division within the Church, Eusebius wrote: 'And so more sweetly pleasing to God than any musical instrument would be the symphony of the people of God, by which, in every church of God, with kindred spirit and single disposition, with one mind and unanimity of faith and piety, we raise melody in unison in our psalmody.'[50] Athanasius in the next generation wrote: 'Monasteries in the mountains, like tabernacles, filled with saintly choirs reciting psalms, devoutly reading, fasting, praying, rejoicing in the hope of things to come, and labouring to give alms while maintaining love and harmony among themselves.'[51] John Chrysostom too, wrote of

[46] Tertullian, *On the [Lord's] Prayer* 3.
[47] Exhortation to the Greeks 9.
[48] Homily 36, *On 1 Corinthians*, PG 61.313.
[49] Ambrose, On Psalm 1, PL 14.925.
[50] Attributed to him: On Psalm 91.4, PG 23.1173.
[51] Life of St Anthony 44, PG 26.908.

the monks: '[At daybreak] all stand forming a sacred choir ... they stand and sing the prophetic hymns with great harmony and well ordered melody'.[52]

THE BONDS OF WISDOM

Wisdom was seen as the mother of the angels, transforming mortals into her children by anointing them with herself. Oil was the sacrament of Wisdom, originally given to the prophets, priests and kings of the ancient temple, but extended in the Church to all the baptized. Christians were the anointed ones. By definition, Wisdom was their mother. She was the Mother of the Messiah, and must have been the mysterious woman of Isaiah's prophecy of Immanuel. The only known pre-Christian Hebrew text of Isaiah 7.11 reads: 'Ask a sign of the *Mother* of the LORD your God ...',[53] rather than 'Ask a sign of the LORD your God', and there is no proof that this was a unique and deviant reading. Some people in the time of Jesus read Isaiah's prophecy that way.

This is corroborated by the vision of the harlot in Revelation. By following the temple pattern of type and dark antitype presented in wordplay, the ancient Lady reappears. The harlot in John's vision was the corrupted second temple, wearing on her forehead the name Babylon the great, mother of harlots and of earth's abominations (Rev. 17.5). In the Hebrew that underlies the present Greek text of Revelation, these could have been the words *qdšm*, which means both male prostitute and holy one, and *mšhyt*, ruin or corruption, very similar to *mšyh*, messiah, anointed one. The harlot was the mother of prostitutes and corruptions, and the Lady was the mother of holy ones and anointed ones. The prophets had described Jerusalem as a harlot: her harlotry had brought destruction (Ezek. 23.20), and, with bitter wordplay, Isaiah described the new temple as a bed, *miškab*, on a lofty mountain, when it should have been *miškan*, the dwelling place of the LORD (Isa. 57.7). The great theme of Isaiah was 'How the faithful city has become a harlot' (Isa. 1.21). The harlot in Revelation had replaced the Lady, who returned as the heavenly city when the harlot had been burned. When the oil was 'lost' in the seventh century BCE, so too were the angels and anointed ones, their vision

---

[52] *On 1 Timothy*, Homily 14; PG 62 576.

[53] In the complete Isaiah scroll from Qumran, 1Q Isaᵃ; see my book, *The Great High Priest*, London: T&T Clark, 2003, pp. 240–1.

and their song.[54] When the Lady returned and gave birth to her son (Rev. 12.1–6), so too did the vision that held all things together (Prov. 29.18).[55]

Wisdom held all things together in harmony, *harmozousa*. That is how the Greek translated the mysterious word *'amon* in Proverbs 8.30, often rendered 'master craftsman.' The Jews of Egypt who had cherished the figure of Wisdom,[56] and for whom the Greek translation was made, must have had a reason for describing her in this way. The Wisdom of Solomon, another text from Egypt, described Wisdom in similar terms: 'Though she is but one, she can do all things, and while remaining in herself she renews all things, in every generation she passes into holy souls and makes them friends of God and prophets (Wisd. 7.27). Philo, also in Egypt, described the angels as the powers of God throughout the creation, bound fast with invisible bonds that should never be loosed. He also described the powers as a choir: 'There is in the air a most holy choir of bodiless souls, whom the sacred scriptures call angels. The whole army is drawn up in connected ranks to serve and minister to the Leader who set them up in order, and, as is right and proper, to follow him as their Leader ...' (*Tongues* 174). It seems that the Mother of the angels was the bond that held them in harmony, and their unity and order were described as harmony in the musical sense.[57]

The angels sang, as Job knew, and their music expressed and maintained the harmony of creation. There were far more singing angels in the Hebrew Scriptures than appear in the surface text. The Targums gave the sense of the Hebrew as it was understood in the synagogues, and wherever 'the heavens' rejoice, this was translated as 'the angels' rejoicing. 'Let the angels on high rejoice' was the Targum to 1 Chronicles 16.31, where the biblical text has 'Let the heavens rejoice.' Psalm 19.1–3 describes the silent praise of the angels throughout creation, and Psalm 148 shows how the praise of the angels was linked to establishing the order of creation. Since Day One was the state of unity, the song of the angels had to express this, and any defect was punished. The Hekhalot Rabbati describes the song: 'with one voice, with one speech, with one knowledge, with one

---

[54] See above p. 126.

[55] Literally 'When there is no prophetic vision, the people unravel ...'

[56] See above pp. 214ff.

[57] In Philo, Wisdom and Logos are equivalent terms. See my book, *The Great Angel*, London: SPCK, 1992, pp. 130–32. He used Wisdom imagery of the Logos, who holds all things together 'so that the universe may send forth a harmony' (*On Planting* 10).

sound ... when they sing the hymn of sanctification before the king of the kings of kings',[58] just as the temple priests had sung 'with one voice' to bring the Glory of the LORD to the temple (2 Chron. 5.13). The Hekhalot Zutarti depicts the seraphim glorifying the LORD, and his servants singing a new song: 'They install you as King for ever, and you shall be called One for ever and ever.'[59]

The angels who broke the harmony were destroyed (3 Enoch 40.3). When Enoch ascended through the heavens he saw the rebel angels in the fifth heaven, and they were silent. 'Their faces were dejected and their mouths were always silent, *for there is no liturgy in the fifth heaven*' (2 Enoch 18.2–3). In the sixth heaven, however, he saw the archangels whose duty was to uphold all the commandments and supervise the heavenly singing: 'They harmonise all existence, in heaven and on earth' (2 Enoch 19.3–4). Finally, when he heard the 'Holy, Holy, Holy' of the seventh heaven, Enoch was anointed with the sweet myrrh oil and transformed into an angel (2 Enoch 22).

[58] HR #185ff., in Schaefer, op. cit n. 28 above, p. 27.
[59] HZ #418, ibid., p. 61.

ENVOI

If only we knew what Basil knew when he wrote about the tradition of the apostles handed down in a mystery!

He knew authentic Christian tradition and teachings not recorded in the Bible: signing with the cross, anointing, the words of the epiclesis. 'A whole day would not be long enough to go through all the unwritten mysteries of the Church' (*On the Holy Spirit* 67).

All the mysteries concerned worship, and the overall pattern, as we have seen, can be traced back to the temple. As the Church lost touch with these roots, the practices acquired new explanations. The world of the temple also faded from view, and much that had been authentic temple tradition was identified as Platonism.

The details of this sketch need to be filled in, but there is enough here, I trust, to show where the roots of Christian worship and its world view are to be found.

'New facts alone do not make a new theory; and new facts alone do not destroy an outlived theory ... The facts that proved that planetary motions depended on the sun have been staring into the face of astronomers throughout the ages — but they preferred to look away' (Arthur Koestler, *The Act of Creation*, London: Hutchinson, 1964, p. 235).

BIBLIOGRAPHY

Primary Sources

Details of English translations are given where they are available.

Abbreviations

ACW *Ancient Christian Writers*

ANF *Ante-Nicene Fathers*, ed. A. Roberts and J. Donaldson, T&T Clark, Edinburgh, 1868–72, reprinted Eerdmans: Grand Rapids, 1950–52.

ANT *The Apocryphal New Testament*, tr. M. R. James, Oxford: Clarendon Press (1924) 1980.

CCSL *Corpus Christianorum Series Latina*

CG *Coptic Gnostic Library*

CWS *Classics of Western Spirituality*

FC *Fathers of the Church*

LCL *Loeb Classical Library*

NPNF *Nicene and Post Nicene Fathers*

OTP *The Old Testament Pseudepigrapha*, 2 vols, ed. J. H. Charlesworth, Garden City: Doubleday, and London: Darton, Longman and Todd, 1983, 1985.

PG *Patrologia Graeca*

PL *Patrologiae Latinae*

SC *Sources Chrétiennes*

Jewish Apocrypha and Pseudepigrapha

1 Enoch is extant in Ethiopic but Aramaic fragments have been found at Qumran and Greek fragments are also known. It has five sections: The Book of the Watchers, the Parables, the Astronomy Book, the Dreams Visions and the Admonitions. Fragments of all sections except the Parables have been found at Qumran. The earliest Qumran Enoch material dates from the third century BCE, but Enochic literature must be much older. The Book of Isaiah presupposes knowledge of something very similar. Jude, a member of Jesus' family, quoted from this text (Jude 14). Text and tr. M. A. Knibb, *The Ethiopic Book of Enoch*.

A New Edition in the Light of the Aramaic Dead Sea Fragments, Oxford, 1978, also tr. in OTP 1 and R. H. Charles *The Book of Enoch,* Oxford, 1912.

2 Enoch, also known as *The Book of the Secrets of Enoch,* is extant in Slavonic but, as most early religious texts in Slavonic were translated from Greek, 2 Enoch was probably a Greek text. It is impossible to date, but affinities with ideas known in the first century CE suggest that its sources could be ancient. Tr. in OTP 1, also R. H. Charles and W. R. Morfill, *The Book of the Secrets of Enoch,* Oxford, 1896, and A. Vaillant, *Le livre des secrets d'Hénoch: texte slave et traduction française,* Paris (1952) 1976.

The Book of Jubilees, also known as *The Little Genesis,* mentioned in the Damascus Document (CD XVI), is a writing with priestly interests possibly dating from early in the second century BCE. The fullest text has survived in Ethiopic but there are fragments in Greek, Syriac and Latin. The original was in Hebrew, and fragments have been found at Qumran and Masada. Tr. in OTP 2.

The Testament of the Levi is part of the Testaments of the Twelve Patriarchs which purport to be the final words of the twelve sons of Jacob, originating perhaps in the early years of the second century BCE but with later Christian additions. The earliest surviving texts are in Greek, but Aramaic fragments of similar material have been found at Qumran. Tr. in OTP 1, also R. H. Charles, *The Greek Versions of the Testaments of the Twelve Patriarchs,* Oxford, 1908 and *The Testaments of the Twelve Patriarchs,* London, 1908.

The Assumption of Moses, also known as *The Testament of Moses,* purports to be Moses' final words to Joshua, and as such is related to Deuteronomy 31–34. Only one Latin text is known which seems to have been translated from an earlier Greek. The original must have been written in Hebrew or Aramaic, probably in the first century CE, as there are thinly veiled references to Herod the Great in chapter 7. Tr. in OTP 1, also E. M. Laperrousaz, *Le Testament de Moïse (généralement appelé 'Assomption de Moïse'). Traduction avec introduction et notes,* Paris, 1970.

The Letter of Aristeas was written in Greek, probably by an Alexandrian Jew, and describes the translation of the Septuagint in the mid third century BCE. It also gives an account of the temple and the high priest. Josephus used it in *Antiquities 12,* but it is impossible to date the work. Tr. in OTP 2.

Life of Adam and Eve is a Latin text which largely corresponds to a Greek text known as *The Apocalypse of Moses.* They elaborate on the story of Adam and Eve and probably derive from a Hebrew original written in the early second century CE. Tr. in OTP 2, also L. S. A. Wells in *The Apocrypha and Pseudepigrapha of the Old Testament*, vol. 2, ed. R. H. Charles, Oxford, 1913.

The Apocalypse of Abraham, extant only in Slavonic, is thought to be a first-century CE Hebrew text. Tr. in OTP 1.

Qumran Texts

English translations of most of the non-biblical texts in G. Vermes, *The Complete Dead Sea Scrolls in English*, London, 1997.

1 QIsa^a The Complete Isaiah Scroll in M. Burrows, J. C. Trever and W. H. Brownlee, The Dead Sea Scrolls of St Mark's Monastery I, New Haven, 1950.

Other Jewish Writers

Philo of Alexandria (about 20 BCE – 50 CE) was from a wealthy and influential family; he headed the community's embassy to the Emperor Caligula in 40 CE. Jerome said that Philo was of a priestly family (*On Illustrious Men* XI) and he was probably correct. He was aware of the older priestly traditions of Israel, and much in his writings that is identified as Platonism, e.g. the heavenly archetypes, the second mediator God, is more likely to have originated in the priestly traditions of the first temple. Text and tr. F. H. Colson, G. H. Whitaker and R. Marcus in LCL, 12 vols, 1929–1963.

Flavius *Josephus* was the Roman name of Joseph ben Matthias (about 35–100 CE), a man of royal and high priestly blood. At the start of the revolt against Rome he commanded troops in Galilee, but changed sides and served as a translator for the Romans. He later lived in Rome under the patronage of the emperor, and wrote *The Jewish War*, originally in Aramaic, but only the Greek version survives. Although an eyewitness, he was hardly an impartial observer. Text and tr. H. St. J. Thackeray, LCL, 3 vols (1927) 1997. He later wrote *The Antiquities of the Jews*, the first half based on the Hebrew Scriptures and the remainder a valuable source for the later period. Text and tr. Marcus, LCL, 9 vols, 1963–1969. Josephus also wrote an autobiography *Life*, and an apologetic piece *Against Apion* which describes the antiquity of Israel and the ideals of the Law. Text and tr. by H. St. J. Thackeray in LCL, 1956–65. An older and interesting translation of the works of Josephus was made by William Whiston, published London, 1844.

Rabbinic texts

The *Mishnah,* a name derived perhaps from the Hebrew word for repeat or learn, perhaps from the fact that it was 'second' in relation to the Law, is the collection of religious law from the end of the second temple period attributed to R. Judah ha Nasi. The Mishnah comprises six sections, each subdivided into Tractates. Tr. H. Danby *The Mishnah,* Oxford, (1933) 1989.

Gemara, the 'completion' of the study, was added to each section of the Mishnah and thus the Talmud 'study' was formed. *The Palestinian Talmud,* the Yerushalmi, is the commentary on the Mishnah developed in Palestine, and contains additional material only loosely connected to the Mishnah. Compiled perhaps in the early fifth century, it does not cover the whole of the Mishnah. Tr. as *The Talmud of the Land of Israel,* ed. J. Neusner, Chicago and London, 1989–. The Babylonian Talmud, a longer work including other material taught in the rabbinic schools, was probably compiled in the early sixth century CE. Tr. I. Epstein, *The Babylonian Talmud,* 35 vols, Soncino, London, 1935–1952, reprinted 1961.

The Fathers According to R. Nathan, tr. A. Cohen, can be found in the Minor Tractates of the Talmud, vol. 1, London, 1965.

Tosefta means addition, a supplement to the Mishnah. Tr. in *Tosefta,* ed. J. Neusner, New York, 1979–.

Midrashim

Genesis Rabbah, an exegetical midrash compiled in Palestine perhaps in the early fifth century CE, became part of the mediaeval Midrash Rabbah, the Great Midrash. Tr. H. Freedman, 2 vols, London (1939) 1961.

Exodus Rabbah is in two parts: the first is an exegetical midrash on Exodus 1–10 and the second a homiletic midrash on Exodus 12–40. Exodus 11 is not covered. Dating is uncertain, but it was known in its present combined form in the twelfth century. Tr. S. M. Lehrman, London, (1939) 1961.

Leviticus Rabbah is a homiletic midrash and was probably compiled in the fifth century CE from the traditions of scholars in Palestine. Tr. J. Israelstam and J. J. Slotki, London, (1939) 1961.

Numbers Rabbah is a composite work: the first and longer part covers Num. 1–7; the second part deals more briefly with Num. 8–36. The two were combined by the thirteenth century. Tr. J. J. Slotki, London (1939) 1961.

Song of Songs Rabbah is an exegetical midrash. Some date the compilation to the mid sixth century, but it seems to contain much older material which reflects early Jewish Christian controversies. Tr. M. Simon, London (1939) 1961.

Mekhilta of Rabbi Ishmael is a commentary on parts of Exodus, some of which is attributed to teachers of the mid second century CE. Text and tr. J. Z. Lauterbach, 3 vols, Philadelphia 1933–5.

Targums

The *Targums* are Aramaic translations (and expansions) of biblical texts, representing Babylonian (Onkelos) and Palestinian traditions. It is not possible to date them because they are the written deposit of an oral tradition and contain material from many periods. There are English translations in the Aramaic Bible series published by T&T Clark, Edinburgh.

T. Neofiti *Genesis* by M. McNamara 1992.
T. Pseudo-Jonathan *Genesis* by M. Maher 1992.
T. Neofiti 1 *Exodus*, tr. M. McNamara with notes by C. T. R. Hayward; and T. Pseudo-Jonathan *Exodus*, tr. and notes by M. Maher in one volume, 1994.
T. Neofiti 1 *Leviticus*, tr. M. McNamara with notes by C. T. R. Hayward, 1994.
T. Onqelos *Numbers*, tr. and notes B. Grossfeld, 1988.
The Isaiah Targum, by B. Chilton, 1987.

Merkavah Texts

3 Enoch, also known as *The Hebrew Enoch*, (but its original title was probably *Sepher Hekhalot*), contains material attributed to the early second century CE R. Ishmael. It is the deposit of a school of tradition with Palestinian roots and probably reached its present form in the fifth/sixth century CE. Tr. P. Alexander in OTP 1.

Hekhalot Rabbati (The Greater Palaces) and *Hekhalot Zutarti* (The Lesser Palaces) are similar collections of texts which Schaefer holds to be earlier than 3 Enoch. There is also *Merkavah Rabbah*, (The Great Chariot). Texts in P. Schaefer *Synopse zur Hekhalot Literatur*, Tübingen: Mohr, 1981, translated extracts in P. Schaefer,

The Hidden and Manifest God. Some Major Themes on Early Jewish Mysticism New York, 1992. I do not know of any complete translation into English.

The *Zohar* claims to be R. Simeon ben Yohai's commentary on the Pentateuch, but the earliest evidence for its existence is from 13th century Spain. *Zohar*, tr. H. Sperling and M. Simon, 5 vols, London and Bournemouth, 1949.

Early Christian Texts

Ambrose (339–397 CE) was Bishop of Milan. *On the Psalms* PL 14: tr. *Commentary of St Ambrose on Twelve Psalms*, I. M. NiRiain, Dublin: Halcyon Press, 2000.

The Apostolic Constitutions is a collection of materials on church order in eight books, compiled perhaps at the end of the 4th century. It is based on the *Didache*, the *Didascalia* and the *Apostolic Tradition* of Hippolytus. PG 1; tr. ANF 7.

Athanasius (297–373 CE) was Bishop of Alexandria.
On the Incarnation, PG 26; tr. NPNF 2.4, also R. W. Thomson Oxford: Oxford University Press, 1971.
Festal Letters, PG 26.
Life of St Antony, PG 26; tr. CWS, R. C. Gregg, New York, 1979.

The *Letter of Barnabas*, written after the fall of Jerusalem in 70 CE, was traditionally attributed to Barnabas the Levite from Cyprus who was Paul's companion on his first missionary journey (Acts 4.36; 13.2). The Greek text was rediscovered in 1859 in the Sinai Codex. PG 2; tr. ANF 1, also M. Staniforth in *Early Christian Writings. The Apostolic Fathers*, Harmondsworth, 1968.

Basil of Caesarea (330–379 CE) known as 'the Great', became Bishop of Caesarea in Cappodocia in 370 CE.
On the Holy Spirit, PG 32; tr. NPNF 2.8

Clement was Bishop of Rome at the end of the first century. His letter to Corinth is known as 1 Clement. PG 1; tr. ANF 8, also M. Staniforth in *Early Christian Writings. The Apostolic Fathers*, Harmondsworth, 1968.

Attributed to Clement of Rome are the *Clementine Recognitions* which describe how Clement was converted to Christianity and travelled with St Peter. Opinions vary as to the date and value of this work. PG 1; tr. ANF 8.

Clement of Alexandria (died c. 214 CE). According to Eusebius (*History* 6.6, 13) he settled in Alexandria as a pupil of Pantaenus and eventually succeeded him as head of the Catechetical School there, where he taught Origen. He fled to Asia Minor during the persecution of Severus in 202 CE.

Miscellanies, PG 8–9; tr. ANF 2.

Exhortation to the Greeks, PG 9; tr. ANF 2.

Excerpts from Theodotus, text and tr. R. P. Casey, *Studies and Documents 1*, London, 1934.

Cosmas was a sixth-century Egyptian Christian who had travelled as far as India, hence 'Indicopleustes'. PG 88; tr. J. W. McCrindle, *A Christian Topography*, London: The Hakluyt Society, 1897.

Cyril of Alexandria was bishop there 412–444 CE.

Letters, PG 77; tr. J. I. McEnerney, FC 76, 77.

Cyril of Jerusalem was bishop there 349–387 CE.

Catecheses, PG 33; tr. NPNF 2.7, also F. L. Cross, London: SPCK, 1966; also *Catecheses 1–12*, tr. L. P. McCauley and A. A. Stephenson FC 2; and

Catecheses 13–18 and Mystagogical Lectures (i.e *Catecheses* 19–23) tr. L. P McCauley and A. A. Stephenson, FC 64.

The Didache or 'The Teaching of the Lord through the Twelve Apostles to the Nations' is a manual of church life, possibly from the first century. It was rewritten as Bk 7 of the Apostolic Constitutions and parts survive in Coptic, Ethiopic, and Latin. There is a complete Greek text dated 1056. Eusebius (*History* 3.25) said that it was orthodox teaching but not part of the canon. Text and tr. A. Milavec, *The Didache*, New York, 2003, also tr. ANF 1, and M. Staniforth in *Early Christian Writings. The Apostolic Fathers*, Harmondsworth, 1968.

The Didascalia is an early third-century Greek text from Syria, which survives in Syriac and parts in Latin. There are Ethiopic and Arabic versions, and it became the basis for books 1–6 of the Apostolic Constitutions. R. H. Connolly, *Didascalia Apostolorum. The Syriac Version Translated and Accompanied by the Verona Latin Fragments*, Oxford, 1929.

Dionysius the Areopagite, known as Pseudo-Dionysius, lived around 500 CE in Syria, but was identified with the Athenian Dionysius of Acts 17.34.

On the Ecclesiastical Hierarchy, PG 3; tr. CWS, C. Luibheid in *Pseudo-Dionysius. The Complete Works*, New York, 1987.

Egeria's Travels is an early fifth century travel diary rediscovered in 1884, describing the pilgrimage sites, the great churches of the Holy Land, and the celebration of the Holy Week. CCSL 175; tr. and ed. J. Wilkinson, *Egeria's Travels*, 3rd edn Warminster, 1999.

Ephrem 'the Syrian', founded a school of biblical and theological studies in Edessa and died in 373 CE. *St Ephrem's Commentary on Tatian's Diatessaron*, C. McCarthy, Oxford: Oxford University Press, 1993.

Epiphanius became bishop of Salamis on Cyprus in 367 CE. He wrote the *Panarion*, meaning the Medicine Chest, against the eighty heresies which he believed were contrary to Nicene orthodoxy. It contains quotations from works which have not survived elsewhere. PG 41; tr. F. Williams, *Panarion Book 1 (1–46)*, Leiden: Brill, 1987.

Eusebius (c. 260–340 CE), bishop of Caesarea, preserved in his writings quotations from many texts which no longer survive. The first draft of his *Church History* was written before he became a bishop c. 313 CE, but he revised the work in the light of later developments. *The Preparation of the Gospel* and its companion *The Proof (Demonstration) of the Gospel* were written later in response to the philosopher Porphyry's attack on Christianity.
Church History and *Martyrs of Palestine*, PG 20; tr. H. J. Lawlor and J. E. Oulton *The Ecclesiastical History and Martyrs of Palestine*, 2 vols, London, 1927, also G. A. Williamson, *The History of the Church*, Harmondsworth, 1965.
The Preparation of the Gospel, PG 21; tr. E. H. Gifford, Oxford, 1903.
Proof of the Gospel, PG 22; tr. W. G. Ferrar, London, 1920.
Life of Constantine, PG 20; tr. A. Cameron and S. G. Hall, Oxford, 1999.
In Praise of Constantine, PG 20 tr. NPNF 2.1

Germanus was patriarch of Constantinople 715–703 CE. *On the Divine Liturgy*, PG 98; tr. P. Meyendorff, New York: St Vladimir's Seminary Press, 1999.

Gregory of Nazianzus, 'the theologian', was bishop of Constantinople 379–381 CE. *On the Pascha*, PG 44; tr. NPNF 2.7; Poems, PG 37.

Gregory, bishop of Nyssa (372–395 CE) was the younger brother of Basil the Great. *Letters*, PG 46; tr. NPNF 2.5, *Life of Moses*, PG 44; tr. CWS, A. J. Malherbert, New York, 1978.

Hermas was a visionary who lived in Rome and recorded his visions from c. 90 CE. *The Shepherd,* (his guiding angel was dressed as a shepherd), was written in Greek and included in the Sinai Codex. PG 2; tr. ANF 1; also text and tr. K. Lake in *The Apostolic Fathers,* vol. 2, LCL (1913) 1948.

Hippolytus (c. 160–235 CE), was a schismatic bishop at Rome who was exiled to Sardinia. He was the last major scholar in the Roman church to write in Greek. *Hippolytus of Rome Contra Noetus,* PG 10; tr. ANF 5, also tr. R. Butterworth, London: University of London Press, 1977. *On Daniel,* PG 10; tr. ANF 5, *and Refutation,* PG 10; tr. ANF 5. *The Canons of Hippolytus* survive only in an Arabic version; ed. P. F. Bradshaw, tr. C. Bebawi, Nottingham: Grove Books, 1987.

Ignatius became the second bishop of Antioch (Eusebius, *History* 3.36) about 69 CE and died a martyr in Rome c. 107 CE. En route to Rome he wrote seven letters to churches in Asia Minor, which were collected by Polycarp, Bishop of Smyrna (Ep. Poylcarp to the Philippians 13.2). PG 5; tr. ANF 1; also M. Staniforth in *Early Christian Writings. The Apostolic Fathers,* Harmondsworth, 1968.

Irenaeus was born in Smyrna where he knew Polycarp and learned from him about the teachings of John. He studied in Rome and then went as bishop to Lyons. His work *The Proof of the Apostolic Preaching* (also known as *The Demonstration*) was lost for centuries but an Armenian version was discovered in 1904, tr. J. A. Robinson, *St Irenaeus. The Demonstration of the Apostolic Preaching,* London, 1920. His major five-volume work, *Against Heresies,* is a refutation of gnosticism in all its aspects. It is extant in a Latin translation but fragments of the original Greek survive as quotations in other works. Text, PG 7; tr. ANF vol 1.

The Ascension of Isaiah is a composite work comprising the Martyrdom of Isaiah (chs 1–5) and The Vision of Isaiah (chs 6–11), but these sections are themselves composite. Although probably written in Hebrew and then translated into Greek and other languages, the entire text survives only in Ethiopic. A pre-Christian Hebrew text about the martyrdom of Isaiah has been expanded by Christian visionary material, some of which clearly describes the Church in the first century. The Christian additions show a remarkable similarity to the teaching attributed to James in Eusebius, *History* 2.23 and *Clementine Recognitions* 1.66–70. Epiphanius, *Panarion* I.36.16 attributes to James an otherwise unknown book used by the Ebionites, *The Ascents of*

James, which has probably survived in these portions of the Ascension of Isaiah. In OTP 2.

Infancy Gospel of James, an early Christian text telling of the birth and childhood of Mary, was known to Origen. In ANT.

Jerome (c. 347–420 CE) was head of a monastery near Bethlehem for over thirty years and was appointed by Pope Damasus to prepare a revised Latin text of the Bible, which eventually became the Vulgate. The prefaces to the biblical texts can be found in the Vulgate itself. Between 393 and 406 CE he wrote a series of commentaries on biblical texts.

Letters, PL 22; tr. NPNF 2.3; also C. C. Mierow, ACW 33, Westminster, Maryland, 1963, and F. A. Wright, LCL (1933) 1963.
On Isaiah, PL 24.
On Zephaniah, PL 25.
On Matthew, PL 26; French tr. E. Bonnard, *Commentaire sur S.Matthieu* SC 259, Paris, 1979.

John Chrysostom (347–407 CE), born in Antioch, was a great preacher and interpreter of the Bible. He became bishop of Constantinople in 398 CE, but ecclesiastical and court politics led to his expulsion, and he died in exile.

On Priesthood, PG 48; tr. NPNF 1.9, also G. Neville, London: SPCK, 1977.
Homilies On 1 Timothy, PG 62; tr. NPNF 1.13.
On Psalms, PG 55; tr. R. C. Hill, 2 vols, 1998, 2000.
Against Judaising Christians, PG 48; tr. P. W. Harkins, FC 68.
On Hebrews, PG 63; tr. NPNF 1.14.
On 1 Corinthians, PG 61; tr. NPNF 1.12.

John of Damascus, died c. 750 CE, was a monk of Mar Saba near Jerusalem. *On the Divine Images*, PG 95; tr. NPNF 2.9, also D. Anderson, Crestwood: St Vladimir's Seminary, 1980.

Justin was born of a Roman family who lived near Shechem in Samaria. He lived for a while in Ephesus where his dialogue with the Jew Trypho is set, some time after the end of the Bar Kochbar revolt in 135 CE. He moved to Rome where he wrote his First Apology, addressed to the Emperor Antoninus Pius, and his Second Apology addressed to the Roman senate. His defence of Christianity eventually led to his execution c. 165 CE. *Dialogue with Trypho* and *Apology*, PG 6; both tr. ANF 1.

Lactantius who died about 325 CE, came from North Africa. He was a teacher of Latin rhetoric and tutor to the Emperor Constantine's son. *The Divine Institutes, 1–8*, PL 6; tr. ANF 7; also tr. M. F. McDonald, FC 49.

Maximus the Confessor (580–662 CE) was a Greek monk and mystic who was exiled and tortured for his faith. *The Church's Mystagogy*, PG 91; tr. CWS, G. C. Berthold in *Maximus Confessor. Selected Writings*, New York, 1985.

Melito, bishop of Sardis at the end of the second century. *Homily on the Passion*, text and tr. S. G. Hall, Oxford: Clarendon Press, 1979.

Methodius, died c. 311, bishop of Olympus who opposed Origen. *The Symposium* is his only work to survive in Greek; others survive mainly in Old Church Slavonic. PG 18; tr. ANF 6.

Narsai, a Nestorian, became head of the school of Edessa in 451 CE. Ecclesiastical politics forced him to flee to Nisibis where he taught until his death in c. 503 CE. *The Liturgical Homilies of Narsai*, tr. R. H. Connolly, Cambridge, 1909.

Novatian was a bishop in Rome in the mid third century. *On the Trinity*, CCSL 4; tr. R. J. DeSimone FC 67.

Origen was the greatest biblical scholar in the early Church, both as textual critic and as exegete. Forced by ecclesiastical politics to flee from his home city of Alexandria, he settled in Palestine, where he died some time after June 251, as the result of torture during the Decian persecution. ANF 4.
First Principles, PG 11; tr. G. W. Butterworth, London, 1936.
Against Celsus, PG 11; tr. H. Chadwick, Cambridge, 1953.
Homilies on Genesis and Exodus, PG 12; tr. R. E. Heine, FC 7.
Homilies on Leviticus 1–16, PG 12 tr. G. W. Barkley, FC 83.
On Numbers, PG 12; French tr. A. Méhat, SC 29.
Homilies on Jeremiah, PG 13; tr. J. C. Smith, FC 97.
Homilies on Ezekiel, PG 13; French tr. M. Borret, *Homélies sur Ézéchiel*, SC 352.
On John 1–10, PG 14; tr. R. E. Heine, FC 80.
On John 13–32 PG 14 tr. R. E. Heine, FC 89.

Serapion was bishop of Thmuis in Egypt in the mid fourth century. *Bishop Serapion's Prayer Book*, tr. NPNF 2.2, also J. Wordsworth, London: SPCK, 1923.

The Odes of Solomon are a collection of hymns on baptismal themes, written originally in Syriac or perhaps Hebrew at the end of the first century CE. There are similarities to the Qumran Hymns and to the Fourth Gospel. Text and tr. in J. H. Charlesworth, *The Odes of Solomon*, Oxford, 1973, translation only in OTP 2.

Sozomen, fifth-century historian, born in Palestine but moved to Constantinople. *Church History*, PG 67; tr. E. Walford, London: H. G. Bohn, 1855.

Tertullian, late second century, came from North Africa but moved to Rome. He was the first major Christian writer to use Latin. *On Fasting*, PL 2; *On Baptism* and *On the Lord's Prayer*, PL 1 all tr. ANF 3.

Theodoret was Bishop of Cyrrhus, and died about 460 CE.
Commentary on the Psalms, PG 80; tr. NPNF 2.3; also R. C. Hill, FC 101, 102.

The Acts of Thomas, originally written in Syriac early in the third century, were combined by the Manichaeans with the Acts of John, the Acts of Paul, the Acts of Peter and the Acts of Andrew, as a substitute for the canonical Acts of the Apostles. Tr. in ANT.

Gnostic Texts

Twelve papyrus books of Gnostic texts and fragments of a thirteenth were found at Nag Hammadi in Egypt in 1945, and are known as the Coptic Gnostic Library. Most of the Gnostic texts cited in this book are from this collection. There is still much to be learned about the so-called Gnostics, and much to be unlearned. They regarded themselves as the guardians of true Christianity, and so the label 'heretic' should not be applied with too much confidence. The Gospel of Thomas shows Jesus in his original setting as a temple mystic, for example, and the pair of texts known as the Letter of Eugnostos and the Wisdom of Jesus Christ show how an older text, rooted in the priestly Wisdom tradition, was 'adopted' as the teaching of Jesus. The pre-supposition which makes Plato a major influence on Philo also masks the Hebrew roots of gnosticism (see my *The Great Angel*, 1992). English translations in *The Nag Hammadi Library in English*, ed. J. M. Robinson, Leiden, 1996. Critical editions of the original texts in *The Coptic Gnostic Library*, Leiden. Of the texts cited in this book:

Nag Hammadi Codex I, 2 vols, ed. H. W. Attridge, 1985, contains the Apocryphon of James and The Tripartite Tractate.

Nag Hammadi Codex II.2-7, 2 vols, ed. B. Layton, 1989, contains The Gospel of Thomas, The Gospel of Philip, On the Origin of the World.

Nag Hammadi Codices III.3-4 and V.1, ed. D. M. Parrott, 1991, contains The Letter of Eugnostos.

Nag Hammadi Codices XI, XII and XIII, ed. C. W. Hedrick, 1990, contains A Valentinian Exposition.

Other Classical texts

The Greek Anthology, text and tr. W. R. Paton, LCL 2 vols, 1916.

Hecataeus of Abdera who lived in the fourth century BCE is quoted in *Diodorus Siculus* 40.3.5-6, text and tr. F. R. Walton, LCL 12 vols, 1967.

Pliny the Younger, *Letters,* text and tr. B. Radice, LCL 2 vols, 1969.

Procopius, lived in the first half of the sixth century, and was court historian for Justinian. *History of the Wars,* and *Buildings,* text and tr. H. B. Dewing, LCL 7 vols, 1914–40.

BIBLIOGRAPHY OF SECONDARY SOURCES MENTIONED IN THE TEXT.

Anderson, R., 'À la recherche de Théophile', in 'Saint Luc, évangéliste et historien', *Dossiers d'Archéologie* 279 (2002–3), 64–71.
Barker, M., *The Great Angel: A Study of Israel's Second God,* London: SPCK, 1992.
  The Risen Lord. The Jesus of History as the Christ of Faith, Edinburgh: T&T Clark, 1996.
  The Revelation of Jesus Christ, London: T&T Clark, 2000.
  The Great High Priest, London: T&T Clark, 2003.
  The Hidden Tradition of the Kingdom of God, London: SPCK, 2007.
  'Hezekiah's Boil', *Journal for the Study of the Old Testament* 95 (2001), 31–42.
  'The New Church', *Sourozh,* February 2007.
Barr, J., *The Garden of Eden and the Hope of Immortality,* Minneapolis: Fortress Press, 1993.
Bentzen, A., *King and Messiah,* London: Lutterworth Press, 1955.
Bernard, J. H., *The Odes of Solomon,* Cambridge: Cambridge University Press, 1912.
Blaauw, S de, 'The Solitary Celebration of the Supreme Pontiff', in *Omnes Circumadstantes,* ed. C. Caspers and M. Schneiders, Kampen: Kok Pharos, 1994.

Black, M., *The Book of Enoch or 1 Enoch*, Leiden: Brill, 1985.

Boccaccini, G., *Roots of Rabbinic Judaism*, Grand Rapids: Eerdmans, 2002.

Bradshaw, P. F., *The Search for the Origins of Christian Worship*, London: SPCK, 1992.

Brightman, F. E., *Liturgies Eastern and Western*, Oxford: Clarendon Press, 1896.

Brock, S. P., 'A letter attributed to Cyril of Jerusalem on the Rebuilding of the Temple', *Bulletin of the School of Oriental and African Studies*, 40 (1977), 267–86.

'Baptismal Themes in the Writings of Jacob of Serugh', *Symposium Syriacum*, 1976, Christiana Analecta 205 (1978), 325–47.

'The Syrian Baptismal Rites', *Concilium* 122 (1979), 98–104.

Cantalamessa, R., *Easter in the Early Church*, tr. J. M. Quigley and J. T. Lienhard, Collegeville, Minn.: The Liturgical Press, 1993.

Casey, M., 'The original Aramaic Form of Jesus' Interpretation of the Cup', *Journal of Theological Studies* 41 (1990) 1–12.

Charlesworth, J. H., *The Odes of Solomon*, Oxford: Clarendon Press, 1973.

Chilton, B. D., *The Glory of Israel. The Theology and Provenance of the Isaiah Targum*, Sheffield: Journal for the Study of the Old Testament Supplement 23, 1983.

Connolly R. H., *Didascalia Apostolorum*, Oxford: Clarendon Press, 1929.

The Liturgical Homilies of Narsai, Cambridge: Cambridge University Press, 1909.

Cowley, A. E., *Aramaic Papyri of the Fifth Century BC*, Oxford: Clarendon Press, 1923.

Davies, G. I., *Ancient Hebrew Inscriptions*, Cambridge: Cambridge University Press, 1991.

Dillistone, F. W., *The Christian Understanding of the Atonement*, Philadelphia: Westminster Press, 1968.

Douglas, M., 'The Stranger in the Bible', *Archives de Sociologie Europeanne*, XXXV (1994), 283–96.

'Atonement in Leviticus', *Jewish Studies Quarterly* 1 (1993–4), 109–30.

Jacob's Tears. The Priestly Work of Reconciliation, Oxford: Oxford University Press, 2004.

Ehrman, B. D., *The Orthodox Corruption of Scripture. The Effect of Early Christological Controversies on the Text of the New Testament*, Oxford: Oxford University Press, 1993.

Fletcher-Louis, C. H. T., *All the Glory of Adam. Liturgical Anthropology in the Dead Sea Scrolls*, Leiden: Brill, 2002.

Gelston A., *The Eucharistic Prayer of Addai and Mari*, Oxford: Clarendon Press, 1992.

Halperin, D. J., *The Faces of the Chariot. Early Jewish Responses to Ezekiel's Vision*, Tübingen: Mohr, 1988.

Harrison, J. M., *A New Temple for Byzantium*, Austin: University of Texas Press, 1989.

Hayward, C. T. R., *Interpretations of the Name Israel in Ancient Judaism and some Early Christian Writings*, Oxford: Oxford University Press, 2005.

Hurowitz, V. A., 'Solomon's Golden Vessels and the Cult of the First Temple', in *Pomegranates and Golden Bells*, ed. D. Wright and others, Winona Lake, Ind: Eisenbrauns, 1995, 151–64.

Hurtado, L., 'The Binitarian Shape of Early Christian Worship', in *The Jewish Roots of Christological Monotheism*, ed. C. C. Newman and others, Leiden: Brill, 1999, 187–213.

Idel, M., *Kabbalah. New Perspectives*, New Haven and London: Yale University Press, 1988.

James, E. O., *Christian Myth and Ritual. A Historical Study*, London: John Murray, 1933.

Kimelman, R., 'Birkat Ha Minim and the Lack of Evidence for Anti-Christian Prayer in Late Antiquity', in E. Sanders, ed., *Jewish and Christian Self Definition*, vol. 2, London: SCM Press, 1981.

Kuhnel, B., 'Jewish Symbolism of the Temple and the Tabernacle and Christian Symbolism of the Holy Sepulchre and the Heavenly Tabernacle', *Journal of Jewish Art*, 12–3 (1986–7), 147–168.

From the Earthly to the Heavenly Jerusalem. Representations of the Holy City in Christian Art of the First Millennium, Freiburg: Herder, 1987.

Lang, B., *Sacred Games. A History of Christian Worship*, New Haven and London: Yale University Press, 1997.

Marmorstein, A., 'Philo and the Names of God', *Jewish Quarterly Review* 22 (1931), 295–306.

Marx, A., *Les Offrandes végétales dans l'Ancien Testament*, Leiden: Brill, 1994.

Maxwell, W. D., *An Outline of Christian Worship. Its Development and Forms*, Oxford: Oxford University Press, 1936.

McVey, K., 'The Domed Church as Microcosm: Literary Roots of an Architectural Symbol', *Dumbarton Oaks Papers* 37 (1983).

Mettinger, T. N. D., The Dethronement of Sabaoth, Lund: CWK Gleerup, 1982.

Meyers, E. M., 'Early Judaism and Christianity in the Light of Archaeology', *Biblical Archaeologist* 51 (1988), 69–79.

Neusner, J., *The Incarnation of God. The Character of Divinity in Formative Judaism*, Philadelphia: Fortress Press, 1988.

Oesterley, W. O. E., *The Jewish Background of the Christian Liturgy*, Oxford: Oxford University Press, 1925.

Olson, D., *1 Enoch. A New Translation*, North Richland Hills, Tex.: Bibal Press, 2004.

Oppenheim, A. L., 'The Golden Garments of the Gods', *Ancient Near Eastern Studies* 8 (1949), 172–93.

Patai, R., *The Hebrew Goddess*, 3rd edn, Detroit: Wayne State University Press, 1990.

Quasten, J., *Music and Worship in Pagan and Christian Antiquity*, Washington DC: National Association of Pastoral Musicians, 1983.

Ratcliff, E. R., *Liturgical Studies*, London: SPCK, 1976.

Ruis-Camps J., and Read-Heimerdinger, J., *The Message of Acts in Codex Bezae*, London: T&T Clark, 2006.

Schaefer, P., *The Hidden and Manifest God*, New York: State University of NY Press, 1992.

Schiffman, L., *Who was a Jew? Rabbinic and Halakhic Perspectives on the Jewish-Christian Schism*, Hoboken, NJ: KTAV, 1985.

Segal A. F., *Two Powers in Heaven*, Leiden: Brill, 1978.

Smith, J. Z., 'The Prayer of Joseph', in *Religions in Antiquity. Essays in Memory of E. R. Goodenough*, ed. J. Neusner, Leiden: Brill, 1970, 253–94.

Spiegel, S., *The Last Trial*, New York: Schocken Books, 1967.

Spinks, B. D., *The Sanctus in the Eucharistic Prayer*, Cambridge: Cambridge University Press. 1991.

Stec, D. M., *The Targum of Psalms*, London: T&T Clark, 2004.

Westcott, B. F., *The Gospel According to St John*, London: John Murray, 1903.

Wilkinson, J., *Egeria's Travels*, Warminster: Aris and Phillips, 3rd edn 1999.

  Jerusalem Pilgrims before the Crusades, Warminster: Aris and Phillips, 2002.

Winkler, G., 'The Original Meaning of the Pre-baptismal Anointing and its Implications' *Worship* 52.1 (1978), 24–45.

INDEX OF BIBLICAL AND ANCIENT TEXTS

257

INDEX OF PERSONS, PLACES AND SUBJECTS